MicroPython Projects

A do-it-yourself guide for embedded developers to build a range of applications using Python

Jacob Beningo

BIRMINGHAM - MUMBAI

MicroPython Projects

Copyright © 2020 Packt Publishing

Commissioning Editor: Richa Tripathi
Acquisition Editor: Alok Dhuri
Content Development Editor: Digvijay Bagul
Senior Editor: Rohit Singh
Technical Editor: Gaurav Gala
Copy Editor: Safis Editing
Project Coordinator: Francy Puthiry
Proofreader: Safis Editing
Indexer: Manju Arasan
Production Designer: Alishon Mendonsa

First published: April 2020

Production reference: 1160420

Published by Packt Publishing Ltd.
Livery Place
35 Livery Street
Birmingham
B3 2PB, UK.

ISBN 978-1-78995-803-4

www.packt.com

Subscribe to our online digital library for full access to over 7,000 books and videos, as well as industry leading tools to help you plan your personal development and advance your career. For more information, please visit our website.

Why subscribe?

- Spend less time learning and more time coding with practical eBooks and Videos from over 4,000 industry professionals

- Improve your learning with Skill Plans built especially for you

- Get a free eBook or video every month

- Fully searchable for easy access to vital information

- Copy and paste, print, and bookmark content

Did you know that Packt offers eBook versions of every book published, with PDF and ePub files available? You can upgrade to the eBook version at www.packt.com and as a print book customer, you are entitled to a discount on the eBook copy. Get in touch with us at customercare@packtpub.com for more details.

At www.packt.com, you can also read a collection of free technical articles, sign up for a range of free newsletters, and receive exclusive discounts and offers on Packt books and eBooks.

Contributors

About the author

Jacob Beningo is an independent consultant who specializes in microcontroller-based embedded systems. He has advised, coached, and developed systems across multiple industries, including the automotive, defense, industrial, medical, and space sectors. Jacob enjoys working with companies to help them develop and improve their processes and skill sets. He publishes a monthly newsletter, *Embedded Bytes*, and blogs for publications about embedded system design techniques and challenges. Jacob holds bachelor's degrees in electrical engineering, physics, and mathematics from Central Michigan University and a master's degree in space systems engineering from the University of Michigan.

A lot of effort goes into writing a book and it is often the culmination of months, if not years, of hard work and this book is no exception. The project nature of this book brought about its own challenges and it would not have been possible without the dedication and hard work of colleagues, reviewers, and editors. My colleague, Lorenzo Rizzello, was fantastic in helping me pull together the theory and operations for the object detection chapter. I want to thank all of you!

About the reviewer

Bhaumik Vaidya is an experienced computer vision engineer and mentor. He has worked extensively on OpenCV in solving computer vision problems. He got a gold medal in his master's degree and is now doing a PhD in the acceleration of computer vision algorithms built using OpenCV and deep learning libraries on GPUs. He has a background in teaching and has guided many projects in computer vision and **very-large-scale integration** (**VLSI**). He has previously worked in the VLSI domain as an ASIC verification engineer, and so has very sound knowledge of hardware architectures as well. Bhaumik, along with his PhD mentor, has also received an NVIDIA Jetson TX1 embedded development platform as a research grant from NVIDIA.

Packt is searching for authors like you

If you're interested in becoming an author for Packt, please visit `authors.packtpub.com` and apply today. We have worked with thousands of developers and tech professionals, just like you, to help them share their insight with the global tech community. You can make a general application, apply for a specific hot topic that we are recruiting an author for, or submit your own idea.

Preface

Embedded systems developers have traditionally mostly used C when programming, or if they are daring and cutting edge, they've pushed the envelope by using C++. Over the last decade, a lot has changed in the way that we design and build embedded systems and in the way that software is developed in general. Python has become a dominant language in many computer and server applications, with many young and new developers learning Python first over any other language. This makes Python a unique and interesting choice to develop embedded systems.

MicroPython Projects explores how developers can leverage Python to develop applications that use a slimmed-down version Python known as MicroPython. MicroPython came into existence back in 2013 and has been steadily evolving and growing an active and innovative community around it. MicroPython allows developers to work at a higher level of abstraction, focusing on the application early while leaving low-level processor details behind an interface, which makes it easy for even non-software developers to quickly write applications that control and interface with the hardware.

This book will walk you through the background of developing applications using MicroPython and will help developers to get familiar with some design patterns and formulate ideas for their own projects.

Who this book is for

This book is for embedded systems developers or anyone who is interested in building embedded systems using MicroPython.

I expect that the reader has a basic understanding of electronics and Python while some experimentation with MicroPython will be helpful.

I've tried throughout the book to reinforce the software development process, which I often find lacking in developers who are designing their own product or working on open source software. No matter what your current skill level, readers will get an understanding of where and when to use MicroPython, along with techniques and patterns they can directly apply to their own projects and some ideas on how to expand the projects that are in this book.

What this book covers

Chapter 1, *Down the Rabbit Hole with MicroPython*, takes you through embedded software development and where MicroPython fits in. In this chapter, we look at how to decide what language to use, along with some general best practices.

Chapter 2, *Managing Real-Time Tasks*, helps you explore the different techniques that developers can use to schedule tasks in their MicroPython-based system.

Chapter 3, *Writing a MicroPython Driver for an I/O Expander*, explains how to write your own driver for an external device.

Chapter 4, *Developing an Application Test Harness*, takes you through different methods that can be used to test our MicroPython-based application and presents several different options for developers interested in such activities.

Chapter 5, *Customizing the MicroPython Kernel Start Up Code*, helps you to get behind the scenes with MicroPython by examining and making changes to the MicroPython kernel. In this chapter, we focus on the startup code that developers looking to produce a production system might need to modify.

Chapter 6, *A Custom Debugging Tool to Visualize Sensor Data*, helps you explore how you can transport sensor and debugging information from our device to a computer that then visualizes what is happening on our system. This can be critical to monitoring key variables, debug statements, or just creating a sensor dashboard.

Chapter 7, *Device Control Using Gestures*, helps you learn how we can interface a gesture sensor with a development board and write an application that will detect gestures.

Chapter 8, *Automation and Control Using Android*, helps you learn how we can use an ESP32 microcontroller to create a sensor node that can transmit sensor data and receive commands from an Android template. This project is easily extensible for **Internet-of-Things (IoT)** applications and device control.

Chapter 9, *Building an Object Detection Application Using Machine Learning*, demonstrates the use of an OpenMV camera module powered by MicroPython to build an application that can detect objects in an image.

Chapter 10, *The Future of MicroPython*, explores the future of MicroPython and where we might expect to see it go in the coming years.

Appendix A, *Downloading and Running MicroPython Code*, explains the process of getting code onto the board and running it.

To get the most out of this book

This book assumes that the reader has a basic understanding of Python and that they have at least built a few embedded systems projects previously. The material is written so that a beginner will not have any problems and a more experienced embedded software developer will be able to quickly learn how to write MicroPython-based applications. I also assume that you are able to read flowcharts and basic wiring diagrams. The reader should also understand how to use a Git repository and install software on their computer.

Software/hardware covered in the book	OS requirements
PyCharm	Windows, Linux, macOS
PuTTY	Windows, Linux, macOS
Linux Virtual Machine	Windows, Linux, macOS
Python 3.x	Windows, Linux, macOS
Anaconda Terminal	Windows, Linux, macOS
Simple TCP Socket Tester	Windows, Linux, macOS
OpenMV IDE	Windows, Linux, macOS
Pyboard	-
RobotDyn I2C 8-bit PCA8574 I/O expander	-
Adafruit RGB Pushbutton PN: 3423 or equivalent	-
STM32L4 IoT Discovery Node	-
Robotdyn I2C 8-bit PCA8574 I/O expander	-
USB to UART Converter	-
Adafruit ADPS9960 breakout board	-
MicroPython supported development board	-
ESP32 WROVER-B	-
OpenMV Camera Module	-

The projects are not necessarily designed to be done in order. With that in mind, I would recommend that developers read the first two chapters in order before jumping to the project that is most interesting to them. These chapters give the background on MicroPython and how to schedule tasks. After that, it's up to the developer to decide on the order. As strange as this may sound, I would also encourage readers to make sure they read the last chapter as well, which introduces the pyboard-D, which may be the development board they decide to go with for most of their experimentation.

If you are using the digital version of this book, we advise you to type the code yourself or access the code via the GitHub repository (link available in the next section). Doing so will help you avoid any potential errors related to the copying and pasting of code.

Download the example code files

You can download the example code files for this book from your account at `www.packt.com`. If you purchased this book elsewhere, you can visit `www.packtpub.com/support` and register to have the files emailed directly to you.

You can download the code files by following these steps:

1. Log in or register at `www.packt.com`.
2. Select the **Support** tab.
3. Click on **Code Downloads**.
4. Enter the name of the book in the **Search** box and follow the onscreen instructions.

Once the file is downloaded, please make sure that you unzip or extract the folder using the latest version of:

- WinRAR/7-Zip for Windows
- Zipeg/iZip/UnRarX for Mac
- 7-Zip/PeaZip for Linux

The code bundle for the book is also hosted on GitHub at `https://github.com/PacktPublishing/MicroPython-Projects`. In case there's an update to the code, it will be updated on the existing GitHub repository.

We also have other code bundles from our rich catalog of books and videos available at `https://github.com/PacktPublishing/`. Check them out!

Download the color images

We also provide a PDF file that has color images of the screenshots/diagrams used in this book. You can download it here: `https://static.packt-cdn.com/downloads/9781789958034_ColorImages.pdf`.

Conventions used

There are a number of text conventions used throughout this book.

`CodeInText`: Indicates code words in text, database table names, folder names, filenames, file extensions, pathnames, dummy URLs, user input, and Twitter handles. Here is an example: "Create new modules for each module that will be tested with `_tests.py` appended to the filename."

A block of code is set as follows:

```
def system_init():
    print("Initializing system ...")
    print("Starting application ...")
```

When we wish to draw your attention to a particular part of a code block, the relevant lines or items are set in bold:

```
try:
        PushButton = RGB_Button.DeviceIO.Read()
except Exception as e:
        sys.print_exception(e)
        print("Exiting application ...")
        sys.exit(0)
```

Any command-line input or output is written as follows:

```
pip install pySerial
```

Bold: Indicates a new term, an important word, or words that you see onscreen. For example, words in menus or dialog boxes appear in the text like this. Here is an example: "See the **MicroPython documentation | Quick reference for the pyboard | MicroPython tutorial for the pyboard | 3. Getting a MicroPython REPL prompt** for details."

 Warnings or important notes appear like this.

 Tips and tricks appear like this.

Get in touch

Feedback from our readers is always welcome.

General feedback: If you have questions about any aspect of this book, mention the book title in the subject of your message and email us at customercare@packtpub.com.

Errata: Although we have taken every care to ensure the accuracy of our content, mistakes do happen. If you have found a mistake in this book, we would be grateful if you would report this to us. Please visit www.packtpub.com/support/errata, selecting your book, clicking on the Errata Submission Form link, and entering the details.

Piracy: If you come across any illegal copies of our works in any form on the Internet, we would be grateful if you would provide us with the location address or website name. Please contact us at copyright@packt.com with a link to the material.

If you are interested in becoming an author: If there is a topic that you have expertise in and you are interested in either writing or contributing to a book, please visit authors.packtpub.com.

Reviews

Please leave a review. Once you have read and used this book, why not leave a review on the site that you purchased it from? Potential readers can then see and use your unbiased opinion to make purchase decisions, we at Packt can understand what you think about our products, and our authors can see your feedback on their book. Thank you!

For more information about Packt, please visit packt.com.

Table of Contents

Down the Rabbit Hole with MicroPython 1

The C programming language has dominated the embedded systems industry for half a century! C has been extraordinarily successful, but it is no longer meeting the needs of embedded software developers. In this chapter, we will begin to explore the programming language landscape for embedded systems and how Python, particularly MicroPython, is quickly becoming a good fit for a wide range of applications.

The following topics will be covered in this chapter:

- The embedded software language menagerie
- The case for MicroPython
- Use cases for MicroPython
- Evaluating whether MicroPython is right for you
- Selecting the right development platform
- MicroPython development processes and strategies
- Useful resources

The embedded software language menagerie

In the history of the embedded software industries, for the most part, developers writing software for microcontroller-based systems have had very few software languages to choose from. At the dawn of the computer age, developers were stuck using low-level assembly language that forced them to learn the instruction set for each microcontroller device that they used. While highly effective and efficient, reading, maintaining, or even understanding assembly language was quite difficult and cumbersome.

Between 1969 and 1973, Dennis Ritchie developed the C programming language while working at Bell Labs and forever changed the way that software was developed. The C programming language caught on, and while general-purpose computing systems have moved on to other object-oriented languages, C has been the dominant language to use with microcontrollers for several different reasons. They include the following:

- It is a high-level programming language that doesn't require developers to understand target-specific assembly language.
- The ability to access low-level registers and hardware features.
- The capability to create high-level software abstractions.
- Cross-platform compilation (write the software once and deploy it to multiple targets).
- Software that is reusable and portable.

The C language is so popular and successful that it has dominated the embedded software industry as the language of choice for almost half a century. The popularity of C has remained despite major software design paradigm shifts, such as object-oriented design, and new languages being available, such as C++. C fills an important niche that allows developers to efficiently develop software that interacts at the *bit and byte* levels in the hardware.

While C has been extremely popular among developers, over the past several years, its popularity has been waning for several different reasons. Some of these reasons are listed as follows:

- First, the C language has several sticky spots in its specification that can result in developers either getting confused about what the code is doing or that results in different behavior when compiled for a different target. This has caused additional standards such as MISRA-C to be developed, which create a *safe* subset of C features that developers can use in their software.

- Second, the C language is no longer taught to university students in many parts of the world. In fact, even C++ is no longer taught at university! Students who want to learn a programming language are often presented with Java or Python as the language of choice, which means that any would-be embedded developers have to learn C on the job. When learning C on the job, the chances are that the developer will not be aware of the gotchas and issues with the C language, resulting in buggy, low-quality code that requires additional time and money to make production-ready.
- Next, C is a relatively low-level and verbose programming language. It is quite easy to cause incredibly hard-to-find bugs from memory leaks, buffer overflows, or accidentally accessing an array out-of-bounds. Most modern languages provide explicit protection against these issues with features such as memory management and managed pointers (if pointers exist at all!).
- Finally, most development teams use an object-oriented approach to software development when they develop their software architectures. While good software architecture is language agnostic, it can be much more difficult to write object-oriented code in a language such as C. It's often overlooked that C does provide perfect encapsulation and a mechanism for inheritance, but multiple inheritance and polymorphism are far more complicated and error-prone to pull off.

Because of these reasons, over the last few years, there has been a slow push to begin moving away from using C as the language of choice for embedded applications.

In fact, there has been a small explosion in the number of languages that can be used to develop embedded software. These range from the traditional compiled languages, such as Assembly or C, to C++ or Java, or to even more recent scripting languages such as Python or Squirrel. There are even visual programming languages that allow developers to generate high-level concepts and then generate low-level code such as MATLAB.

Every other year, ASPENCORE performs an embedded industry survey that polls a few thousand developers in the embedded systems industry. In the last survey, in 2019, it was found that only 56% of these projects were developed using the C programming language, while 22% of projects were developed using C++. The remaining 22% was a mix of several other languages, including Python. The complete breakdown can be seen in the following diagram. The menagerie of languages demonstrates how developers are desperately grasping at new languages and techniques that can be used to write their software in a more effective and modern manner. What's interesting is that if you compare these results to the 2017 results, the response for Python has doubled from 3% to 6%. Bear in mind, though, that the responses for C and C++ have stayed exactly the same, so while Python has grown more popular, it is not stealing any market share from C or C++.

The breakdown of programming languages used for embedded systems in 2019 is shown in the following image:

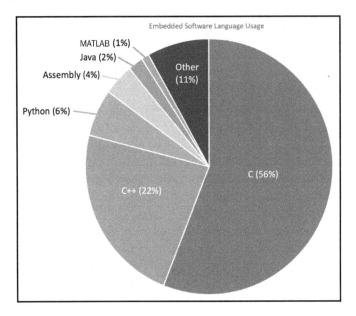

The preceding pie chart is from a survey done by `https://www.embedded.com/`. Note that this is for all embedded systems and includes application processors, not just microcontrollers (*ASPENCORE Embedded Systems Survey, 2019,* `www.embedded.com`).

The case for MicroPython

As developers have started to look for alternative programming languages, the opportunity for Python to become a popular embedded language has dramatically risen. Python has several characteristics that make it an interesting choice for an embedded language. These include, but certainly aren't limited to, the following:

- It is taught at many universities around the world.
- It is easy to learn (I've seen elementary students write Python code).
- It is object-oriented.
- It is an interpreted scripting language that removes compilation.
- It is supported by a robust community, including many add-on libraries that minimize reinventing the wheel.

- It includes error handling (something that C didn't get the memo on).
- It is easily extensible.

Python has actually become the go-to language for developers working on popular application processors such as the Raspberry Pi board.

Python itself, though, has several challenges a developer must consider before using it on a microcontroller:

- First, microcontrollers are resource-constrained devices and, typically, don't have a lot of memory or processing power. This means that the Python interpreter would have to be rewritten so that it could easily fit on a microcontroller with a few hundred kilobytes of flash storage and be able to function in sub-200 MHz environments.
- Second, microcontrollers are used in real-time systems. This means that there needs to be a mechanism to handle interrupts, which doesn't directly exist in Python.
- Third, the Python interpreter would need to be ported to each microcontroller architecture and target in order to operate efficiently.

These three considerations could be quite challenging if a developer decided to undertake them alone. Thankfully, this effort has already been undertaken by the MicroPython community, as described by the project itself:

> *"MicroPython is a lean and efficient implementation of the Python 3 programming language that includes a small subset of the Python standard library and is optimized to run on microcontrollers and in constrained environments."*
>
> *– https://micropython.org/*

MicroPython aims to bring the best of the Python world to embedded systems and loosen our reliance on developing software in C (even though, under the hood, MicroPython is written in C!).

Use cases for MicroPython

It's important to bear in mind that, just like any programming language, there are specific situations where MicroPython is best suited, and other situations where using MicroPython would be a disaster. In general, I have found that there are three different use cases where MicroPython really shines.

They include the following:

- **Do-it-yourself** (**DIY**) projects
- Rapid prototyping
- Low-volume production products

Let's examine each of these use cases in detail.

Use case #1 – DIY projects

MicroPython is extremely well suited for developers who are looking to create a hobbyist or one-off project. As we discussed earlier, Python is a simple scripting language that is very easy to learn. This makes MicroPython extremely accessible to developers who are looking to experiment and create a DIY project such as a MIDI player, robot, drone, or home automation system. The possibilities for its use are really only limited by the imagination of the developer.

There are also, at least, a dozen different low-cost development boards that support MicroPython natively. Being low cost makes it extremely easy to just order a board and, when it arrives, fire it up and start programming with MicroPython. In `Chapter 5`, *Customizing the MicroPython Kernel Start Up Code*, we will show you how to customize the MicroPython kernel and deploy it on your own custom development board.

Finally, if you were to select your favorite search engine, you would find that not only are there a lot of examples on how to use MicroPython in different applications but there are also a lot of examples on how to use Python in general. These resources help to build up a great ecosystem around which a sole developer could create their own projects in the comfort of their own home. Throughout this book, we will also examine the most popular and useful resources, which you can also refer to at leisure.

Use case #2 – rapid prototyping

The use of MicroPython is not limited to DIY engineers. MicroPython fits the bill quite nicely for engineering teams that are looking to develop a rapid prototype or proof of concept. The MicroPython kernel abstracts out the low-level microcontroller hardware, which allows developers to start developing application code or even test code from the first day of a development cycle. This makes it particularly well suited for prototyping.

In a prototyping environment, developers could assemble hardware components for their system and develop scripts to show that the end system that they want to create is actually viable. From the issues that they encounter when prototyping in MicroPython, they should then be able to extrapolate the potential issues they will encounter during development. This will then help them to get a handle on issues such as the following:

- Development costs
- Time to market
- Major engineering hurdles
- Resources that are required

With these types of activities worked out, the development of production code can go much smoother, and the schedule and project costs will be far more accurate.

In addition to proving that a product concept is viable, developers can also use MicroPython to interface with new sensors and devices that need to be understood for development. For example, if I need to write a C driver for an I2C I/O expander chip, I will often create or buy a development board for the chip and connect it to one of my MicroPython boards. I can then write simple Python scripts to interact with the chip, which allows me to do the following:

- Explore the chip registers.
- Exercise the device's peripherals.
- Monitor I2C bus communication to understand what *good* communication looks like.

Utilizing MicroPython in this manner provides us with an in-depth understanding of the device that we are interfacing with. The result is a better-written driver that is created faster because we can utilize a working example to compare our production driver with. Having that working example dramatically decreases the time spent on debugging.

Use case #3 – low-volume production products

MicroPython is still a relatively new programming language for microcontrollers compared to C or C++, which means that it does still carry some risk with it for use in production systems. For example, using MicroPython in mass production could result in issues such as the following:

- A longer programming production cycle
- More costly microcontrollers (to handle the larger MicroPython kernel)
- Difficulty in securing the application firmware properly

- Having to manage firmware updates
- Ensuring robust operation and recovery from failure modes

It's not impossible to use MicroPython for high-volume products, but these issues and several others can make such deployments more difficult, at least at the time of writing this book. However, for products that are going to be low volume – that is, maybe a few dozen a year or several hundred to a thousand units – MicroPython could be a really good fit.

MicroPython does allow a team to develop software much faster than if they were writing in C/C++ at a much lower layer of the software stack. Developers can make use of error-handling capabilities, which can help to decrease the time that is spent on debugging a system. Python is so easy to learn that hardware engineers can write basic Python scripts to monitor their hardware and speed up the development process. In general, MicroPython has the potential to help small businesses and low-volume manufacturers decrease costs and time to market.

There have been several real-world examples where MicroPython has been used in production systems. For example, with one of my clients that works in the space industry, developing small satellites for Earth-imaging applications, we used MicroPython to control the spacecraft's **Electronic Power Supplies** (**EPS**). MicroPython fit well because of the following factors:

- These systems were very low volume.
- The business was a start-up and didn't have a large budget for software engineers.
- The development time was short for the project.
- They had a small software team that was focused on other software priorities within the satellite system and mission.
- They could tolerate a greater level of product risk to offset costs and schedules.

Using MicroPython to develop the EPS software turned out to be more manageable for their team since most of the team understood and could write Python code even though they did not know C. The end results were extraordinarily successful.

Using MicroPython in space systems and other commercial products goes beyond just one company that I have personally encountered. The European Space Industry has been evaluating using MicroPython in their own satellite systems. I have also encountered several other start-ups and entrepreneurs using MicroPython to develop their consumer electronics products. This only helps to show that not only can MicroPython be used in such cases, but there is growing interest in using MicroPython in production systems.

Evaluating whether MicroPython is right for you

So far, we have discussed several use cases for MicroPython and when using it could be a big problem. Even if a project we are working on falls within the sanctioned use cases, MicroPython may still not be the best fit. Just like with any project, we need to objectively evaluate whether MicroPython is the right language to use. Let's examine how we can evaluate whether MicroPython is right for us.

There are several steps that can be followed to evaluate whether a programming language meets the needs of a development team or developer:

1. Identify the key language features needed
2. Evaluate the team's programming skills
3. Ascertain the business results the language might achieve

Let's discuss each of these in more detail.

First, it's important to identify the language features that are needed and will be utilized by the development team. For example, it would not be uncommon for a development team to want a language that is the following:

- Object-oriented
- Has built-in error handling
- Has free and available third-party libraries
- Has a strong ecosystem
- Prevalent examples of its use can be found on the internet

If a team required just these bullet points, MicroPython would already be a front runner as the preferred language choice along with C++.

Second, a team's programming skills really need to be evaluated to determine whether the language that is being used fits with the team. There are several skills that need to be reviewed, such as the following:

- The team's general understanding of programming principles and processes
- Language-specific skill level: beginner, intermediate, or expert

When a team is full of electrical engineers with no formal programming experience, using a language such as Python can be the right choice. We have already discussed that Python is easy to learn, but electrical engineers can use Python scripts to monitor their hardware and get the system working even if the code isn't intended for production. That code can then later be tossed to a software team that makes the software production-ready based on the working, functional examples.

Finally, the business ramifications for the language need to be examined. These could include items such as the following:

- Risk tolerance for security vulnerabilities
- Cost savings from needing fewer embedded developers
- Impact on time to market
- Overall system quality and customer reactions

Once all these factors have been reviewed, only then can a developer decide whether MicroPython is acceptable for them to use in their development cycle.

Selecting the right development platform

There are quite a few options available to developers who are interested in working with MicroPython. To date, MicroPython has been ported to approximately a dozen different microcontroller architectures. Each architecture then supports a range of development boards, putting the options for developers at nearly 50 different development boards. With so many different options, it can be a bit challenging to decide which one makes the most sense for your project.

While there are many different ways to go about selecting a development platform, we are going to walk through a simple process that includes this:

1. Surveying the available architectures
2. Identifying boards of interests within those architectures
3. Creating a **Kepner-Tregoe** (**KT**) matrix to objectively evaluate the best board for the application

This simple process will ensure that you select a development platform that works best for what you want to do with MicroPython.

Surveying the available architectures

The easiest way to survey the available microcontroller architectures is to visit the MicroPython Git repository. The repository is located at `https://github.com/micropython/micropython/tree/master/`.

From the repository's root, navigate to the `ports` folder. The `ports` folder contains a list of all the available microcontroller architectures that run MicroPython and can be viewed as follows:

bare-arm	py/objdict: Make .fromkeys() method configurable.
cc3200	stm32,esp8266,cc3200: Use MICROPY_GC_STACK_ENTRY_TYPE to save some RAM.
esp32	esp32/modsocket: For socket read only release GIL if socket would block.
esp8266	esp8266/machine_uart: Add rxbuf keyword arg to UART constructor/init.
minimal	py/objdict: Make .fromkeys() method configurable.
nrf	nrf/bluetooth: Update BLE stack download script.
pic16bit	all: Update Makefiles and others to build with new ports/ dir layout.
qemu-arm	qemu-arm/test_main: Include setjmp.h because it's used by gc_collect.
stm32	stm32/main: Make thread and FS state static and exclude when not needed.
teensy	teensy: Add own uart.h to not rely on stm32's version of the file.
unix	unix/modos: Rename unlink to remove to be consistent with other ports.
windows	windows: Remove remaining traces of old GNU readline support.
zephyr	py/objstr: Make str.count() method configurable.

It's not a bad idea at this point to browse around the repository and see which microcontroller architectures are supported. At the end of the day, you'll want to choose an architecture that is well supported but also one that you are familiar with, in case you need to dive into the MicroPython kernel. For most developers interested in writing code at the Python level, diving into the MicroPython kernel is something they will probably rarely, if ever, do.

Identifying boards of interest

From the `ports` list, the architecture that is supported the most is the STM32 family. There are several reasons as to why STM32 is supported so well:

- STMicroelectronics provides a low-level driver framework that makes it easy to support multiple STM32 devices all using the same APIs.
- All the official MicroPython development boards, starting with the PYB1.0, were based on the STM32, which built up knowledge around these processors through early adopters.
- There is more support for MicroPython within the STM community than within other microcontroller architecture communities.

Developers will, therefore, find that there are quite a few options to choose from within the STM32 ports, in boards folder, as shown in the following two figures. Different STM32 development boards that are supported by MicroPython, including the Nucleo boards from STMicroelectronics, are shown in the following image:

B_L475E_IOT01A	stm32/Makefile: Allow a board to config either 1 or 2 firmware sections.
CERB40	stm32/boards: Update pins.csv to include USB pins where needed.
ESPRUINO_PICO	stm32/Makefile: Allow a board to config either 1 or 2 firmware sections.
HYDRABUS	stm32/Makefile: Allow a board to config either 1 or 2 firmware sections.
LIMIFROG	stm32/Makefile: Allow a board to config either 1 or 2 firmware sections.
NETDUINO_PLUS_2	stm32/boards: Update pins.csv to include USB pins where needed.
NUCLEO_F091RC	stm32/boards/NUCLEO_F091RC: Enable USART3-8 with default pins.
NUCLEO_F401RE	stm32/Makefile: Allow a board to config either 1 or 2 firmware sections.
NUCLEO_F411RE	stm32/Makefile: Allow a board to config either 1 or 2 firmware sections.
NUCLEO_F429ZI	stm32/can: Allow CAN pins to be configured per board.
NUCLEO_F446RE	stm32/Makefile: Allow a board to config either 1 or 2 firmware sections.
NUCLEO_F746ZG	stm32/boards: Update pins.csv to include USB pins where needed.
NUCLEO_F767ZI	stm32/boards: Ensure USB OTG power is off for NUCLEO_F767ZI.
NUCLEO_H743ZI	stm32/system_stm32: Introduce configuration defines for PLL3 settings.
NUCLEO_L432KC	stm32/boards/NUCLEO_L432KC: Specify L4 OpenOCD config file for this MCU.
NUCLEO_L476RG	stm32/Makefile: Allow a board to config either 1 or 2 firmware sections.

Here are different STM32 development boards that are supported by MicroPython, including the discovery boards from STMicroelectronics and the flagship PY board (PYB) from the creators of MicroPython:

OLIMEX_E407	stm32/boards: Update pins.csv to include USB pins where needed.
PYBLITEV10	stm32/Makefile: Allow a board to config either 1 or 2 firmware sections.
PYBV10	stm32/boards: Add configuration for putting mboot on PYBv1.x.
PYBV11	stm32/boards: Add configuration for putting mboot on PYBv1.x.
PYBV3	stm32/boards: Update pins.csv to include USB pins where needed.
PYBV4	stm32/can: Allow CAN pins to be configured per board.
STM32F411DISC	stm32/boards: Update pins.csv to include USB pins where needed.
STM32F429DISC	stm32/boards/STM32F429DISC: Enable UART as secondary REPL.
STM32F439	stm32/can: Allow CAN pins to be configured per board.
STM32F4DISC	stm32/boards: Update pins.csv to include USB pins where needed.
STM32F769DISC	stm32/main: Add configuration macros for board to set heap start/end.
STM32F7DISC	stm32/main: Add configuration macros for board to set heap start/end.
STM32L476DISC	stm32/boards/STM32L476DISC: Enable external RTC xtal to get RTC working.
STM32L496GDISC	stm32/boards: Add config files for new board, STM32L496GDISC.

Take a few minutes to browse the MicroPython Git repository and look at the different architectures and the boards that are available in each architecture. Open up a web browser and use your favorite distributor, such as Adafruit, Arrow, Digikey, Mouser, or SparkFun, to see which boards are available and what some of their key features are. In fact, it can be useful to create a simple table with the parameters so that you can later go back and select the right board for your project. For example, you may want to track parameters like the following:

- Board name
- Processor used
- Flash
- RAM
- Processor speed (remember, higher clocks = more energy consumed)
- On-board features that are worth noting

I've put together my own table for several boards that I've found to be interesting and that could be used for the projects in this book, as listed in the following table. While you review this table, note the vast differences in available features and memory! MicroPython can be run on very resource-constrained devices with as little as 128 KB of flash (maybe less!). Following is a short list of interesting development boards that already support MicroPython:

Board	Processor	Flash (KB)	RAM (KB)	On-board features
PYB V4	STM32F405RG	1024	192	Accelerometer, SD card, LEDs, and user and reset switches
Adafruit HUZZAH ESP8266	ESP8266	1024	80	Wi-Fi
BBC micro:bit	MKL26Z128VFM4	128	16	Accelerometer, Bluetooth LE, Magnetometer, and user switch
IoT Discovery Board	STM32L4	1024	128	Accelerometer, barometer, Bluetooth, Gyroscope RF, microphone, Magnetometer, and humidity and temperature sensors
NUCLEO_F429ZI	STM32F429ZI	2048	256	LED and user switch
NUCLEO_F746ZG	STM32F746ZG	512	320	LED and user switch

You have probably noticed that quite a few boards on my list are STM32 devices. The reason for this is that I am very familiar with the STM32 family and use it (and many other architectures) in my professional development efforts. While I work with a lot of different microcontroller vendors, the STM32 is the flagship for MicroPython, so it will have the most supported features and makes a really good choice.

Note that we are looking at boards that already exist in order to get started with developing projects for this book. It may very well be that you plan to create your own custom board. In this case, the exact board you want to create will not exist, but you will want to find a board that already supports your processor or has features that you want to include on your custom board.

In a later chapter, I will walk you through how to create your own custom board!

Selecting a development board using a KT matrix

A KT matrix is one of my favorite decision-making tools. For nearly any engineering decision where I believe there could be team contention, or where I want to make an objective decision in which my personal biases are removed, I create a KT matrix.

A KT matrix is a decision-making technique that uses a decision matrix to force a ranking among possible alternative solutions (`https://www.projectmanagement.com/wikis/ 233054/Forced-Ranking--A-K-A---Kepner-Tregoe--Decision-Matrix-`). Developers can identify criteria that are used to make the decision and provide a weight on how important each criterion is. Each member of a team (even a one-man team) can then objectively rank how well an option meets that criteria. Once each criterion is ranked, the weights are calculated and a numeric value results. The option with the highest value is the objective choice that best fits the criteria.

Now, I know this sounds interesting, so let's apply this technique to help us choose a development board. When selecting a development board, there are going to be several different criteria that need to be considered. For example, we might want to consider the following:

- Development board cost (sadly, this is usually the first and only criteria most developers and teams consider, which is completely flawed)
- Board features
- Processor clock speed and memory
- Community support around the board
- Available board examples
- Existing libraries and features for devices that might be interfaced
- Easily expandable

As you can imagine, we can have as many, or as few, criteria as we so choose.

Once we identify which ones we do want to consider, we can put them in the first column of a spreadsheet. In the second column, we would list the weight of how important that criteria is. I personally like to use a ranking from 1 – 5, where 5 is *can't live without* and 1 is basically not important (like how an engineer feels about doing something). The remaining columns are then used to list the development board but also the responses from each person in the team.

If I were to build such a matrix for three development boards and a team of two members, the resulting matrix would look something like the upcoming table. In this example, the team is evaluating how well the boards compare when considering different aspects of cost, the ecosystem, board features, and the engineer.

Each aspect is broken up into small subtopics. For example, board features that are being evaluated can include the following:

- Accelerometer
- Magnetometer
- Temperature sensor
- Humidity sensor
- Wi-Fi
- Bluetooth
- Arduino headers for shields

These may not all be important to be on board and could be external. The importance is adjusted using the weight. The KT matrix designed to evaluate which development board best fits a fictional application is shown as follows:

	Criteria	Weight	PYB V4			BBC micro:bit			IoT Discovery Board		
			Rating 1	Rating 2	Weighted Rating Total	Rating 1	Rating 2	Weighted Rating Total	Rating 1	Rating 2	Weighted Rating Total
Cost	Development Board	5	5	5	50	5	5	50	4	4	40
	External Sensors	5	3	4	35	3	3	30	5	5	50
	Lowest cost to get up to speed (Training)	3	5	5	30	5	5	30	5	5	30
EcoSystem	Highest adoption rate in target industry	4	5	5	40	4	4	32	3	3	24
	Most architectures supported	4	5	5	40	3	3	24	5	5	40
	Largest and most vibrant forum community (fast to respond)	3	5	5	30	4	4	24	4	5	27
	Fastest technical support available	4	4	4	32	4	4	32	4	4	32
	Highest quality professional training available	3	3	3	18	3	3	18	3	3	18
	Example projects and source available	5	5	5	50	4	3	35	4	3	35
Features	Accelerometer	5	5	5	50	5	5	50	5	5	50
	Magnetometer	3	0	0	0	5	5	30	5	5	30
	Temperature Sensor	3	3	3	18	0	0	0	5	5	30
	Humidity sensor	3	0	0	0	0	0	0	5	5	30
	Wi-Fi onboard	5	0	0	0	5	5	50	5	5	50
	Bluetooth	5	0	0	0	0	0	0	5	5	50
	Arduino headers	5	0	0	0	5	5	50	5	5	50
Engineer	Least amount of stress to implement	2	4	4	16	4	4	16	4	4	16
	Most fun / interesting	1	3	3	6	5	3	8	5	3	8
	Minimized labor intensity	5	4	5	45	5	5	50	5	5	50
	Least deadline constrained to get up to speed	3	4	4	24	4	4	24	4	4	24
	Most internal resources available	2	3	3	12	3	3	12	3	3	12
	Total	78	66	68	496	76	73	565	93	91	696
			PYB V4			BBC micro:bit			IoT Discovery Board		

After each member of the team has had a chance to review the criteria and rate it, we can see that, in this fictional example, the **IoT Discovery board** wins out over the other boards. That's not because the IoT Discovery board is better, rather it was only better based on my requirements for my fictional application.

MicroPython development processes and strategies

Developing embedded software using MicroPython can be quite a bit different than developing software using C/C++; however, at the same time, there are many tried and true development techniques and processes that still carry through. For example, when developing a MicroPython application, the software development life cycle doesn't change just because a different programming language is being used.

The **Software Development Life Cycle**, which is sometimes referred to as **SDLC**, defines best practices that developers should follow when developing software. These processes are usually grouped into five main categories:

1. Requirements
2. Design
3. Implementation
4. Testing
5. Maintenance

There are two really good resources that you can review, which provide a great overview of how software should be developed. It can be found and downloaded for free by performing a simple web search. The first is the IEEE **Software Engineering Body of Knowledge** (**SWEBOK**). The **SWEBOK** is a free download from IEEE, which covers the best practices that engineers should be following when they develop software along with processes and strategies.

Second, Renesas offers a Synergy Software Quality Handbook that they developed when they were creating their Renesas Synergy™ Platform. Their quality guide describes the processes that they used to develop and validate their software. This document has several gems that both professional and novice software developers will find extremely interesting and worth implementing in their own software development processes.

As you go through this book and either follow along with the projects or leverage the materials for your own projects, there are several processes and strategies that you should be following. These include the following:

- Using revision control
- Clearly documenting the software
- Leveraging the **Read-Eval-Print Loop** (**REPL**) serial interface
- Understanding the firmware update process

Throughout this book, we will be demonstrating and discussing these topics further but let's take a moment to briefly discuss them now.

Before starting any project, it is highly recommended that you create a revision control repository for the project. This can be done using popular online repositories such as GitHub or Bitbucket. The reason we want to use a revision control system is that, as the software is developed, we want to be able to save snapshots of the code base that are in working order. If we break something in the code, accidentally delete it, or discover a bug, we can use the revision control system to revert our code back to a good known base or compare our code with a previous version to hunt down a bug.

There will potentially be two different types of projects that you will want to create a repository for: kernel code and application code. Managing kernel code can be tricky because we must pull from the MicroPython mainline and any changes we make will either need to be pushed back and approved to enter the kernel, or we will need to manage updates from the mainline back into our own version. As you might imagine, this can be messy; however, we will discuss best practices to manage this when we create our own MicroPython board.

As we work through our application code, we also want to make sure that we clearly document the software. Python is an easy language to read, but it's also easy to write code that is completely perplexing and difficult to understand. Make sure that as you develop your software you include code comments to help you understand what the code is doing. While you are writing the software, it will make sense, but come back a week, month, or year later and that code could easily make no sense to you.

Personally, I prefer to document all my Python code using comments that are compatible with Doxygen. Doxygen is a tool that can generate software documentation by parsing source files that are commented in very specific ways. Doxygen is beyond the scope of this book, but I would recommend that you check out the Doxygen website and review my Doxygen articles and free templates, which can be downloaded from www.beningo.com. You might also want to review my book, *Reusable Firmware Development, Chapter 5, Documenting Firmware with Doxygen*, for a full explanation on how to use Doxygen for embedded software development.

As you should already know, the REPL is an interactive MicroPython prompt that allows a developer to access and interact with their development board running MicroPython. A REPL example that shows the MicroPython prompt can be seen in the following screenshot. The REPL allows developers to work from the MicroPython prompt and test out APIs and functions or execute their application script so that the board can run autonomously. The REPL can also be used to transfer files and perform advanced functions. Throughout this book, we will be using the REPL in detail to test out our modules and perform ad hoc programming.

Mastering the REPL is beyond the scope of this book. If you are currently not familiar with it, I highly recommend that you review the MicroPython tutorials and documentation to fully understand everything that can be done through the REPL. The REPL provides developers with an interactive Python Terminal to interact with the kernel modules and scripts:

```
● ● ● ● 🖥 beningo — screen /dev/tty.usbmodem3476355133332 115200 ▪ SCREEN — 8...
MicroPython v1.9.4-788-gf874e8184 on 2019-01-24; PYBv1.0 with STM32F405RG
Type "help()" for more information.
>>> []
```

Finally, firmware updates for MicroPython applications are extremely simple. Python application code is stored in plain text format internally on flash or externally on an SD card or eMMC device. Updating the application simply requires that a developer copy their latest code to their development board. The general process that I use to update firmware is as follows:

1. Stop any executing threads and applications.
2. Copy the new files to the development board.
3. Perform a soft reset using *Ctrl + D*.

At that point, the new firmware is installed, and the development board memory and peripheral have been set back to their default states. Commands can then be entered through the prompt or the application could be configured to start automatically. There are some ports that have USB, while others only have a serial interface. A few ports provide developers with over-the-air (Wi-Fi) update capabilities. We can even compile our application into the kernel code, which is often referred to as **frozen**. We can even convert our application modules into bytecode (mpy files) and place those on our filesystem. We will discuss all of these details throughout the book.

Useful development resources

There are several resources that you will want to make sure that you have on hand to develop your MicroPython-based projects. In many instances, these are the same tools that you would want to have whether you are a hobbyist or a professional developer. At a minimum, I would recommend that you purchase or download the following:

- Male to female 6" jumpers (https://www.sparkfun.com/products/9140)
- Male to male 6" jumpers (https://www.sparkfun.com/products/8431)

- Female to female 6" jumpers (`https://www.sparkfun.com/products/8430`)
- A terminal application such as Tera Term, or PuTTY
- A high-speed micro SD card (if your development board supports one)

I would highly recommend that you also pick-up a logic analyzer such as an 8-channel Saleae Logic. I've also found that using an SPI/I2C bus tool such as a Total Phase Aardvark can be a major time-saver to test and understand different sensors and ICs that will be integrated with the microcontroller. Developers who are interested in MicroPython kernel development will also want to pick-up a good debugger such as a SEGGER J-Link or a Keil U-Link.

As far as development boards go, each project will describe the specific board that was used to create the project. These may vary from one project to the next, but the source code is fully available and can be modified to work with any available development board with a little extra effort. I enjoy working with and experimenting with different boards, so there will be several that we will use throughout the book. Part of this, undoubtedly, stems from my work as a consultant, where I am often evaluating and analyzing what's currently available in the industry and determining where the industry is going.

Summary

Python has taken the software world by storm due to its elegant simplicity, ease to learn, but also its ability to easily scale and adapt to changing industry conditions. Python has found its way into the resource-constrained environment of microcontroller applications through MicroPython. In the rest of this book, we will explore how we can learn and leverage MicroPython for DIY and product development projects through several hands-on projects.

The projects in this book vary in terms of the skill level required to complete and understand them. Whether you are new to programming or a skilled professional, I will walk you through the design process that's required to complete projects successfully. In order to make sure that no reader is left behind, I will periodically point out useful resources to get up to speed on topics that might otherwise be outside the scope of this book but that will be helpful in completing the projects.

In the next chapter, we will examine several techniques developers can use for real-time scheduling and design our own cooperative scheduler.

Questions

1. What Python features make it a competing choice for use in embedded systems?
2. What three use cases does MicroPython match well with?
3. What business ramifications should be evaluated for using MicroPython?
4. What microcontroller architecture is supported the most by MicroPython?
5. What decision-making tool can be used to remove human bias?
6. What five categories make up the SDLC?
7. What key combination in the REPL will produce a soft reset?
8. What workbench resources do you need to develop a MicroPython project? Are you currently missing any?

Further reading

1. ASPENCORE Embedded Systems Survey, 2017, `www.embedded.com`
2. Know how to use a KT Matrix at `https://www.projectmanagement.com/wikis/233054/Forced-Ranking--A-K-A---Kepner-Tregoe--Decision-Matrix-`
3. *Reusable Firmware Development* by Jacob Beningo
4. MicroPython Tutorials, located at `https://docs.micropython.org/en/latest/pyboard/tutorial/index.html`

2
Managing Real-Time Tasks

Embedded systems need a way to schedule activities and respond to events in an efficient and deterministic manner. MicroPython offers developers several methods to achieve task scheduling.

In this chapter, we will review the methods that are most commonly used by developers and how to use `uasyncio` to schedule our own real-time tasks.

The following topics will be covered in this chapter:

- The need for real-time scheduling
- MicroPython scheduling techniques
- Writing a scheduling loop with `uasyncio`

Technical requirements

The example code for this chapter can be found in this book's GitHub repository: `https://github.com/PacktPublishing/MicroPython-Projects/tree/master/Chapter02`

In order to run the examples, you will require the following hardware and software:

- Pyboard Revision 1.0 or 1.1
- Pyboard Series-D
- Terminal application (such as PuTTy, RealTerm, or a Terminal)
- A text editor (such as VS Code or PyCharm)

The need for real-time scheduling

A real-time embedded system is a system with a dedicated purpose. The real-time system may operate standalone or it may be a component or subsystem of a larger device. Real-time systems are often event-driven and must produce the same output and timing when given the same initial conditions. A real-time system might be built using a microcontroller system that uses a bare-metal scheduler or a **real-time operating system** (**RTOS**) to schedule all of its system tasks. Alternatively, it could be built using a **System on Chip** (**SoC**) or **Field Programming Gate Array** (**FPGA**).

Every embedded system is not necessarily a real-time system. An application processor such as Raspberry Pi using Raspbian or Linux would not be a real-time system because, for a given set of inputs, while the system may give the same output, the time taken can vary wildly due to the multitasking nature of the system. General-purpose operating systems often interrupt tasks to handle OS-related functions, which results in the computing time being variable and non-deterministic.

There are several characteristics that can be used to identify a real-time embedded system:

- They're event-driven as they do not poll inputs.
- They're deterministic because when given the same initial conditions, they produce the same outputs in the same time frame.
- They're resource-constrained in some manner; for example, clock speed, memory, or energy consumption.
- They use a dedicated microcontroller-based processor.
- They may use an RTOS to manage system tasks.

Real-time system types

Real-time systems can be subdivided into two categories: soft real-time and hard real-time systems. Both types require that the system executes in a deterministic and predictable manner. However, they differ in what happens if a deadline is missed. A soft real-time system that misses a deadline is considered to be annoying to its users. It's undesirable for the deadline to be missed and may decrease the usefulness of the system after the deadline, but it's not critical. A hard real-time system, on the other hand, will dramatically decrease its usefulness after a deadline and results in a fatal system fault.

An example of a soft real-time system is a **Human Machine Interface** (**HMI**) with a touch controller that is controlling a home furnace. There may be a deadline where the system needs to respond to user input within 1 second of the screen being touched. If a user goes and touches the screen but the system doesn't respond for 3 or 4 seconds, the result is not world ending, but it may make the user complain about how slow the system is.

A hard real-time system could be an electronic braking system that needs to respond to a user pressing the brake pedal within 30 milliseconds. If a user were to press the brake and it took 2 seconds for the brakes to respond, the outcome could be critical. The system's failure to respond could result in injury to the user and dramatically decreases the usefulness of the embedded system.

It is possible to have an embedded system that has a mix of hard and soft requirements. The software in an embedded system is often subdivided into separate tasks based on function and timing requirements. We might find that the user interface on a system is considered to have soft real-time requirements, while the actuator control task must have hard real-time requirements. The type of system that is being built will often factor in the type of scheduler that is used in the solution.

Now, let's explore the different scheduling architectures that can be used with MicroPython to achieve real-time performance.

MicroPython scheduling techniques

When it comes to real-time scheduling using MicroPython, there are five common techniques that developers can employ. These techniques are as follows:

- Round-robin scheduling
- Periodic scheduling using timers
- Event-driven scheduling
- Cooperative scheduling
- MicroPython threads

We'll discuss them in detail in the subsequent sections. In the rest of this chapter, we will build example projects to explore several of these scheduling paradigms. We will also give special treatment to the `uasyncio` library at the end of this chapter, which is a powerful library for scheduling in MicroPython.

Round-robin scheduling

Round-robin scheduling is nothing more than an infinite loop that is created with a `while` loop. Inside the loop, developers add their task code and each task is executed sequentially, one after the other. While round-robin is the easiest and simplest scheduling paradigm to implement, there are several problems that developers will encounter when using it. First, getting the application tasks to run at the right rates can be difficult. Any code that is added or removed from the application will result in changes to the loop timing. The reason for this is that there is now more or less code to execute per loop. Second, each task has to be designed to recognize that there are other tasks, which means that they cannot block or wait for an event. They must check and then move on so that the other code has the opportunity to use the processor.

Round-robin scheduling can also be used with interrupts to handle any real-time events that might be occurring in the system. The loop handles all the soft real-time tasks, and then the hard real-time tasks are allocated to interrupt handlers. This helps to provide a balance that ensures each type is executed within a reasonable period of time. Round-robin is a good technique for beginners who are just trying to get a simple application up and running.

As we discussed earlier, adding or removing code affects the loop time, which can affect how the system performs. Round-robin schedulers can handle soft real-time tasks. Any events or hard real-time requirements need to be handled using interrupts. I often refer to this as round-robin scheduling with interrupts. A flowchart showing round-robin scheduling with interrupts can be seen in the following diagram:

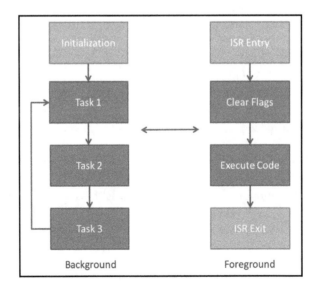

The main round-robin loop is often referred to as the background loop. This loop constantly executes in the background when there are no interrupts executing. The interrupts themselves are referred to as the foreground and handle any hard real-time events that need to be handled by the system. These functions trump background tasks and run immediately. It's also important to note that MicroPython handles clearing the interrupt flags for developers, so while they are shown in the preceding diagram, this detail is abstracted and handled by the MicroPython kernel.

In C, an application that uses round-robin scheduling might look something like the following:

```
int main (void)
{
    // Initialize the Microcontroller Unit (MCU) peripherals
    System_Init();
    while(1)
    {
        Task1();
        Task2();
        Task3();
    }
    // The application should never exit. Return 1 if
    // we do reach this point!

    return 1;
}
```

In this example, the code enters into the main function, initializes the microcontroller, and then enters into an infinite while loop that calls each task in order. This is a design pattern that every embedded software developer will have seen early in their career and should be quite familiar with.

Implementing round-robin in MicroPython is very similar:

1. First, it's important to recall that the application entry for MicroPython is located within main.py. To access any peripherals, the pyb library needs to be imported into the application (or the machine library for code that can be ported across MicroPython ports).
2. Second, any initialization and task functions need to be defined above the main loop. This ensures that they are defined before they are called by the Python interpreter.
3. Finally, an infinite loop is created using a while True statement. Each defined task is entered into this loop. The loop's timing can be controlled and tuned using pyb.delay().

Building a task manager using round-robin scheduling

Let's look at an example application that generates an LED **railroad** lights pattern. From a hardware perspective, this requires the use of two LEDs on the pyboard, such as the blue and yellow LEDs (on the pyboard series-D, you might use the green and blue LEDs). I prefer to use these because when we save new code to the pyboard, the red LED is used to show that the filesystem is being written to, and we don't want to interfere with that indicator. If we want one LED to be on while the other is off and then toggle them back and forth, we will need to initialize the blue LED to be on and the yellow to be off. We can then create two separate tasks, one to control the yellow LED and the other to control the blue LED. The Python code for this is as follows:

```
import pyb     # For uPython MCU features
import time

# define LED color constants
LED_RED = 1
LED_GREEN = 2
LED_BLUE = 3
LED_YELLOW = 4

def task1():
    pyb.LED(LED_BLUE).toggle()

def task2():
    pyb.LED(LED_GREEN).toggle()
```

However, the application is not complete until we initialize the LEDs and schedule the tasks to run. The following code shows the LED railroad application's initialization and task execution being written using round-robin scheduling. The `main` loop is delayed by `150` milliseconds, as well as each loop using the `sleep_ms` method from the `time` module. Importing `time` actually imports the `utime` module, but importing `time` can make porting code a little bit easier:

```
# Setup the MCU and application code to starting conditions
# The blue LED will start on, the yellow LED will be off
pyb.LED(LED_BLUE).on()
pyb.LED(LED_GREEN).off()

# Main application loop
while True:
    # Run the first task
    task1()

    # Run the second task
    task2()
```

```
# Delay 150 ms
pyb.delay(150)
```

These two code blocks, when combined, provide us with our first MicroPython application. Running the application on the pyboard can be done by copying the `main.py` script onto the development board. This can be done either directly, through a Python IDE such as PyCharm, or manually using the following steps:

1. Connect the pyboard to your computer with a USB cable.
2. Open your Terminal application and connect to the pyboard (refer to the **MicroPython documentation ǀ Quick reference for the pyboard ǀ MicroPython tutorial for the pyboard ǀ 3. Getting a MicroPython REPL prompt**, for details).
3. In the serial Terminal, press *Ctrl + C* to interrupt any currently running scripts.
4. Copy the script to the pyboard USB drive. While the copy is in progress, the red LED will be lit up.
5. Once the red light has gone off, the pyboard flash system will be updated.
6. In the Terminal, press *Ctrl + D* to perform a soft reset.

 For additional methods regarding how to deploy the application and develop within the PyCharm environment, refer to the `Appendix`, *Downloading and Running MicroPython Code*.

Now, you should see the blue and green LEDs toggling back and forth.

Periodic scheduling using timers

There may be applications where every task that needs to be executed is periodic, such as a push button that needs to be sampled every 10 milliseconds; a display that needs to be updated 60 times per second; or a sensor that is sampled at 10 Hz or interrupts when a value has gone out of range. In purely periodic systems, developers can architect their software to use periodic timers to execute tasks. Each timer can be set up to represent a single task that is executed at the desired rate. When the timer interrupt fires, the task executes.

When using periodic timers for task scheduling, it's important to keep in mind that the task code will be executed from an interrupt handler. Developers should follow best practices for using interrupts, such as the following:

- Keep ISRs short and fast.
- Perform measurements to understand interrupt timing and latency.

- Use interrupt priority settings to emulate pre-emption.
- Make sure that task variables are declared as volatile.
- Avoid calling multiple functions from an ISR.
- Disable interrupts as little as possible.
- Use `micropython.schedule()` to schedule a function to execute as soon as the MicroPython scheduler is able to.

When using periodic timers to schedule tasks, some of these best practices can be bent slightly. However, if the developer carefully monitors their task timing, bending the rules shouldn't be an issue. If it is, then any hard real-time activity can be handled by the interrupt task and then a round-robin loop can be notified to finish processing the task at a later time.

Timers guarantee that the task will be executed at a regular interval, no matter what is being executed, assuming that a higher-priority interrupt is not executing. The key thing to remember is that these tasks are executed within an interrupt, so the tasks need to be kept short and fast! Developers who use this method should handle any high-priority activity in the task and then offload the rest of the task to the background. For example, a task that handles an incoming byte over a **Universal Asynchronous Receiver/Transmitter (UART)** device can process the incoming byte by storing it in a circular buffer and then allowing a background task to later process the circular buffer. This keeps the interrupt task short and sweet while allowing the lower-priority processing to be done in the background.

Interrupts within MicroPython are also special in that they are **garbage collector (gc)** locked. What this means to a developer is that you cannot allocate memory in an ISR. All memory, classes, and so on need to be allocated before being used by the ISR. This has an interesting side effect in that if something goes wrong while executing an ISR, the developer has no way of knowing what went wrong! To get traceback information in situations where memory can't be allocated, such as in ISRs, developers can use the MicroPython emergency exception buffer. This is done by adding the following line of code to either the top of `main.py` or `boot.py`:

```
micropython.alloc_emergency_exception_buf(100)
```

This line of code is used to allocate `100` bytes to store the traceback information for ISRs and any other tracebacks that occur in areas where memory cannot be allocated. If an exception occurs, the Python traceback information is saved to this buffer and then printed to the REPL. This allows a developer to then figure out what they did wrong and correct it. The value of `100` is recommended as the buffer size by the MicroPython documentation.

When considering using timers for tasks, it's also important to recognize that each time an interrupt fires on an Arm Cortex®-M processor, there is a 12–15 clock cycle overhead to switch from the main code to the interrupt and then again to switch back. The reason for this overhead is that the processor needs to save and restore context information for the application when switching into and out of the interrupts. The nice thing is that these transitions, while they consume clock cycles, are deterministic!

Building a task manager using periodic scheduling

Setting up a timer to behave as a periodic task is exactly the same as setting up a timer in MicroPython for any other purpose. We can create an application very similar to our round-robin scheduler using timers by initializing a timer for each task in the application. The first timer will control the blue LED, while the second will control the green LED. Each timer will use a callback function to the task code that will be executed when the timer expires.

We can use the exact same format for our code that we used previously. We will initialize the blue LED as on, and the green LED as off. This allows us to let the timers free-run and generate the railroad pattern that we saw earlier. It's important to note that if we let the timer free-run, even if we stop the application in the REPL, the timers will continue to execute! The reason for this is that the timers are hardware peripherals that will run until the peripheral is disabled, even if we exit our application and return to the REPL. I mention this because any print statements you add to your callback functions will continue to populate the REPL, even after you halt the program, which can make it difficult to work or determine the state of the application.

When using timers to set up tasks, there is no need for an infinite `while` loop like we saw with the round-robin applications. The timers will just free-run. If the infinite loop is not added to `main.py`, background processing will fall back to the system REPL and sit there instead. I personally still like to include the `while` loop and some status information so that I know whether the MicroPython interpreter is executing code. In this example, we will put a sleep delay in the `main` loop and then calculate how long the application has been running.

The Python code for our tasks is identical to the round-robin example, except for the addition of the emergency exception buffer, as shown here:

```
import micropython # For emergency exception buffer
import pyb         # For uPython MCU
import time

micropython.alloc_emergency_exception_buf(100)
```

```
LED_RED = 1
LED_GREEN = 2
LED_BLUE = 3
LED_YELLOW = 4

def task1(timer):
    pyb.LED(LED_BLUE).toggle()

    return

def task2(timer):
    pyb.LED(LED_GREEN).toggle()

    return
```

Instead of calling the task code directly, we set up two timers – time 1, and timer 2 – with a frequency of 5 Hz (period of 200 milliseconds) and set up the callback function to call the tasks. The code to accomplish this is as follows:

```
pyb.LED(LED_BLUE).on()
pyb.LED(LED_GREEN).off()

# Create task timer for Blue LED
TimerBlueLed = pyb.Timer(1)
TimerBlueLed.init(freq=5)
TimerBlueLed.callback(task1)
print("Task 1 - Blue LED Toggle initialized ...")

# Create task timer for Green LED
TimerGreenLed = pyb.Timer(2)
TimerGreenLed.init(freq=5)
TimerGreenLed.callback(task2)
print("Task 2 - Green LED Toggle initialized ...")
```

The only code that's necessary for this example is the code for the main loop, which will do nothing more than print out how long our application has been running. To accomplish this, we need to sample the application start time using the time module's `ticks_ms` method and store it in `TimeStart`. We can then use `time.ticks_diff` to calculate the elapsed time between the current tick and the application start tick. The final piece of code is as follows:

```
TimeStart = time.ticks_ms()

while True:
    time.sleep_ms(5000)
    SecondsLive = time.ticks_diff(time.ticks_ms(), TimeStart) / 1000
    print("Executing for ", SecondsLive, " seconds")
```

Once the code is on the pyboard and executing, the REPL should display the information shown in the following screenshot. It shows timer-based task scheduling, which prints the current execution time in the REPL and toggles between the blue and green LEDs at 5 Hz. At this point, you know how to use timers to schedule periodic tasks:

```
MPY: sync filesystems
MPY: soft reboot
Task 1 - Blue LED Toggle initialized ...
Task 2 - Green LED Toggle initialized ...
Executing for   5.0   seconds
Executing for   10.0  seconds
Executing for   15.0  seconds
Executing for   20.0  seconds
Executing for   25.0  seconds
Executing for   30.0  seconds
Executing for   35.0  seconds
Executing for   40.0  seconds
Executing for   45.0  seconds
Executing for   50.0  seconds
Executing for   55.0  seconds
Executing for   60.0  seconds
Executing for   65.0  seconds
```

At this point, we are ready to examine some additional scheduling paradigms that are not completely mainstream within MicroPython, such as thread support.

MicroPython thread mechanism

The last scheduling paradigm that developers can use to schedule tasks is the MicroPython thread mechanism. In a microcontroller-based system, a thread is essentially a synonym for a task. There are some minor differences, but they are beyond the scope of this book. Developers can create threads that will contain task code. Each task could then use several different mechanisms to execute their task code, such as the following:

- Waiting on a queue
- Waiting on time using a delay
- Periodically monitoring for a polled event

The thread mechanism has been implemented directly from Python 3.x and provides developers with an easy method for creating separate tasks in their application. It is important to recognize that the Python thread mechanism is **NOT** deterministic. This means that it will not be useful for developing software that has a hard real-time requirement. The MicroPython thread mechanism is also currently experimental! Threads are not supported in all MicroPython ports and for the ones that are, a developer usually needs to enable threads and recompile the kernel in order to have access to the capability on offer.

For additional information on threads and their behavior, please refer to the *Further reading* section at the end of this chapter.

Starting with MicroPython version 1.8.2, there is support for an experimental threads module that developers can use to create separate threads. Using the threads module is not recommended for developers who are just getting started with MicroPython for several reasons. First, by default, threading is not enabled in the MicroPython kernel. Developers need to enable threading and then recompile and deploy the kernel. Second, since the threading module is experimental, it has not been ported to every MicroPython port yet.

If threads aren't officially supported and not recommended, why are we even talking about them? Well, if we want to understand the different scheduling mechanisms available to us with MicroPython, we need to include the mechanisms that are even experimental. So, let's dive in and talk about threading with MicroPython (even though you may not be able to run a threading application until you have learned how to recompile the kernel, which you will do in Chapter 5, *Customizing the MicroPython Kernel Start Up Code*).

When a developer creates a thread, they are creating a semi-independent program. If you think back to what a typical program looks like, it starts with an initialization section and then enters into an infinite loop. Every thread has this structure! There is a section to initialize the thread and its variables, followed by an independent loop. The loop itself can be periodic by using `time.sleep_ms()` or it can block an event, such as an interrupt.

Advantages of using threads in MicroPython

From an organizational standpoint, threads can be a good choice for many MicroPython applications, although similar behavior can be achieved using the `asyncio` library (which we will talk about shortly). There are several advantages that threads provide, such as the following:

- They allow a developer to easily break up their program into smaller constituents that can be assigned to individual developers.
- They help us improve the code so that it's scalable and reusable.
- They provide us with a small opportunity to decrease bugs in an application by breaking the application up into smaller, less complex pieces. However, as we mentioned previously, more bugs can be created by developers who are unfamiliar with how to use threads properly.

Considerations when using threads in MicroPython

For a Python programmer, before using threads in a MicroPython application, it makes a lot of sense to consider the potential consequences before immediately jumping to threads. There are a few important considerations that a developer needs to contemplate:

- Threads are not deterministic. When a Python thread is ready to execute, there is no mechanism in place for one thread to be executed before another.
- There is no real mechanism for controlling time slicing. Time slicing is when the CPU is shared between multiple threads that are currently ready to execute.
- To pass data around the application, developers may need to add additional complexities to their design, such as the use of queues.
- Developers who are not familiar with designing and implementing multi-threaded applications will find that inter-thread communication and syncing is full of pitfalls and traps. More time will be spent debugging and new developers will find that the other methods we've discussed are more appropriate for their applications.
- Support for threading is currently experimental in MicroPython (see `https://docs.micropython.org/en/latest/library/_thread.html`).
- Threads are not supported on all MicroPython ports, so the applications may be less portable than expected.
- Threads will use more resources than the other techniques we've discussed in this chapter.

Building a task manager using threads

Despite a few drawbacks to using threads, they can be a very powerful tool for developers who understand how to use them in the context of a real-time embedded system. Let's take a look at how we can implement our railroad blinky LED application using threads. The first step to developing the application is to create our threads, just like how we created our tasks in the previous examples. In this case, though, there are several key modifications that are worth noting.

First, we need to import the threading module (`_thread`). Second, we need to define a thread as a regular function declaration. The difference here is that we treat each function like a separate application where we insert a `while True` statement. If the thread were to exit the infinite loop, the thread would cease operating and not use any more CPU time.

In this example, we're controlling the LED toggling time by using the `time.sleep_ms` function and setting our thread loop time to `150` milliseconds, just like we did in the previous examples. Our code now looks as follows:

```
import micropython # For emergency exception buffer
import pyb          # For uPython MCU features
import time         # For time features
import _thread      # For thread support

micropython.alloc_emergency_exception_buf(100)

LED_RED = 1
LED_GREEN = 2
LED_BLUE = 3
LED_YELLOW = 4

def task1():
    while True:
        pyb.LED(LED_BLUE).toggle()
        time.sleep_ms(150)

def task2():
    while True:
        pyb.LED(LED_GREEN).toggle()
        time.sleep_ms(250)
```

We can initialize the system the exact same way that we did before by initializing the blue LED to on and the green LED to off. The difference in our thread application is that we want to write some code that will spawn off our two threads. This can be done with the following code:

```
pyb.LED(LED_BLUE).on()
pyb.LED(LED_GREEN).off()

_thread.start_new_thread(task1, ())
_thread.start_new_thread(task2, ())
```

As you can see, we're using the `_thread.start_new_thread` method here. This method requires two parameters. The first is the function that should be called when the thread is ready to run. In this case, these are our `Led_BlueToggle` and `Led_YellowToggle` functions. The second parameter is a tuple that needs to be passed to our threads. In this case, we have no parameters to pass, so we just pass an empty tuple.

Before running this code, it's useful to note that the rest of the script is the same as the code in our timer example. We create an infinite loop for the script and then report how long the application has been running for. As a reminder, the code for this is as follows:

```
TimeStart = time.ticks_ms()

while True:
    time.sleep_ms(5000)
    SecondsLive = time.ticks_diff(time.ticks_ms(), TimeStart) / 1000
    print("Executing for ", SecondsLive, " seconds")
```

An interesting question to ask yourself as you run the threaded code is, *How long will it take before these LEDs are no longer blinking in an alternating pattern?* Since the threads are not deterministic, over time, there is the potential for these threads to get out of sync and for the application to no longer behave the way that we expect it to. If you are going to run the code, let it run for a while, over several hours, a day, or even a week, and observe the application's behavior.

Event-driven scheduling

Event-driven scheduling can be an extremely convenient technique for developers whose systems are driven by events that are happening on the system. For example, the system may need to respond to a user button press, an incoming data packet, or a limit switch being reached by an actuator.

In event-driven systems, there may be no need to have a periodic background timer; instead, the system can just respond to the event using interrupts. Event-driven scheduling may have our common infinite `while` loop, but that loop will do nothing or put the system into a low-power state until an event occurs. Developers who are using event-driven systems can follow the interrupt best practices that we discussed earlier and should also read the MicroPython documentation on ISR rules, which can be found at `https://docs.micropython.org/en/latest/reference/isr_rules.html`. It's important to note that when you do use interrupts, MicroPython automatically clears the interrupt flag for the developer so that using interrupts is simplified.

Cooperative scheduling

Cooperative scheduling is a technique that developers can leverage to achieve task periodicity without using a timer for every task. Cooperative schedulers are one of the most widely used schedulers throughout embedded system history. A quick look at any of the embedded.com embedded systems surveys will easily show that.

A cooperative scheduler often uses a single timer to create a system tick that the scheduler then uses to determine whether the task code should be executed. The cooperative scheduler provides a perfect balance for developers who need periodicity, simplicity, flexibility, and scalability. They are also a stepping stone toward an RTOS.

So far, we have examined the methods that developers can use in MicroPython to schedule activities. In the next section, we will discuss how we can use the `asyncio` library to cooperatively schedule tasks. This method is perhaps the most commonly used method by MicroPython developers due to its flexibility and precise timing beyond the methods that we have already examined.

Cooperative multitasking using asyncio

So far, we have examined how we can schedule tasks in a MicroPython-based system using round-robin, timers, and threads. While threads may be the most powerful scheduling option available, they aren't deterministic schedulers and don't fit the bill for most MicroPython applications. There is another scheduling algorithm that developers can leverage to schedule tasks within their systems: cooperative scheduling.

A cooperative scheduler, also known as cooperative multitasking, is basically a round-robin scheduling loop that includes several mechanisms to allow a task to yield the CPU to other tasks that may need to use it. The developer can fine-tune the way that their application behaves, and their tasks execute without adding the complexity that is required for a pre-emptive scheduler, like those included in an RTOS. Developers who decide that a cooperative scheduler fits their application best will need to make sure that each task they create can complete before any other task needs to execute, hence the name *cooperative*. The tasks cooperate to ensure that all the tasks are able to execute their code within their requirements but are not held to their timing by any mechanism.

Developers can develop their own cooperative schedulers, but MicroPython currently provides the `asyncio` library, which can be used to create cooperatively scheduled tasks and to handle asynchronous events in an efficient manner. In the rest of this chapter, we will examine `asyncio` and how we can use it for task scheduling within our embedded applications.

Introducing asyncio

The `asyncio` module was added to Python starting in version 3.4 and has been steadily evolving ever since. The purpose of `asyncio` is to handle asynchronous events that occur in Python applications, such as access to input/output devices, a network, or even a database. Rather than allowing a function to block the application, `asyncio` added the functionality for us to use coroutines that can yield the CPU while they wait for responses from asynchronous devices.

MicroPython has supported `asyncio` in the kernel since **version 1.11** through the `uasyncio` library. Prior versions still supported `asyncio`, but the libraries had to be added manually. This could be done through several means, such as the following:

- Copying the `usyncio` library to your application folder
- Using `micropip.py` to download the `usyncio` library
- Using `upip` if there is a network connection

If you are unsure whether your MicroPython port supports `asyncio`, all you need to do is type the following into the REPL:

```
import usyncio
```

If you receive an import error, then you know that you need to install the library before continuing. Peter Hinch has put together an excellent guide regarding `asyncio` with instructions for installing the library that you can find at `https://github.com/peterhinch/micropython-async/blob/master/TUTORIAL.md#0-introduction`.

It's important to note that the support for `asyncio` in MicroPython is for the features that were introduced in Python 3.4. Very few features from the Python 3.5 or above `asyncio` library have been ported to MicroPython, so if you happen to do more in-depth research into `asyncio`, please keep this in mind to avoid hours of debugging.

The main purpose of `asyncio` is to provide developers with a technique for handling asynchronous operations in an efficient manner that doesn't block the CPU. This is done through the use of coroutines, which are sometimes referred to as **coros**. A coroutine is a specialized version of a Python generator function that can suspend its execution before reaching a return and indirectly passes control to another coroutine. Coroutines are a technique that provides concurrency to a Python application. Concurrency basically means that we can have multiple functions that appear to be executing at the same time but are actually running one at a time in a cooperative manner. This is not parallel processing but cooperative multitasking, which can dramatically improve the scalability and performance of a Python application compared to other synchronous methods.

The general idea behind `asyncio` is that a developer creates several coroutines that will operate asynchronously with each other. Each coroutine is then called using a task from an event loop that schedules the tasks. This makes the coroutines and tasks nearly synonymous. The event loop will execute a task until it yields execution back to the event loop or to another coroutine. The coroutine may block waiting for an I/O operation or it may simply sleep if the coroutine wants to execute at a periodic interval. It's important to note, however, that if a coroutine is meant to be periodic, there may be jitter in the period, depending on the timing for the other tasks and when the event loop can schedule it to run again.

The general behavior for how coroutines work can be seen in the following diagram, which represents an overview of using coroutines with the `asyncio` library. This diagram is a modified version of the one presented by Matt Trentini at *Pycon AU* in 2019 during his talk on `asyncio` in MicroPython:

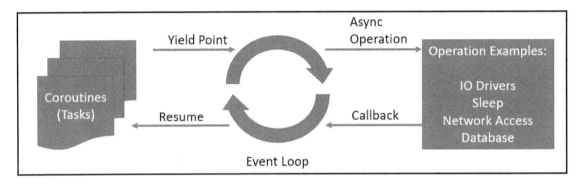

As shown in the preceding diagram, the **Event Loop** schedules a task to be executed that has 100% of the CPU until it reaches a yield point. A **yield point** is a point in the coroutine where a blocking operation (asynchronous operation) will occur and the coroutine is then willing to give up the CPU until the operation is completed. At this point, the event loop will then schedule other coroutines to run. When the asynchronous event occurs, a callback is used to notify the **Event Loop** that the event has occurred. The **Event Loop** will then mark the original coroutine as ready to run and will schedule it to resume when other coroutines have yielded the CPU. At that point, the coroutine can resume operation, but as we mentioned earlier, there could be some time that elapses between the receipt of the callback and the coroutine resuming execution, and this is by no means deterministic.

Now, let's examine how we can use `asyncio` to rewrite our blinky LED application using cooperative multitasking.

A cooperative multitasking blinky LED example

The first step in creating a railroad blinky LED example is to import the `asyncio` library. In MicroPython, there is not an `asyncio` library exactly, but a `uasyncio` library. To improve portability, many developers will import `uasyncio` as if it were the `asyncio` library by importing it at the top of their application, as follows:

```
import uasyncio as asyncio
```

Next, we can define our LEDs, just like we did in all our other examples, using the following code:

```
LED_RED = 1
LED_GREEN = 2
LED_BLUE = 3
LED_YELLOW = 4
```

If you look back at our example of writing a thread-based application, you'll recall that our `task1` code looked as follows:

```
def task1():
    while True:
        pyb.LED(LED_BLUE).toggle()
        time.sleep_ms(150)

 def task2():
    while True:
        pyb.LED(LED_GREEN).toggle()
        time.sleep_ms(150)
```

This is important to review because creating a coroutine will follow a similar structure! In fact, to tell the Python interpreter that our tasks are asynchronous coroutines, we need to add the `async` keyword before each of our task definitions, as shown in the following code:

```
async def task1():
    while True:
        pyb.LED(LED_BLUE).toggle()
        time.sleep_ms(150)
async def task2():
    while True:
        pyb.LED(LED_GREEN).toggle()
        time.sleep_ms(150)
```

The functions are now coroutines, but they are missing something very important: a yield point! If you examine each of our tasks, you can tell that we really want our coroutine to yield once we have toggled our LED and are going to wait 150 milliseconds. The problem with these functions as they are currently written is that they are making a blocking call to time.sleep_ms. We want to update this with a call to asyncio.sleep_ms and we want to let the interpreter know that we want to relinquish the CPU at this point. In order to do that, we are going to use the await keyword.

The await keyword, when reached by the coroutine, tells the event loop that it has reached a point in its execution where it will be waiting for an event to occur and it is willing to give up the CPU to another task. At this point, control is handed back to the event loop and the event loop can decide what task should be executed next. Using this syntax, our task code for the railroad blinky LED applications would be updated to the following:

```
async def task1():
    while True:
        pyb.LED(LED_BLUE).toggle()
        await asyncio.sleep_ms(150)
async def task2():
    while True:
        pyb.LED(LED_GREEN).toggle()
        await asyncio.sleep_ms(150)
```

For the most part, the general structure of our coroutine/task functions remains the same. The difference is that we define the function as async and then use await where we expect the asynchronous function call to be made.

At this point, we just initialize the LEDs using the following code:

```
pyb.LED(LED_BLUE).on()
pyb.LED(LED_GREEN).off()
```

Then, we create our event loop.

Creating the event loop for this application requires just four lines of code. The first line will assign the asyncio event loop to a loop variable. The next two lines create tasks that assign our coroutines to the event loop. Finally, we tell the event loop to run forever and our coroutines to execute. These four lines of code look as follows:

```
loop = asyncio.get_event_loop()
loop.create_task(task1())
loop.create_task(task2())
loop.run_forever()
```

As you can see, we can create any number of tasks and pass the desired coroutine to the `create_task` method in order to get them into the event loop. At this point, you could run this example and see that you have an efficiently running railroad blinky LED program that uses cooperative multitasking.

Going further with asyncio

Unfortunately, there just isn't enough time to discuss all the cool capabilities that are offered by `asyncio` in MicroPython applications. However, as we progress through this book, we will use `asyncio` and its additional capabilities as we develop our various projects. For those of you who want to dig deeper right now, I would highly recommend checking out Peter Hinch's `asyncio` tutorial, which also covers how you can coordinate tasks, use queues, and more, with `asyncio`. You can find the tutorial and some example code at `https://github.com/peterhinch/micropython-async/blob/master/TUTORIAL.md#0-introduction`.

Summary

In this chapter, we explored several different types of real-time scheduling techniques that can be used with a MicroPython project. We found that there are many different techniques that a MicroPython developer can leverage to schedule activities in their application. We found that each of these techniques has its place and varies based on the level of complexity a developer wants to include in their scheduler. For example, MicroPython threads can be used, but they are not fully supported in every MicroPython port and should be considered an in-development feature.

After looking at several techniques, we saw that the `asyncio` library may be the best choice for developers looking to get started with MicroPython. Python developers are already familiar with it and `asyncio` provides developers with cooperative scheduling capabilities that can provide them with the ability to handle asynchronous events in an efficient, non-blocking manner. This allows developers to get more out of their applications while wasting fewer cycles.

In the next chapter, we will explore how we can write drivers for a simple application that uses a push button to control the state of its RGB LEDs.

Questions

1. What characteristics define a real-time embedded system?
2. What four scheduling algorithms are commonly used with MicroPython?
3. What best practices should a developer follow when using callbacks in MicroPython?
4. What process should be followed to load new code onto a MicroPython board?
5. Why would a developer place `micropython.alloc_emergency_exception_buf(100)` in their application?
6. What reasons might deter a developer from using the `_thread` library?
7. What keywords indicate that a function is being defined as a coroutine?

Further reading

Here is a list of references you can refer to:

- `https://www.smallsurething.com/private-methods-and-attributes-in-python/`
- `https://hackernoon.com/concurrent-programming-in-python-is-not-what-you-think-it-is-b6439c3f3e6a`
- `https://realpython.com/async-io-python/`
- `https://realpython.com/async-io-python/`

3
Writing a MicroPython Driver for an I/O Expander

The ability to design and implement a driver is an important skill in embedded software development. Whether the driver is for an internal peripheral or for external sensors and **input/output** (**I/O**) capabilities, developers need to design and construct drivers that are flexible and scalable.

In this chapter, we will explore how to properly design drivers by implementing a project that uses an external I/O chip to interface with an RGB LED pushbutton. We will design a MicroPython driver to perform I/O using the external chip and to drive the RGB LEDs using the pyboard's **Pulse Width Modulation** (**PWM**) channels.

The following topics will be covered in this chapter:

- The RGB pushbutton I/O expander project requirements
- The hardware and software architecture design
- Creating the class outline
- Project construction
- Testing and verification

Technical requirements

The example code used in this chapter can be found at the following GitHub location: `https://github.com/PacktPublishing/MicroPython-Projects/tree/master/Chapter03`

To be able to run the examples and build your own scheduler, you will need to have the following hardware and software:

- Pyboard revision 1.0 or 1.1
- A RobotDyn I2C 8-bit PCA8574 I/O expander module, or equivalent
- An Adafruit RGB pushbutton PN: 3423, or equivalent
- A breadboard
- 6" jumpers
- A Terminal application (PuTTy, RealTerm, Terminal, or one of many others)
- A text editor, such as PyCharm

The RGB pushbutton I/O expander project requirements

The primary goal for this project is to gain experience with developing a driver for external chips using MicroPython. In order to gain this experience, we will select hardware that allows us to expand the I/O capabilities of the pyboard and connect an RGB pushbutton to the expanded I/O. Before we jump into selecting components or writing any code, we first need to define the requirements for this project. We have two different sets of requirements that need to be considered: hardware and software. Let's look at each set of requirements individually.

Hardware requirements

The hardware requirements for this project are relatively loose. As we saw in the last chapter, we can list out our requirements and, within the requirements, define any constraints that we want. In general, we want our requirements to be general enough that engineers can make engineering decisions on what they use. We don't want to tie their hands completely by saying, for example, that they must use a specific pushbutton or microcontroller (even though we may do this for our own purposes in this book). They should be able to review the requirements and then perform a trade study on which technologies and hardware help them to best meet their requirements.

For our pushbutton project, we can define a few simple requirements:

- The hardware needs to be based on a microcontroller that supports MicroPython.
- A pushbutton needs to be used to accept user input.
- The pushbutton needs to be capable of displaying a multitude of colors through RGB LEDs.
- The hardware needs to support the pushbutton through an external I/O expander chip in order to reserve I/O on the MicroPython board for future expansion.

As you can see from these four requirements, you can select nearly any MicroPython-capable microcontroller, your own I/O expansion chips, and even your own RGB pushbutton! The hardware requirements for this project are quite relaxed, which is not always the case in every project.

Software requirements

The software requirements for this project are also straightforward:

- The RGB LED will display, on startup, the color red in a pattern that starts with a 0% duty cycle and increases by 2.5% every 25 milliseconds. When the duty cycle reaches 100%, the intensity will decrease by 2.5% every 25 milliseconds and then the cycle will repeat.
- Pressing the pushbutton will change the color based on the number of times it has been pressed:
  - The first press: Green
  - The second press: Blue
  - The third press: White
  - The fourth press: Red
  - The fifth press: Repeat pattern
- The software needs to be written so that it contains two scalable and reusable drivers:
  - An I/O expander driver
  - An RGB pushbutton driver

Again, these requirements demonstrate the features that need to be implemented and we leave the implementation details up to the developer's best judgment.

The hardware and software architecture design

At this stage in the project, we've discovered the requirements for the project. We are now going to develop the hardware and software architecture. The best way to picture an architecture is through a map that is general enough to provide directions to where we need to head but does not provide enough details to restrict how we get there. The architecture should be flexible so that we can deal with any changing requirements on the fly.

For our purposes, we will use this section to first explore the high-level architecture and then develop the detailed design that we can use to construct the project in the next section.

The hardware architecture

When it comes to the hardware architecture, the best way to understand the main pieces and how they connect and interact with each other is to create a hardware block diagram. The block diagram can be generated using several different methods. The first, and my preferred method, is to use the schematic capture tool. These tools often have high-level organizational elements that allow a schematic page to be represented as a block.

Interconnects can be created between the blocks, which then shows how the blocks interact with each other and also provides an easy way to navigate the schematic project. **Altium** is a tool that has such features but, unfortunately, it's a professional development tool and probably outside the price point for most individuals and readers of this book. Some alternatives that you might consider include **Eagle** or **Altium CircuitMaker**.

Another method that can be used is to create the block diagram in a program such as Microsoft PowerPoint. While this method is not as functional as creating the architecture in a schematic capture program, it does produce a *pretty picture* that is easier to look at, analyze, distribute, and use in presentations and books. We are going to use this method in this book.

The architecture for our RGB pushbutton and I/O expander project is quite simple and contains only four elements:

- The pushbutton
- RGB LEDs
- An I/O expander
- A MicroPython board

When developing the architecture, we want to place these components in our diagram and then identify what the inputs and outputs for each block look like. The result should be an architectural diagram similar to the one shown here:

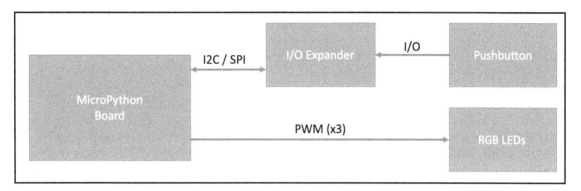

Notice that, in our diagram, we aren't listing out specific parts yet. Also, we are constraining which interfaces are being used and showing the flow of data through the system using arrows.

Detailed hardware design

Now that we understand the high-level hardware architecture, we can start to dive into the details. The first step is to perform a trade study and select the different components we are going to use in our design. Since this project is just about an RGB pushbutton and an I/O expander, we can start by specifying that we are going to use the MicroPython hardware we have around the lab and the pyboard.

Next, we need to examine the I/O expanders that we can use with our pushbutton. If we look back at our requirements, there really isn't too much there to constrain us, so we will use the best practices. We will select an I/O expander that uses an I2C bus in order to limit the number of pins used and to provide flexibility to expand the design later. We also want to find an I2C device that is easy to use. If you do a search for I/O expanders on your favorite supplier website, such as Digi-Key, Mouser, SparkFun, or Adafruit, you might come across the PCA8574. The PCA8574 is an 8-bit I/O expander that, by default, sets the eight I/O lines to inputs. It has no internal registers, which will dramatically simplify the software implementation. We could use a standard development board for the PCA8574 or buy an adapter board, but I found that the RobotDyn PCA8574AD I2C 8-bit I/O expander module had a great footprint and cost for the expansion I/O module.

Finally, we need to select our RGB pushbutton. Again, we don't have any major requirements for the pushbutton. It doesn't have to work with automotive voltages or withstand outside environments. You can select whatever pushbutton meets your own interests. There are two pushbuttons that I have evaluated and found to be interesting. Let's examine them in a little more detail.

Selecting a pushbutton

The first is the Schurter Inc. 3-101-399 RGB pushbutton switch, which is a single-pull, single-throw capacitive switch. This switch comes with all the leads already attached, so they simply need to be connected to the pyboard. Since the switch does use capacitance, there is no physical movement on the switch. This makes it interesting in an instance where a button is pressed repeatedly and there would usually be concern about wearing out the switch. On the other hand, if it is going to be used in environments where a gloved hand would be used, the capacitive technology would not work.

The second switch is the Adafruit Rugged Metal pushbutton (product ID 3423). This switch supports a maximum voltage of 6 volts. The switch also does not come with the leads preinstalled, so there is a little bit of soldering that needs to be done in order to get the switch hooked up to the development board. The switch is also a mechanical switch but is designed for industrial use and, since it does not need extra electronics for capacitance sensing, it is nearly half the cost of the Schurter button.

While both switches look like they would work perfectly for our application, it's important to really dig into the component datasheets. I discovered that the Schurter button provides a constant current source to its RGB LEDs. This means that if we try to PWM the LEDs, the onboard electronics will actually average out the signal and provide a steady brightness level for the LEDs. This means that we will not be able to meet our requirement for dimming the LEDs. Therefore, the Schurter pushbutton, while interesting, does not meet our requirements.

The I/O expander schematic

At this point, we have all the information that we need to develop a detailed schematic diagram for our project, as follows:

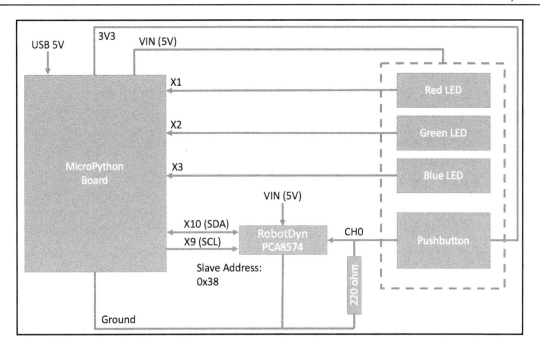

This design is fairly straightforward. First, the pyboard is supplied 5 volts through the **USB** or **VIN** pin. The 5-volt power rail is used to power the LEDs and the RobotDyn PCA8574. The pyboard onboard regulator also converts this rail into a 3.3-volt power rail that is used as the pushbutton power supply.

Next, the negative side of the LEDs, the **cathode**, is connected to the **X1**, **X2**, and **X3** pins. These pins are associated with an internal timer that allows us to generate a PWM signal on them. When these pins provide a 100% duty cycle, the LEDs will turn off. Providing a 0% duty cycle will turn them on. While this seems backward, it's the result of the hardware components. To switch this around in the hardware, a transistor can be placed between the LED and the pyboard pin, which inverts the signal. This would also allow more current to flow through the LEDs, which would make them brighter, but would also potentially require a current limiting resistor in series with the diode. In order to minimize the hardware, we will resolve this later in the software.

Finally, we have the RobotDyn PCA8574. The PCA8574 is connected to the pyboard through **X9** and **X10** with the I2C slave address set to its default value of **0x38** (56 decimal). If there were other I2C devices onboard, we could adjust the address as needed. When the pushbutton is released and not pressed, it provides 3.3 volts to the PCA8574 input channel 0, which is read as a high state. We used a 220-ohm resistor, which could be scaled to 1 or 10K to minimize the leakage current, to pull the voltage to ground and show that it is in a pressed state.

The software architecture

In order to develop any piece of software, a developer usually requires the use of at least three different diagrams. The full list of diagrams can be found in the UML standard, which is referenced at the end of this chapter in the *Further reading* section. To create our pushbutton application, we require three diagrams:

- An **application flowchart**
- A **state diagram**
- A **class diagram** (for our API and driver design)

Let's start by examining the flowchart, which can be seen here:

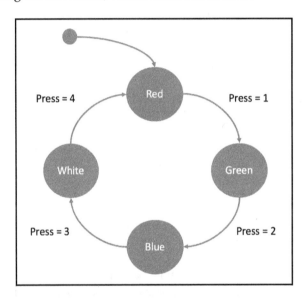

The best way to proceed with any design is to keep things simple. For our RGB pushbutton application, all we need to do is read the switch and update the PWM state periodically. The switch characteristics are fine to debounce at 25 milliseconds and updating the PWM duty cycle at this rate is below the human perception threshold, so it will have a smooth appearance as it changes. For these reasons, we are just going to use a simple round-robin scheduler to accomplish our task.

As seen in the preceding diagram, we can start by initializing the application and then move into the main program loop. This loop reads the button and then processes its state. If the button has just been released, it will increment the system state, which is shown in a state diagram that we will discuss shortly. After processing the button, a new PWM value is generated and sent to the LEDs.

Now, at this point, you are probably starting to realize that this flow chart is demonstrating the high-level behavior of the application. As the designer, we can decide how deep into the details we want to get. We can say that this is good enough and move on to other diagrams that we find useful or we could literally dive into every path and branch we want the software to take. For this project, we will keep the diagrams at a high level and allow our implementation to fill in the details.

A moment ago, we mentioned that we need more than one diagram to fully understand the software that we are designing. The second diagram that is useful for developers is the **state diagram**. This allows us to view the application as a series of states that occur and the events that can transition from one state to the next. The following diagram shows the different states that the system will generate on the RGB LEDs based on the number of times that the button has been pressed:

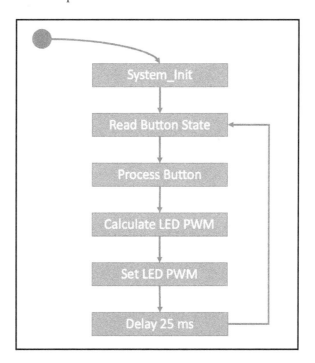

As seen in the state diagram, the application will start with the red LED on. Pressing and releasing the button once will result in the red LED turning off and the blue LED turning on. Each press of the button will change the color state up until the states repeat with red. A variable is used to track how many times the button has been pressed, which then changes the color that is displayed.

The final diagram that will be useful for us to create in order to understand the software and its organization is the **class diagram**. We discussed in the previous chapter how we can use the class diagram to not only design our object-oriented structure but also to define our APIs. The design of our RGB pushbutton application can be seen here:

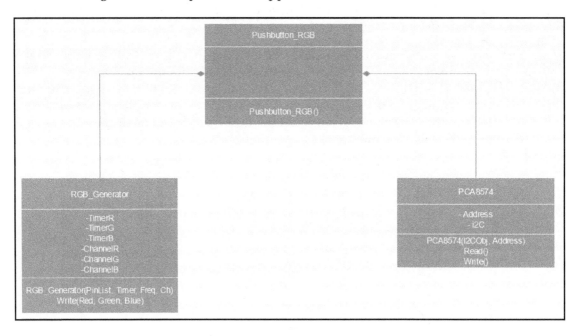

The way we are going to design our interface and drivers is by providing a single class, the RGB_Pushbutton class, which is a composition of RGB_Generator and a RobotDynPCA8574 class. RobotDynPCA8574 will handle the I2C communication with the I/O expander and RGB_Generator will handle the PWM generation for the LEDs. When composed together, there are only two functions that we need to concern ourselves with.

Firstly, RGB_Set takes three duty cycle values between 0 and 100 that represent the red, green, and blue LEDs. During instantiation, the class object requires the pinlist be provided for which pins the LEDs are connected to, the timer that will be used to generate the PWM along with its frequency, and the PWM channels that will be used. This provides everything required to generate the PWM for each LED.

Secondly, the read method will be used to read the state of all eight channels on the I/O expander. This provides a quick and easy way to get the overall status of the channels by the most efficient means necessary.

Armed with our hardware and software architecture designs, we are now ready to start building the project and implementing our software.

Project construction

Now that the design for the hardware and the software has been thought through, we are ready to start building. There are different ways that we can go about building the project.

First, we could assemble one piece of hardware at a time and develop the software for that piece and, once it's working, add additional pieces. This is a great approach and one that I often use on more complex projects because it allows us to focus on just a single feature. Each feature can be developed and tested, with integration coming later.

Second, we can fully assemble the hardware and then develop the software. This approach is often used for smaller projects that may not have a bunch of moving pieces. For this project, we will use the second approach since we only have the **external I/O expander** and the **pushbutton**.

Building the hardware

For this project, we are going to prototype out the hardware using a breadboard. This will allow us to easily reconfigure and adjust the hardware on the fly without having to take out a soldering iron to make adjustments. No matter how simple or complex a project is, I've always found that breadboarding the circuits first is a great way to improve the odds that the first spin of a **printed circuit board** (**PCB**) will work as expected.

In order to assemble this project, I recommend gathering all of the components listed in the *Technical requirements* section of this chapter. It would also be a good idea to keep the flowchart (of different states that the system will generate on the RGB LEDs based on the number of times that the button has been pressed) readily available. As seen previously in *The I/O expander schematic* section, the schematic diagram tells us where our connections need to be made. With a breadboard and jumpers, it's important to realize that the prototype is going to be messy! When I am professionally developing hardware, I custom-cut every jumper and run the wire right against the breadboard so that the connections can be easily traced and so that the breadboard has a professional polish to it.

As you can see in the following photograph, the fully assembled prototype using pre-manufactured jumpers adds some chaos to the look, but it's still functional and gets the job done:

At this point, you can go ahead and wire up your own setup. Be careful to make sure that you don't accidentally connect anything that is 5V to anything that is a 3.3V input! If you do, it could potentially damage the microcontroller pin. Once you have assembled the board, we are ready to start implementing the software. We will start by developing a driver for the I/O expander.

I/O expander driver construction

For PCA8574, we are going to create a separate file, named PCA8574.py, that includes all the driver capabilities and functions for the I/O expander. We are going to use the PCA8574 class specification from the design of our RGB pushbutton application to guide our driver construction.

The first step is to create our class definition and constructor. The class will be named PCA8574_IO so that we have a little description as to what that chip actually is. The class initialization requires two pieces of information: an object that represents the initialized I2C bus and the slave address of PCA8574. This class can be instantiated multiple times for different addresses if we have more than one device connected to our application. The class definition and initialization is as follows:

```
class Pca8574_Io:

    def __init__(self, i2c_object, slave_address):
        assert slave_address < 256, "Slave Address >= 256!"
```

```
    self.Address = slave_address
    self.I2C = i2c_object
```

Notice that I am also using `assert` to check that the `SlaveAddress` parameter is within the design address ranges of *0-255*. Assertions are good to include during your software development phase. An assertion is basically a sanity check that, at a specific point in a program, checks that the conditions are as you expect them to be. If they are not, then there is a bug in the application. Assertions are normally turned off prior to the final validation testing for production.

Once the class is defined, we need to implement our two methods: `read` and `write`. These methods allow our application to interact directly with the `PCA8574` I/O expander chip. In the implementation, we will wrap our attempts to write and read from the I2C bus in a `try/except` block. The `try/except` block is the equivalent of the C++ `try/catch` statement. Basically, we are telling the code that we are going to try something and we want to watch for any errors that occur and, if they do occur, that we want to respond accordingly. In our code, we are going to use generic `except` cases that catch any error and just print a message that an error occurred. In general, Python coding standards don't like us to have all-encompassing `except` cases, but we are going to do it for now because handling errors will be left to you to investigate on your own.

The implementation of the `read` method is as follows:

```
def read(self):
    try:
        return ord(self.I2C.recv(1, self.Address))
    except:
        print("Unable to retrieve I/O status")
        return 0xFF
```

There are several interesting points that you may notice about this code. First, we are using the MicroPython I2C library `recv` method to receive data from the I2C bus. The `1` numeral is telling the driver that we want to receive one byte of data from the bus at the `self.Address` address. The `ord` function is used to convert the byte that is received into an ordinal number.

The implementation of the `write` function is as follows:

```
def write(self, state):
    assert state < 256, "State >= 256"
    try:
        self.I2C.send(state, self.Address)
    except:
        print("Unable to set I/O state")
```

Again, we are using an assertion here to test that the parameters passed from the higher-level application are meeting our requirements for this function: that the state is to be less than 256.

Now that we have implemented our I/O expander driver, let's construct the driver for driving the LEDs.

RGB driver construction

One of the goals of this project is to drive the RGB LEDs that are located on our pushbutton. In order to do so, we really want to have a class that can drive three different LEDs on different PWMs in a flexible manner. In order to do this, we are going to construct an RGB_Generator class that meets our API requirements from the design of our RGB pushbutton application.

RGB_Generator is interesting in that it requires a fair number of parameters in order to get the PWM set up:

1. First, we are going to pass this class constructor, PinList, which contains the three pins that will be used to drive the LEDs.
2. Second, we are going to pass the Timer modules, which will be used to generate the timing for the PWM signals.
3. Third, we pass in the frequencies that we want the PWM to be generated at.
4. Finally, we have a list of channels that correspond to the timer channel.

These steps sound complicated but, as you can see in the following snippet, the code is actually pretty simple:

```
class RGBGenerator():
    def __init__(self, pinlist, timer, frequency, channels):
        self.TimerR = pyb.Timer(timer[0], freq=frequency[0])
        self.TimerG = pyb.Timer(timer[1], freq=frequency[1])
        self.TimerB = pyb.Timer(timer[2], freq=frequency[2])
        self.R_Ch = self.TimerR.channel(channels[0],
            pyb.Timer.PWM, pin=pinlist[0])
        self.G_Ch = self.TimerG.channel(channels[1],
            pyb.Timer.PWM, pin=pinlist[1])
        self.B_Ch = self.TimerB.channel(channels[2],
            pyb.Timer.PWM, pin=pinlist[2])


    def Write(self, red, green, blue):
        self.R_Ch.pulse_width_percent(red)
```

```
self.G_Ch.pulse_width_percent(green)
self.B_Ch.pulse_width_percent(blue)
```

The constructor for the class starts by setting up the timers that will be used for each of the LEDs. Once the timer is set up, the channel for that timer is configured to be a PWM and the pin that the signal will be generated on is provided to the `Timer` API. It's important to note that the easiest way to use this class is to select the pins and timers that are all grouped together.

Once an `RGB_Generator` object has been created, we can use the `Write` function to set the PWM for each LED. In the design, I've decided to pass each PWM in as a separate parameter, but we could just as easily pass in a list of duty cycles as well. It's really up to the implementer to decide how they want to do this. I chose this approach because when I'm reading code, I can glance at the function call and see each duty cycle without having to track down a list and then it. I thought, from a code-readability viewpoint, it would be easier.

RGB pushbutton driver construction

The RGB pushbutton driver is going to be nothing more than a class that is a composition of `RGB_Generator` and the `PCA8574_IO` class that we have already created. This means that we are not going to add any additional methods to the class. Instead, we are going to use the constructor to initialize an `RGB_Generator` object and a `PCA8574_IO` object. The application code will then pass in the required parameters to initialize these objects. The implementation of this class can be seen in the following code:

```python
from PCA8574 import PCA8574_IO
from LED_RGB import RGB_Generator

class PushButtonRGB:

    # Initializer / Instance Attributes
    def __init__(self, pin    ist, timer, frequency, channels,
        i2cobject, slaveaddress):
            self.RGB = RGB_Generator(pinlist, timer, frequency, channels)
            self.DeviceIO = PCA8574_IO(i2cobject, slaveaddress)
```

As you can see from the preceding code, the constructor instantiates the class objects and then allows the application to interact with both classes through the `PushButton` object.

Now that we have created our driver objects, we are ready to test the drivers and write our application code.

Testing and validation

At this stage in the project, we have created the basic drivers that will control all the low-level hardware devices in our project. We have drivers that allow us to generate PWM signals to drive RGB LEDs and a driver to access the I/O expander chip to write and read its status. At this point, we would normally develop a test harness that could fully test the drivers. This would allow us to discover issues we might have with functionality or boundary conditions. Since developing a test harness is an entire project in itself, we will save the test harness discussion for the next chapter. For now, we will jump ahead and create a test application that meets our project requirements and develop a few simple test cases to make sure that the high-level system meets those requirements.

Developing the test cases

Before we develop our application, we should develop test cases that link our project requirements to behaviors we expect to see at the system level once the application is completed. This can be done at any stage in the development process and will typically be done along with the requirements definition. However, engineering processes can vary dramatically from one team to the next based on the preferred development methods. In many cases, teams will use a sophisticated electronic method for tracing their requirements to test cases at the system level but, for our purposes, we are going to use a simple test case format that can be developed in Microsoft Word.

In any test case, there is important information that we want to make sure we capture. This includes the following:

- The test case number
- The test case objective (why are we doing the test?)
- The conditions that need to occur before the test is performed
- The input that needs to be applied to the system during testing (push a button)
- The expected results (what should we see happen?)
- Who did the testing?
- When was the test performed?
- The software version number that the test is to be performed on

Armed with this information, we can not only perform the test but also, later on, go back and understand the conditions that were used to test the system. If a test case fails, we can easily go back and create the failed condition to remove any defects as well.

The template that I use for simple projects is one that I first started to use when I was an entry-level engineer. I really don't remember anymore if this format came from a book, a website, or if I put it together after reading the **IEEE Swebok** for the first time. Either way, I've found that reading through the requirements and using the following template can be very helpful:

Test Case #: ###	Firmware Version: ##.##.##
Objective: What are we trying to do here?	
Preconditions: - What are the system preconditions?	

Input:
  • System Input
	Expected Results:
	  • What should happen

Testing Results: What happened?	

Tester:
    Jacob Beningo
	Date:
	    02/03/2014

Let's review the software requirements and create a few test cases to test the system behavior. Keep in mind that these are system-level tests and are not designed to be driver-functional or unit tests. We will look at how that can be done in the next chapter. (Keep in mind that you'll notice it looks like these test cases have already been performed. They have, in fact, and I am showing the result with the test case development.)

The first software requirement that we have says that the LED that is lit at startup should vary in intensity from a 0 to 100% duty cycle. We can create a first test case for this requirement as in the following screenshot:

Test Case #: 001	Firmware Version: 1.0.0
Objective: 　　　Verify that the LEDs intensity varies from off to full on in	
Preconditions: 　- Application is started	
Input: 　• None	Expected Results: 　• Should see the LED intensity increase to maximum and then decrease to zero before repeating
Testing Results: After starting up the software, the LED started at 0% intensity and increased over a second and then decreased over a second. See the attached logic analyzer trace to show the PWM output.	
Tester: 　Jacob Beningo	Date: 02/03/2019

Next, we want to create a test case for verifying that when we press the button, the LED color state changes as expected. This requirement actually produces two different test cases. First, we need a test case to verify that the system starts up with the red LED lit. Second, we need a test case that shows that when we press the button the correct color states are displayed. These test cases can be seen in the following two screenshots:

Test Case #: 002	Firmware Version: 1.0.0
Objective: Verify on start-up that the red LED is the initial RGB LED state	
Preconditions: - Application is started	

Input:
   • None
	Expected Results:
	   • Red LED should be illuminated

Testing Results: After starting up the software, the red LED was the first LED to light up and remained lit as expected.	

Tester:
   Jacob Beningo
	Date:
	   02/03/2019

Test Case #: 003	Firmware Version: 1.0.0
Objective: Verify that the when the button is pressed, the LED color changes from the initial red to the following upon each press: 1. First press – Green 2. Second press – Blue 3. Third press – White 4. Fourth press – Red 5. Fifth press – Repeat pattern	
Preconditions: - Application is started	

Input:
   • Press button (observe LED state)
   • Press button 8 times total and observe LED state
	Expected Results:
	   • Should see the LED color change based on the pattern in the objective.

Testing Results: After starting up the software, the LED color was red. Pressing the button 12 times resulted in the following pattern: green, blue, white, red, green, blue, white, red	

Tester:
   Jacob Beningo
	Date:
	   02/03/2019

We could certainly develop dozens of test cases to ensure that our application is perfect no matter what a user does or how they use our driver functions. Sometimes, however, you need to evaluate when the software tests and quality are *good enough*. Otherwise, you can engineer yourself out of business or, if it's a DIY project, you may never finish it. (Keep in mind that I focus on highly reliable and robust real-time systems, so defining *good enough* can be quite challenging.)

Writing the application

Now that we have the system test cases, our low-level drivers, and the hardware ready, it's time to develop the application. We are going to develop the application in five steps:

1. Identify the imports we need.
2. Define the constants.
3. Define the application variables.
4. Initialize the application.
5. Create the main loop.

Let's look at these steps in more detail:

1. First, we want to look at the imports that our application is going to need. By default, we always include the `micropython` and `pyb` libraries. Next, we need to review the classes that we are going to use. We need the `PushButton_RGB` class, which also has dependencies on `Pin`, `Timer`, and `I2C`. The complete list of imports can be seen in the following snippet:

```
import micropython                          # For emergency exception
                                            # buffer
import pyb                                  # For uPython MCU features
from pyb import Pin                         # For pin names
from pyb import Timer                       # For PWM generation
from pyb import I2C                         # For I2C functions
from button_rgb import PushButton_RGB       # For PushButton control
import sys                                  # For exit function
```

2. Next, we want to create useful named constants that will be needed in the application so that we don't end up with **magic numbers** scattered throughout the application. A **magic number** is a numerical value that has special meaning but whose value you don't know without a useful comment describing why that value was chosen. It's best practice not to use magic numbers but to instead create a named variable or constant that describes what that value means.

3. For our application, we need to define constants for the LED PWM, which is the rate at which the PWM changes on each cycle and the direction the duty cycle is going (up or down). Now, I say constants here, but in Python, there is no way to create a true constant. You just define a variable, assign it a value, and then you don't change it. The constants that we need in our application related to driving the LEDs are as follows:

```python
# Defines the PWM value for LED FULL On
LED_FULL_ON = 0

# Defines the PWM value for LED Full Off
LED_FULL_OFF = 100

# Defines the Duty Cycle increment rate
DUTY_CYCLE_CHANGE_RATE = 2.5

# Defines if the LED is brightening
PWM_COUNT_DOWN = True

# Defines if the LED is dimming
PWM_COUNT_UP = False
```

4. In addition to constants for driving the LEDs, we also need constants for managing the pushbutton and the PCA8574. These constants will include the I2C address, the maximum state for the button press counter, and the value that is read for a button that is pressed and not pressed. These constant definitions can be found by reading the datasheet and are implemented as follows:

```python
# Defines PCA7485 don't pressed state
BUTTON_NOT_PRESSED = 0xFF

# Defines PCA7485 button pressed state
BUTTON_PRESSED = 0xFE

# Defines the maximum state supported by the pushbutton application
MAX_SYSTEM_STATE = 4

# Defines the address the I/O expander is on
PCA8574_ADDRESS = 0x38
```

5. With the constants defined, the next step is to create the variables that will be used to control the application. We need to create variables that will track the PWM duty cycle and define the pins and timer channels used to generate the PWM. These variables can be found in the following code:

```
# List object that contains the duty cycle for RGB
# Valid values are 0 - 100. Due to the hardware, the
# duty cycle is reversed! 0% provides a ground which is
# full on to the LED's. 100% is full voltage and LED is off.
DutyCycle = 100

# Defines the pins used to drive the RGB duty cycle
PinList = [Pin('X1'), Pin('X2'), Pin('X3')]

# Defines the timers used to generate the PWM
TimerList = [2,2,2]

# Defines the timer frequency in Hz for the RGB
FrequencyList = [1000, 1000, 1000]

# Specifies the timer channels used to drive the RGB LEDs
TimerChList = [1, 2, 3]
```

The preceding code may seem a little strange to a Python developer. It isn't very common for a Python developer to create lists of parameters and then pass them into functions to initialize objects. While this is done very rarely, I'm doing it this way for electrical engineers and traditional developers so that this code will, for now, look familiar to them. As we progress through this book, we will develop to using more Pythonic-appropriate styles.

6. We also need to define the variables to track the system state, the direction the duty cycle should be moving, and the last state of the button. These variables are defined in the following code:

```
# Holds the button state based on how many times its been
# pressed
System_State = 0

# If 0, the duty cycle is counting down.
# If 1, the duty cycle is counting up.
PwmDirection = 0

# Holds the button state from the last time it was read.
# This is used to determine if the button has been released.
ButtonLastState = False
```

7. Once the variables are defined, the next step is to initialize the application. There are several things we need to do in this step. First, we need to initialize the I2C bus and then scan the bus for slave devices. I like to store the slaves available in a list and then make sure that devices are present before proceeding. If there are no devices present, then an error should be supplied to the user and the application can be exited. This can be seen here:

```
try:
    i2c = I2C(I2C_BUS1, I2C.MASTER, baudrate=100000)
    I2C_List = i2c.scan()

    if I2C_List:
        print("I2C Slaves Present =", I2C_List)
    else:
        print("There are no I2C devices present!
            Exiting application.")
        sys.exit(0)
except Exception as e:
    sys.print_exception(e)
```

8. Next, we can define the object that will be used to interact with the pushbutton. In this case, we are going to instantiate the `PushButton_RGB` class with an `RGB_Button` object, as shown here:

```
try:
    RGB_Button = PushButton_RGB(PinList, TimerList,
        FrequencyList, TimerChList, i2c, PCA8574_ADDRESS)
except Exception as e:
    sys.print_exception(e)
```

When we instantiate the object, we need to provide all the parameters necessary to initialize the class, such as the following:

- `PinList`
- `TimerList`
- `FrequencyList`
- `TimerChList`
- The `i2c` object
- The slave address

9. The last piece of the initialization is to write the RGB states to a known initial condition. In this case, we are turning on the red LED and turning off the green and blue LEDs. Just as before, we want to be able to catch any errors so we will wrap this in a `try`/`except` clause. We have already checked to make sure there is a slave device so there is no longer a reason to check whether there are slave devices present. The code is as follows:

```
try:
    # Make sure that the I2C device is present before proceeding.
    RGB_Button.RGB.Write(LED_FULL_OFF, LED_FULL_OFF, LED_FULL_OFF)
except Exception as e:
    sys.print_exception(e)
```

Finally, we can create the main application loop. The main application loop needs to implement a code that does the following:

- Reads the pushbutton
- Processes the press
- Calculates the PWM
- Writes the LEDs

Let's now implement the code to do the preceding actions:

1. We will start by reading the pushbutton. To read the pushbutton, we need to utilize the `read` function from the `PCA8574` class. This is done through the `DeviceIO` object, which is part of the `RGB_Button` object. We can do this as in the following snippet:

```
# Make sure we have an I2C device to talk to, if so, try to read
from it
try:
    PushButton = RGB_Button.DeviceIO.Read()
except Exception as e:
    sys.print_exception(e)
    print("Exiting application ...")
    sys.exit(0)
```

2. After the button has been read, we need to determine whether the button has been pressed or not. If the last button read was *pressed* and the button now reads *not pressed*, we know that the button has been released. If it has been released, we want to increment the system state and then clear out the PWM duty cycle so that the cycle starts from the beginning. We also want to make sure that if the system state has reached a value equal to or greater than 5, we reset the value back to 0. The code to perform all of this button processing can be seen in the following snippet:

```
# Check the Pushbutton to see if it has been pressed and released.
# When released, move to the next system state.
if PushButton == BUTTON_NOT_PRESSED:
    if ButtonLastState == True:
        ButtonLastState = False
        DutyCycle = LED_FULL_OFF
        System_State += 1

        if System_State >= MAX_SYSTEM_STATE:
            System_State = 0
elif PushButton == BUTTON_PRESSED:
    ButtonLastState = True
```

3. After the button has been processed and the system state has been determined, we need to calculate the next PWM duty cycle value. This is just a matter of incrementing or decrementing the state based on the value of `PwmDirection` and constraining its value between 0 and 100:

```
# The example application will toggle the LED from full on to
# full off and then back again.
if PwmDirection == PWM_COUNT_DOWN:
    DutyCycle -= DUTY_CYCLE_CHANGE_RATE

    if DutyCycle <= LED_FULL_ON:
        PwmDirection = PWM_COUNT_UP
else:
    DutyCycle += DUTY_CYCLE_CHANGE_RATE

    if DutyCycle >= LED_FULL_OFF:
        PwmDirection = PWM_COUNT_DOWN
```

4. Finally, we need to update the LEDs with the calculated duty cycle based on the state that the system is in. This involves nothing more than reading the system state and then calling the `Write` method with the appropriate duty cycle values:

```
# This is a simple "State Machine" that will run different
# colors and patterns based on how many times the button
```

```
        # has been pressed
        try:
            if System_State == 0:
                RGB_Button.RGB.Write(DutyCycle, LED_FULL_OFF, LED_FULL_OFF)
            elif System_State == 1:
                RGB_Button.RGB.Write(LED_FULL_OFF, DutyCycle, LED_FULL_OFF)
            elif System_State == 2:
                RGB_Button.RGB.Write(LED_FULL_OFF, LED_FULL_OFF, DutyCycle)
            elif System_State == 3:
                RGB_Button.RGB.Write(DutyCycle, DutyCycle, DutyCycle)
        except Exception as e:
            sys.print_exception(e)
```

That's it! At this point, you can run the application and you should see a properly behaving pushbutton application! When the application starts, you should see behavior in the Terminal similar to that in the following screenshot:

You can download this from the GitHub repository mentioned at the beginning of the chapter, in the *Technical requirements* section.

Summary

In this chapter, we defined a simple test project that allowed us to expand the I/O capabilities of the pyboard while gaining experience in developing drivers. We integrated these drivers together to control an RGB LED pushbutton, whose color status was controlled by pressing the button. Throughout this chapter, we also discussed the software development life cycle and have been trying to adhere to its principles and major stages to ensure that we create a robust project.

In the next chapter, we are going to explore how we can create a test harness to fully test and integrate drivers. We will be leveraging the drivers that we just created in this chapter to develop and test our harness.

Questions

1. What is a high-level system diagram called?
2. What is a detailed hardware diagram called?
3. What three diagrams did we use in this chapter to define our software architecture?
4. What is it called when two classes are connected together without the use of an inheritance mechanism?
5. What information should be included in test cases?
6. How can a developer create a constant in Python?
7. What line of code should a developer write to find out which addresses have slaves present on the I2C bus?
8. What can be used to catch an exception and print it out?
9. What statement can be written to force an application to exit?
10. What type of setup can be used to fully test and validate the drivers created in an application?

Further reading

1. `www.UML.org`
2. `https://www.computer.org/education/bodies-of-knowledge/software-engineering`

Developing an Application Test Harness

4

In the previous chapter, we developed several modules that will be used in an application project to perform I/O functionality and interact with a user. The question, though, is how can we be certain that those modules we created actually work? We created several tests, but if we make any changes to them, we have to rerun those tests manually. By doing this, we'll find that it is easy to overlook a potential bug. Manual testing is not just time-consuming but also error-prone.

In this chapter, we are going to develop an application test harness that we can use to test our MicroPython modules and ensure they have the fewest number of bugs.

The following topics will be covered in this chapter:

- What a test harness is and why we would want to use one
- Requirements for developing a test harness
- Test harness design
- Test harness construction
- Running the test harness

Technical requirements

The example code for this chapter can be found in this book's GitHub repository: `https://github.com/PacktPublishing/MicroPython-Projects/tree/master/Chapter04`.

To run the examples and your own test harness, you will need the following hardware and software:

- Pyboard Revision 1.0 or 1.1
- RobotDyn I2C 8-bit PCA8574 I/O expander module or equivalent
- Adafruit RGB Pushbutton PN: 3423 or equivalent
- A terminal application (PuTTy, RealTerm, or Terminal)
- A text editor such as Sublime Text

A brief introduction to test harnesses

A **test harness** is a collection of software and data that is used to automatically test application modules under various conditions in order to determine whether they meet the design requirements. A test harness will often consist of three main components, as follows:

- **A test execution engine**: This is a piece of software that interfaces with the application modules under test and provides them with various inputs. After doing this, it monitors their outputs to ensure that the expected result is achieved. The test execution engine is usually written in the same language as the application modules that are under test.
- **A repository of tests**: These are additional software modules that are written that contain the desired conditions under which the modules will be tested. The tests also contain the expected output for those tests so that it can be determined whether the test has actually passed or whether it has failed. If the test fails, the module has not met its design requirements and it is a sign that there is a bug in that module that needs to be resolved.
- **A test reporting mechanism**: This mechanism provides developers with a way to visually monitor whether their application modules have passed or failed the test. The reporting capabilities will vary greatly, based on the test harness that is used. At a minimum, we want the test harness to report any tests that have failed. In a more verbose harness, we would want a report to be generated that states whether the test passed or failed and if it failed, under what conditions it failed, what the inputs were, and what outputs were generated.

A test harness can be a very powerful tool for developers and brings several advantages to the testing process, such as the following:

- Automated testing that then allows developers to focus on other activities
- Allows them to perform regression testing, which can verify that recent changes haven't broken other pieces of code
- Increased code quality

A test harness can be used in several different ways. First, it can be used to perform unit testing. Unit tests are used to test a specific function within an application. When creating unit tests, I like to test the function for preconditions, postconditions, parameter values, and parameter boundary conditions. Unit tests can help verify that each function works. Next, we have **module testing**. This testing goes beyond unit tests in that it tests that the functions can all work together at the module level. Module testing can be thought of as the beginning of integration testing. Finally, we have system integration testing, which can be used to verify that the entire system is working as expected.

As you might have realized, creating and using a test harness for an embedded system can be challenging. At some point, there will be a software layer that has to interact with microcontroller hardware, external integrated circuits, sensors, and other devices. In these situations, developers either have to create a software representation for that hardware device, which is often referred to as a **mock**, or develop tests that include the hardware. When hardware is included in the testing process, these are often referred to as **hardware-in-the-loop** (HIL) tests. These tests require that the microcontroller, sensors, and other devices are all set up and that the test harness interacts with the embedded system. This type of testing can be complicated since it may require setting up logic analyzers, bus sniffers, and other devices that then need to be automated in order to get a test result.

If a test harness sounds like it can be a lot of work, you aren't wrong. Just like any other piece of software, test harnesses can have bugs, and your test results are only as good as the tests that you write! If you write poor tests, then you won't necessarily improve the quality of your software. In fact, you may find that you have giant holes in your tests that only give you a false sense of accomplishment.

The primary goal of this chapter is to create a project that allows us to gain experience with developing and using test harnesses for MicroPython-based applications. We will develop a test harness that will test the modules we developed in the previous chapter and also look at how we can verify that the low-level hardware behaves the way that we expect it to. We will also discuss a simple process that you can follow to develop your test cases that should minimize gaps in your testing.

Test harness requirements

There are several areas where we need to make careful considerations for our test harness. First, we need to consider the hardware requirements. When we develop our test harness, we may need to design and implement a hardware interface that will allow us to not just interact with the system but also verify various communication and control aspects of the software. This requires us to clearly define any additional hardware that will be required.

Second, we need to define what our software requirements will be. These include areas such as how the test harness will be executed, what's needed when it comes to reporting, and the language that will be used to execute our tests. In this section, we will explore these requirements and put together the requirements for the test harness that we will build to test our MicroPython code. Keep in mind that we are going to outline some of the high-level requirements. We aren't building a safety-critical device that requires fully specified requirements, so we will just lay out enough requirements to help guide us through the process.

Hardware requirements

Just as we discussed in the previous chapters, we want to think through the hardware requirements that are necessary to support our test harness. We want requirements that will be general enough so that we don't tie our hands in the design process but also enough so that we have breadcrumbs that lead us in the right direction. For our test harness, which will test our pushbutton project modules from Chapter 3, *Writing a MicroPython Driver for an I/O Expander*, before we develop our hardware requirements, we need to review the hardware that we designed, which can be seen here:

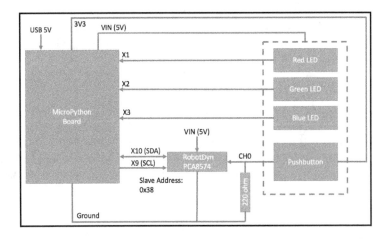

From reviewing our hardware diagram, we can see that there are several hardware requirements that we want to define, as follows:

- The test harness shall be capable of recording the output signals on **X1**, **X2**, and **X3** for manual review and verification.
- The test harness shall monitor I2C communication on **X9** and **X10**.
- The test harness shall replace the **CH0** pushbutton's input with an I/O line that can be controlled by the test harness.

As you can see from these requirements, we are specifying a few high-level needs for our test harness so that it can interface with our device. We could go much further by removing the RobotDyn I/O expander and using something like an Aardvark to directly interface on the I2C bus and then simulate the RobotDyn chip. This would allow us to then simulate various fault conditions and see how our system responds to those faults. These could include faults such as the following:

- A non-responsive slave device
- An invalid response
- I2C bus errors

We can make our test harness as sophisticated or as simple as we want based on our application needs. For us, just making sure that we can communicate with a device and read the input values correctly is about as much as we need for this project.

Software requirements

The software requirements for our test harness need to take into account any external tools that we need to interface with, along with how the test harness will behave. The following are a few thoughts on what our test harness should include:

- The test harness shall be configurable so that it can run a subset of tests or the entire test suite based on the test harness configuration settings.
- The test harness shall be modular to allow test harness features to be reused across multiple projects.
- The test harness shall record how long it takes to perform each test, along with the total test time.

- The test harness shall generate a report that will be saved to the filesystem once the tests are complete. This report will specify the following:
  - Software version under test
  - Test harness version
  - Hardware version
  - Number of tests to execute
  - Test start time
  - Test-specific information, such as the following:
    - Name of test executed
    - Input parameters
    - Expected output
    - Actual output
    - Time to run the test
    - Test stop time
  - Number of tests that pass
  - Number of tests that fail

When developing your own test harness, it's a good idea to think through all the features that you may want the harness to have, but start simple. For example, we've listed quite a few reporting features here, but on our first iteration, just being able to run a test and determine whether it passed or failed might be good enough. Over time, we can build up the test harness so that it's much more sophisticated. Remember, the more complex we make our harness, the greater the chances that we will introduce bugs to the harness that require more time and maintenance. This could become an entire project all on its own.

Test harness design

At this stage in the project, we've discovered what the basic requirements for our test harness are going to be. Now, we are ready to dive deeper into the hardware and software architecture that is necessary to support the test harness. Just like in previous chapters, at this stage, we are going to start with an architecture that will then feed into a more detailed design that is then used in the construction phase. Remember, the architecture should be flexible so that we can deal with any changing requirements on the fly.

The test harness hardware architecture

The hardware architecture for our project requires just a few minor adjustments in order to support our test harness. These updates will provide hardware support so that we can monitor three features:

- The I2C bus
- Triggering the pushbutton
- Reading the PWM channel

We are interested in monitoring these signals for several reasons. First, we want to make sure that we can record the I2C communication that is occurring between the MicroPython board and the RobotDyn I/O expander. This will be used to verify I2C communication. Second, the pushbutton is a mechanical switch that can only be triggered by someone attending the test. We want to automate as much testing as possible! In order to do so, we will add the ability to trigger the pushbutton input using an I/O line. Finally, when the tests are running, we want to be able to verify that the correct PWM channel is running and that the frequency is set correctly. In order to do this, we want to monitor each PWM channel independently.

To accomplish these three monitoring tasks, we need to add two pieces of hardware, as follows:

- An I2C Bus Monitor
- A data acquisition system

The way these pieces of equipment will be added to our hardware architecture can be seen in the following diagram:

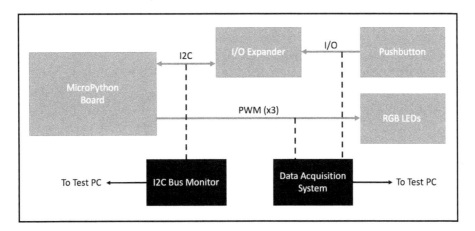

Here, we're adding the hardware components with dashed lines between them. This is to show that these are optional components that are only added to the design for testing and are then removed from the system. Both systems are then interfaced to a test PC that will drive these components and interact with the system.

This is a good time to pause for a moment and consider some of the ramifications for adding monitoring equipment to our hardware. Adding test tools to the hardware can have unintended consequences that make you believe that your system is working as expected but when the test tools are removed, the system suddenly stops working! There have been several times in the past where I've worked on a client project where we had logic analyzers, bus analyzers, and data acquisition systems in the mix and everything worked as expected but as soon as these tools were removed, the system crashed and burned.

When you add extra pieces of equipment to your hardware, especially monitoring equipment, you change the electrical characteristics of your hardware. For example, a tool that monitors the I2C bus will often act as a pull-up for the I2C lines. If there are not properly sized pull-ups on the I2C lines, the monitoring tool can help the I2C bus work as expected. As soon as the I2C bus tool is removed, the improperly sized pull-ups suddenly can't handle it and the I2C bus no longer works.

It's important to recognize that while a test harness will help us automate tests, do regression testing, and many other fabulous activities that can help us speed up development and improve quality, we need to realize that we still need to perform tests on our system in a standalone mode. This will ensure that our test equipment hasn't inadvertently affected the device under test.

The test harness software architecture

There are quite a few options available to us regarding how we can architect the software side of a test harness. At the end of the day, it really comes down to how much complexity we want in our test harness. In our example, I've complexified the test harness by adding external devices that need to monitor the I2C bus, drive an I/O line, and then monitor the PWM signals. Let's examine several different ways that this can be done. The method that we will implement in this project is going to be the lowest cost and least complex method available.

The first test harness software architecture that is available to us is to use a personal computer as the main driver for the test harness and the data collection process. In this architecture, the test groups that we want to execute are stored on the MicroPython board but are executed over a communication link that is driven by a test computer.

In this architecture, our test computer runs a Python script that can either communicate with the REPL or uses a serial link with a custom communication protocol. The reason that the PC script drives the test is so that it can control the test equipment that is monitoring the I2C bus, controlling the pushbutton, and watching the PWM lines. An example of what this software architecture would look like can be seen in the following diagram:

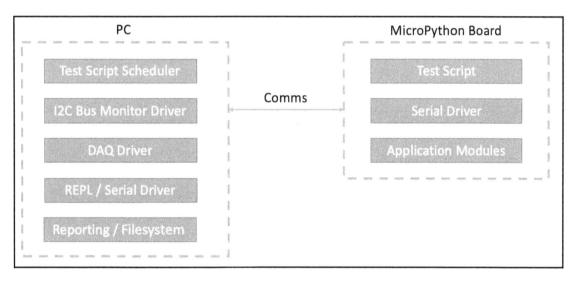

This architecture is fairly complex and would be more beneficial to a professional developer than someone who is developing a DIY project or rapid prototyping. There are several benefits to using this architecture, as follows:

- Easily scalable.
- Can support multiple external test equipment devices.
- Easy access to test data.
- Developers can leverage existing Python libraries to simplify and speed up development.
- Portable for use in other projects.

The second test harness software architecture that is available to us is to build the entire test harness on the MicroPython board and use a second MicroPython board connected to the first to monitor I2C and perform the other monitoring and control activities. This harness removes the need for a personal computer to be involved and it can dramatically decrease the test equipment's cost by building the functionality into a pyboard.

While we are removing costs and complexity, there is still additional work that needs to be done. For example, we would need to develop the capability to monitor I2C while minimizing its impact on the hardware bus and then need to develop a communication protocol that can be used between the two MicroPython boards. This would allow the test harness to let the second board know that it should now trigger a pushbutton, monitor PWM, and so on. These aren't necessarily complex tasks since we needed to add that functionality to the first architecture as well. We are just simplifying the concept and removing more expensive pieces of equipment from the effort.

An overview of this architecture can be seen in the following diagram:

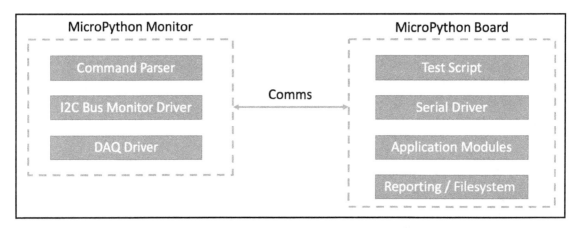

The final architecture that we are going to look at only works if the application that we developed has memory and CPU cycles to spare. In this architecture, we are eliminating all the extra hardware and using spare I/O on the main MicroPython board to control and monitor the testing process. In this architecture, we are putting the entire test harness on the MicroPython board and then calling our test cases and monitoring functions from the same device. This architecture is as follows:

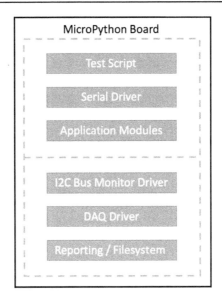

There are some obvious disadvantages to putting the entire test harness on our device, some of which are as follows:

- The test harness can have an impact on testing, depending on the end application.
- The test harness may use too much memory or CPU cycles.
- The complexity of managing multiple functions on a single device.

While these disadvantages do need to be managed, the advantages could dramatically outweigh them. Some of these advantages are as follows:

- Decreased hardware costs
- Decreased overall test harness complexity
- All the code is in a single place

These are just a few examples of how we could architect our test harness software. There are so many other options that we could use and variations of these three types. For example, we could remove the serial communication link and have a MicroPython board that sends all the test data to the cloud over a Wi-Fi link or sends it via Bluetooth. The options are quite limitless.

Now, we are going to look at how we can implement a test harness directly on the MicroPython board. This is the least complex solution but also foundational in that it's a building block to more complex and scalable architectures. Let's get started.

Constructing the test harness

The bulk of the test harness that we will be constructing is going to be software. The modules that we are going to build the test harness for are the modules that we created in Chapter 3, *Writing a MicroPython Driver for an I/O Expander*. We could build a harness that not only includes low-level module testing but also the high-level system behavior; however, I want to convey how we can create a test harness. I will leave the high-level application testing to you as an exercise. The modules that we will be testing are as follows:

- PCA8574.py
- LED_RGB.py
- Button_rgb.py

Let's get started!

Writing the test harness scaffolding

Before we dive in and start developing tests, we should spend a few minutes thinking about how we are going to organize our test harness. I like to create modules that represent the tests for the device under test. For example, if I have a module named PCA8574.py, I will create a separate module named PCA8574_tests.py. As I construct my software module, I will also add tests to make sure that I'm not overlooking anything. There are formalized processes such as **Test-Driven Development** (**TDD**) that can be followed, but I'm not as strict in my own implementations.

Each of the *_tests.py modules will be invoked through another high-level test module called test_harness.py. test_harness.py is called from the main.py module. test_harness.py can be customized during each run for the tests that we want to be executed. The reason we're creating these separate modules is to build modularity and portability into the test harness. There are certainly other ways to construct our harness, but if you want to run tests on the target with a MicroPython implementation, I've found this method to be the most useful. If we're reusing a module, this also makes it easier to bring the test harness component with us to the new application.

For each test function, there are several operations that we want to make sure that we think through and implement. These operations are as follows:

- **Test setup**: Test setup prepares the system for the series of tests that we are about to run. Test setup is really creating the preconditions that are necessary for the tests to execute. For example, if we are going to run a series of tests that use the I2C bus, we might configure an I2C object during the test setup operation, provided that the setup is not part of our tests.

- **Test execution**: Test execution is where our test cases are executed on the processor. This might be where we check the boundary conditions on input parameters or simply verify that we get the expected output from the code under test.

- **Test cleanup**: Once the test cases have been executed, we need to clean up the execution environment and return it to a clean slate. If we don't undo what we just did, then other tests may be starting with unexpected conditions on the processor that could either cause tests to fail, or worse, pass when they should have failed! The cleanup phase might involve deallocating memory and objects and setting I/O lines back to their initial states. In a simple implementation, we could just assume that the test setup phase will configure the system as necessary, but it's always a good idea to be as explicit as possible when developing software.

- **Test reporting**: Finally, the reporting phase is where we release the results from the tests that have just been executed. The output results can be provided in many different ways. For example, a developer could dump the results in a terminal, or they could write the results to a file. No matter the format, it's important that the output is done in such a way that the data can be easily processed. For example, I will often output the test results in a comma-delimited format such as the following:
  Mode Under Test, Test Description, Pass or Fail

  Using this format makes it easier to pull the results into a Python script or Excel spreadsheet for processing.

In a sophisticated test harness, we may create separate functions that perform these operations, but it is certainly possible – and sometimes easier – to implement these operations within a single function.

At this point, we should have enough information to put together the test harness scaffolding and then start to develop our tests. The following steps can now be followed to set up the scaffolding:

1. Create new modules for each module that will be tested with `_tests.py` appended to the filename.
2. In each test module, create a new function with the module name and then `_tests` appended to it. (We will leave these blank for the moment.)
3. Create a `test_harness.py` module with a function named `Tests_Run`.

Now we are ready to add tests to our harness.

Tests for the PCA8574

The PCA8574 is the lowest level component in the application that we developed in `Chapter 3`, *Writing a MicroPython Driver for an I/O Expander*. It makes sense that we should develop the test cases for this module first. As I mentioned earlier, preferably, we would do this while we were developing the module, but in this case, we are adding it after the fact. We want to make sure that we test the module effectively for our application. In this case, there are four tests that we want to perform:

- I2C object creation and initialization
- I2C object creation handling for out-of-range addresses
- **Lowest Significant Bit (LSB)** high read
- **Lowest Significant Bit (LSB)** low read

We could design a series of tests that would check every single I/O line and make sure that it reads properly, but the PCA8574 is a simple device and returns a single 8-bit value for the I/O states. If we are able to successfully read the LSB, then we should not have any issues reading the other bits. (In a commercial product, I would verify all the I/O. For this example, we are streamlining to the minimal necessary tests.)

To run these tests, we want to implement the four operations that we discussed in the previous section:

1. First, we implement the test setup. In PCA8574_tests.py, we begin by populating the PCA8574_Tests function with code that can set up the I2C peripheral. In the following code, you'll notice the code we are using to set up the test is the same code that we used to set up the I2C in the application code:

```
try:
  # Initialize I2C 1
  i2c = I2C(I2C_BUS1, I2C.MASTER, baudrate=100000)
  # returns list of slave addresses
  I2C_List = i2c.scan()

  if I2C_List:
    print("I2C Slaves Present =", I2C_List)
  else:
    print("There are no I2C devices present! Exiting application.")
    sys.exit(0)
except Exception as e: print(e)
```

In many cases, you'll find that there will be code that can be reused between the test harness and the application code.

2. Once we have this setup code in place, it's time to implement the tests that will be executed. We start by testing that we can initialize an I2C object in the range 0 – 255. This object will be created using the I2C address that is detected on the I2C bus during the test setup operation. We wrap our test case in a try/except statement. Any error that is generated when trying to initialize the object will tell us that our test case has failed. The code for this is as follows:

```
# Test that we can initialize the object
try:
        PCA8574_Object = PCA8574_IO(i2c, I2C_List[0])
        print("PCA8574, Object Creation, Passed")
except:
        print("PCA8574, Object Creation, Failed")
```

Notice that as part of the test case, we include the fourth operation, which is to report whether the test passes or fails. We could have just collected the results in an array or dictionary but since we are trying to build test harness functionality bit by bit, we're keeping things simple by just printing the results to the Terminal as the test is executed.

3. The next test that we want to execute is an initialization of the PCA8574 with an invalid address. We want to run this test in order to verify that our assert throws an exception. For this test case, if we reach the exception, then it means that the test has passed, and if we successfully initialize the object, then we have failed the test. The code for this test case is as follows:

```
try:
        PCA8574_Object1 = PCA8574_IO(i2c, 256)
        print("PCA8574, I2C Address Out-of-Bounds, Failed")
except:
        print("PCA8574, I2C Address Out-of-Bounds, Passed")
```

4. Finally, we can create the test cases that check whether we can successfully read a value from the PCA8574 I/O or not. This requires two test cases: one for validating a high input on the LSB and one for validating a low input on the LSB. Don't forget that we need to add code that will control one of the pyboard's I/O lines that will then be connected to the LSB. During the tests, we can change the state of this pin in order to simulate that the button has been pressed. The alternative would be to notify the tester and have them manually press and hold the button. Before we start toggling pins, we need to add some GPIO setup to the test setup portion of our test. The following code shows the code that should be added to the test setup in order to control an I/O that will simulate the I/O state changing from a button press:

```
p_out = Pin('X4', Pin.OUT_PP)
p_out.high()
```

Don't forget that you will also need to import `Pin` from the `pyb` library if you have not already done so.

5. At this point, we are able to write our test code in order to verify that we can successfully read the PCA8574 input states. The code for this is as follows:

```
# Set the switch to not pressed
  p_out.high()
  Result = PCA8574_Object.Read()
  if Result is 0xFF:
          print("PCA8574, LSB I/O - High, Passed")
  else:
```

```
        print("PCA8574, LSB I/O - High, Failed,", Result)

# Set the switch to pressed
p_out.low()
Result = PCA8574_Object.Read()
if Result is 0xFE:
        print("PCA8574, LSB I/O - Low, Passed")
else:
        print("PCA8574, LSB I/O - Low, Failed,", Result)
```

For this example, the only cleanup operation that we are going to apply is to make a call to `p_out.High()` once the testing is complete. This will return the I/O line to the high state. For our purposes, we will leave the I2C bus initialized at this time and any additional tests that may be running can either use its settings or it can set up its own configuration.

Now, we are ready to run the test harness for the first time and see what results we get from our tests. Before doing so, make sure that you import the `PCA8574_test.py` module into your `test_harness.py` script and then import this script into your `main.py` module. This will give you a fully working test harness that allows you to add additional tests by making changes to the `test_harness.py` script.

Running the test harness

Running the test harness on the target will not be any different than running any other MicroPython script. Copy `main.py`, `test_harness`, and the test scripts to the pyboard. From the terminal, you can use *Ctrl* + *C* to terminate any application that is already running. Then, use *Ctrl* + *D* to cause a soft reset to occur on the pyboard. At this point, you should see an output from the test harness similar to the following:

```
>>>
MPY: sync filesystems
MPY: soft reboot
Initializing system ...
Starting application ...
Starting Tests ...
I2C Slaves Present = [56]
PCA8574, Object Creation, Passed
PCA8574, I2C Address Out-of-Bounds, Passed
PCA8574, LSB I/O - High, Passed
PCA8574, LSB I/O - Low, Failed, 255
Testing Completed
```

From the preceding output, we can see that the script has been started and that testing has begun. We can see our test setup operation followed by the execution and reporting operations. We can also see that the first three tests pass successfully but that our final test, the LSB I/O – Low test, fails. From the test report, it looks like the I/O stayed at the high state rather than toggling low.

There are several potential causes for this test failure, some of which are as follows:

- The module under test has a bug,
- The test case is faulty,
- There is a hardware problem.

As it turns out, I did not connect X4 to the PCA8574 board. After making the connection and then rerunning the test harness, you should receive an output similar to the following:

```
>>>
MPY: sync filesystems
MPY: soft reboot
Initializing system ...
Starting application ...
Starting Tests ...
I2C Slaves Present = [56]
PCA8574, Object Creation, Passed
PCA8574, I2C Address Out-of-Bounds, Passed
PCA8574, LSB I/O - High, Passed
PCA8574, LSB I/O - Low, Passed
Testing Completed
```

At this point, all the tests are passing! This should mean that there are no problems with our test harness or the module under test, correct? The truth is, all we have done is written some tests that we expect to pass. We never really tested that these test cases can fail! TDD teaches us that before any test case is made to pass, we should write it and verify that it fails first. This helps us to verify that the test case can actually fail. As you move forward and start to develop test cases for the remaining modules that are part of Chapter 3, *Writing a MicroPython Driver for an I/O Expander*, verify that your tests fail first before you make sure that they return the right result.

Summary

In this chapter, we explored the different methods that we can use to create a test harness for MicroPython modules and application code. While there are many methods available, ranging from very simple to highly sophisticated, we implemented a simple test harness that you can easily leverage and use as the foundation to build even more useful harnesses. The harness that we built used the device under test to simulate system inputs, which allowed us to keep the test harness' costs low and required no additional external hardware.

In the next chapter, we are going to dive deep into the MicroPython kernel and learn how we can customize the startup code and the kernel for our own application needs. As part of this project, we are going to compile our own kernel and deploy it to a development board that doesn't come with MicroPython installed on it by default.

Questions

1. What are the three main components that are part of nearly every test harness?
2. What are the advantages of using a test harness?
3. What are a few examples of faults that we would want a test harness to test for?
4. What are some of the architectures that a test harness can follow?
5. What are the four operations that we need our module tests to perform?

Further reading

- *Test-Driven Development with Python*, Harry Percival
- *Test-Driven Development for Embedded C*, James W. Grenning

5
Customizing the MicroPython Kernel Start Up Code

Developing embedded software using MicroPython is relatively straightforward but there may come a time when there is a need to build a custom-printed circuit board, adjust the default pin settings in the kernel, handle failure modes, or simply build a software library in the MicroPython kernel. In order to do this, a developer will need to be familiar with the MicroPython kernel by examining it and the steps necessary to customize it, which we will do in this chapter.

The following topics will be covered in this chapter:

- An overview of the MicroPython kernel
- Navigating the startup code
- Modifying the default GPIO initialization
- Adding MicroPython modules to the kernel
- Testing the results

Technical requirements

The example code used in this chapter can be found at `https://github.com/PacktPublishing/MicroPython-Projects/tree/master/Chapter05`.

In order to run the examples and build your own custom MicroPython kernel, you will need the following hardware and software:

- A Linux machine or virtual machine
- An STM32L4 IoT Discovery node
- A RobotDyn I2C 8-bit PCA8574 I/O expander module, or equivalent
- An Adafruit RGB pushbutton PN: 3423, or equivalent
- A breadboard
- 6" jumpers
- A generic two-position switch
- A 30-gauge wire-wrapping wire
- A Terminal application (PuTTY, RealTerm, Terminal, or one of many others)
- A text editor, such as Sublime Text

An overview of the MicroPython kernel

The MicroPython kernel is a collection of software libraries, code, and a Python interpreter that comes pre-built on a MicroPython board, such as the pyboard. Someone who is new to MicroPython may not even realize that their Python interpreter is made up of C modules. These modules are compiled and then programmed onto their board, which then reveals the filesystem and REPL that we have become so familiar with. In this chapter, we are going to look more closely at the kernel and explore how we can make our own modifications that will enhance our applications.

Downloading the MicroPython kernel

Before you can get a feel for what it contains, you need to download the kernel so that you can navigate through its directory structure. The kernel is easy to download. I recommend downloading it on a Linux machine or within a Linux virtual machine. The build process for MicroPython is easier in this environment, which we will be going through later on in this chapter.

Make sure that you have Git installed on your machine by typing the following into your Terminal:

```
sudo apt-get install git
```

If Git is already installed, you should see a screen similar to this:

```
beningo@ubuntu:~$ sudo apt-get install git
[sudo] password for beningo:
Reading package lists... Done
Building dependency tree
Reading state information... Done
git is already the newest version (1:2.17.1-1ubuntu0.4).
0 upgraded, 0 newly installed, 0 to remove and 21 not upgraded.
beningo@ubuntu:~$
```

If Git is not installed, it will go through the installation process to install it on your development machine. Once Git is installed, you can use the following command in the terminal to clone MicroPython:

```
sudo clone https://github.com/micropython/micropython.git
```

Once the command is issued, MicroPython will be cloned into a directory called `micropython`, as follows:

```
beningo@ubuntu:~/MicroPython$ git clone https://github.com/micropython/micropyth
on.git
Cloning into 'micropython'...
remote: Counting objects: 40037, done.
remote: Total 40037 (delta 0), reused 0 (delta 0), pack-reused 40036
Receiving objects: 100% (40037/40037), 24.66 MiB | 5.57 MiB/s, done.
Resolving deltas: 100% (28873/28873), done.
Checking connectivity... done.
Checking out files: 100% (2270/2270), done.
```

Congratulations! You now have the MicroPython kernel on your development machine and it's time to jump in and start getting familiar with it.

MicroPython kernel organization

If you navigate to the `micropython` directory where you cloned the MicroPython kernel, you'll find that the kernel is organized as in the following screenshot:

```
beningo@ubuntu:~/micropython$ ls
ACKNOWLEDGEMENTS    CONTRIBUTING.md   drivers    extmod   LICENSE   mpy-cross   py          tests
CODECONVENTIONS.md  docs              examples   lib      logo      ports       README.md   tools
beningo@ubuntu:~/micropython$
```

Upon examination, you'll notice that there are several top-level directories. The information contained in each of these directories can be found in the following table:

Folder	Description
docs	Contains documentation for different major ports.
drivers	Contains external device drivers for items, such as displays, memory devices, radios, and SD cards.
examples	Contains example Python scripts.
extmod	Contains additional (non-core) modules that are implemented in C, such as crypto and filesystems.
mpy-cross	The MicroPython cross-compiler, which generates bytecode from scripts.
ports	Contains all the different architecture ports supported by MicroPython.
py	The Python implementation, which includes the Python core, compiler, libraries, and runtime.
tests	Contains the test framework for MicroPython.
tools	Contains scripts that can be useful for developing the MicroPython kernel.

I recommend that you briefly take some time to explore these directories and get a better feel for what is in these folders. We will spend most of our time in the ports/STM32 directory but there could be tools or modules elsewhere that it would be useful to know about, depending on what you are looking to modify in the kernel.

Becoming familiar with the STM32L475SE_IOT01A port

If you navigate deeper into the ports folder, you'll find that there are now more than a dozen different ports for MicroPython. In my opinion, the **stm32** port is the best supported port, but some of the wireless chips are also good contenders, such as the **esp8266**. You can see that all the architectures that are currently supported in MicroPython are contained within the port's directory, as in the following screenshot:

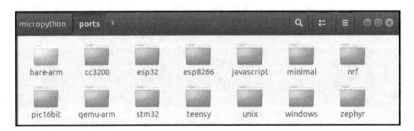

If you open up the **stm32** folder, you'll find a few different items of interest. First, it contains all the drivers and C code modules that are required to drive an STM32 microcontroller. These files are actually generated from the STM32 HAL, which is provided by STMicroelectronics, and are periodically updated as STMicroelectronics makes updates and changes to their HAL. For the most part, you won't need to modify any of these driver files; they just play a supporting role in the microcontroller's peripherals and capabilities.

Next, you'll notice that there are several folders in the `stm32` directory. Most of these again contain the supporting code modules for features such as booting the microcontroller and other advanced features, such as USBs. The folder that is really the most interesting to us is the `boards` folder.

The `boards` folder contains several different types of files and folders, including the following:

- Supported `board` folders, which are all the different boards supported by MicroPython
- STM32 derivative linker files, which define the memory maps for the different processors
- STM32 derivative pin maps, which describe what each pin does on the processor

You can see all the different STM32 boards—and third-party boards that use an STM32 microcontroller—that have currently been ported to MicroPython in the following screenshot:

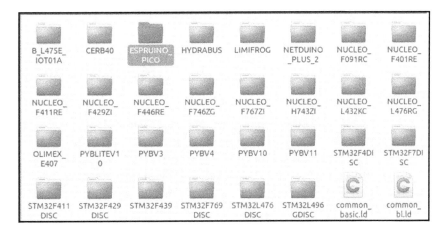

As seen in the preceding screenshot, the `STM32/boards` folder contains all the STM32 MicroPython ports that currently exist.

As you can see, there are more than two dozen different boards supported, including the pyboard, which can be seen in the PYBV3, PYBV4, PYBV10, and PYBV11 folders. Since we have already looked at it, we are going to investigate the STM32L475E_IOT01A development board in more detail in this chapter.

The STM32L475E_IOT01A board is particularly interesting because it includes an onboard Wi-Fi and Bluetooth module in addition to several sensors. The board also has Arduino headers on it for shield expansion and a MOD connector. You can see an overview of the development board in the following photograph:

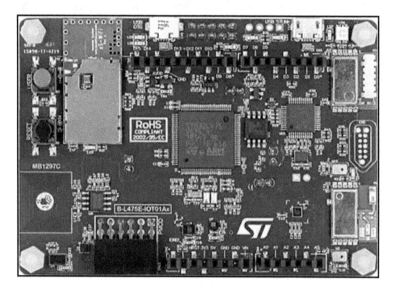

(Image source: STMicroelectronics)

The STM32L475E_IOT01A board supports Arduino headers and includes onboard Wi-Fi and Bluetooth, which makes it a great prototyping environment for MicroPython projects.

Before we dive into this development board, it's useful to first look at some of the files in the board's directory. In the board's directory, you'll notice several different csv and ld files. The ld files are the linker scripts for the microcontroller. If you select one of the ld files and open it, you'll find that it specifies which addresses are RAM and which are flash. You'll also find that there are areas for defining the cache, heap, stack, and any other custom memory regions. For the most part, you won't need to play around with these linker scripts unless you are interested in tuning the size of the heap and the stack. I've found that some of the linker files are a bit conservative or use default settings for a smaller microcontroller and, by reviewing your targets datasheet, you may find that there is extra RAM or features that you can utilize.

For example, I was working with a client on an **Electronic Power Supplies** (EPS) and the target that we selected had an extra bank of zero state RAM that was not being used. I added it to the linker file and was able to utilize it for additional variable or stack space. I also found that if you have a complex application, you may run out of heap space. Heap space is tunable, and you can modify the linker file as needed. The following snippet is from the linker that shows how you can modify _heap_end to get a little more stack space:

```
/* RAM extents for the garbage collector */
_ram_fs_cache_start = ORIGIN(FS_CACHE);
_ram_fs_cache_end = ORIGIN(FS_CACHE) = LENGTH(FS_CACHE);
_ram_start = ORIGIN(RAM);
_ram_end = ORIGIN(RAM) + LENGTH(RAM;
_hesap_start = _ebss; /* heap starts just after statistically allocated
memory */
_heap_end = 0x20014000; /* tunable */
```

The linker script allows a MicroPython kernel developer to adjust how much RAM is allocated to the head, stack, and other features within the system.

Just remember, if you take up more heap space, you'll have less space somewhere else (such as in the stack). If you open a file, such as stm321476af.csv, you can see the pin mappings for that derivative. You'll notice that it provides not only a list but also the functionality options for each pin. These files can be useful in showing the capabilities of the derivative, but generally, you won't need to modify these unless you are adding a new one to the MicroPython code base. You can customize these pin names, which will then change how they are accessed within the MicroPython runtime environment, but this is usually done in a pin file that is located within a specific board directory.

Let's now move on to the board folder. Take a look at the STM32L475E_IOT01A board folder. You'll notice that this directory contains just the following four files:

- mpconfigboard.h
- mpconfigboard.mk
- pins.csv
- stm32l4xx_hal_conf.h

These four files will control the default settings for the MicroPython board, that is, how the development board will function. Let's examine each of these in more detail in the following sections.

mpconfigboard.h

The `mpconfigboard.h` header file contains the definitions for features, such as pin mappings for peripherals, LEDs, and USB, as well as board definitions, such as the board name and the microcontroller target. A very brief example of some of the information that is contained in this file is shown in the following screenshot:

```
#define MICROPY_HW_BOARD_NAME "B-L475E-IOT01A"
#define MICROPY_HW_MCU_NAME "STM32L475"

#define MICROPY_HW_HAS_SWITCH (1)
#define MICROPY_HW_ENABLE_RNG (1)
#define MICROPY_HW_ENABLE_RTC (1)
#define MICROPY_HW_ENABLE_USB (1)
```

In the preceding code, we can see some example definitions from `mpconfigboard.h`, which give the hardware board name and MCU type as well as defining several MicroPython features, such as a user switch and USB. Let's now take a look at the next one:

```
#define MICROPY_HW_LED1 (pin_A5)      // green
#define MICROPY_HW_LED2 (pin_B14)     // green
#define MICROPY_HW_LED_ON(pin)        (mp_hal_pin_high(pin))
#define MICROPY_HW_LED_OFF(pin)       (mp_hal_pin_low(pin))
```

This code shows some more example definitions from `mpconfigboard.h`, which create the pin mappings for the LEDs on the development board and define the function to be used to turn an LED on or off.

mpconfigboard.mk

`mpconfigboard.mk` is the make file for the target board. It contains information including the following:

- The MCU series
- The CMSIS target definition
- An alternate function mapping file for the board
- The linker file to be used
- Memory definitions for flash
- A debug probe configuration file

For the most part, you will not need to modify or even look at this file unless you are creating a custom port, which could happen depending on what it is your designing. You can see an example of the make file in the following snippet:

```
MCU_SERIES = 14
CMSIS_MCU = STM32L475XX
# The stm32l475 does not have a LDC controller which is
# the only difference to the stm32l476 - so reuse some files.
AF_FILE = boards/stm32l476_af.csv
LD_FILES = boards/stm32l476xg.ld boards/common_ifs.ld
TEXT0_ADDR = 0x08000000
TEXT1_ADDR = 0x08004000
OPENOCD_CONFIG = boards/openocd_stm32l4.cfg
```

pins.csv

Next, we have the `pins.csv` file. This file contains the pins that exist on the target and the names that they will have within the MicroPython environment so that they can be accessed through a Python script. Every pin that exists on the processor will need to be in this file with a name. I recommend that you open the file to see everything that is in it. The files are usually quite large but the following screenshot shows an example of how the first eight pins are defined for ports `A0`-`A7`. Again, we can customize the name if we want to:

	A	B
1	PA0	PA0
2	PA1	PA1
3	PA2	PA2
4	PA3	PA3
5	PA4	PA4
6	PA5	PA5
7	PA6	PA6
8	PA7	PA7

The excerpt from `pins.csv` that we can see in the preceding screenshot defines what pins exist on the target and what they will be named.

stm3214xx_hal_conf.h

The `stm3214xx_hal_conf.h` module defines which peripheral modules are defined and enabled within the code base. For example, if the target device supports CAN, the following definition would be created:

```
#define HAL_CAN_MODULE_ENABLED
```

If CAN was not supported by the device, then that definition would be commented out so that it is not included in the code base. A snippet from the `stm3214xx_hal_conf.h` module is shown in the following code:

```
/* ######################### Module Selection ##################### */
/**
  * @brief This is the list of modules to be used in the HAL driver
  */
#define HAL_MODULE_ENABLEd
#define HAL_ADC_MODULE_ENABLED
#define HAL_CAN_MODULE_ENABLED
/* #define HAL_COMP_MODULE_ENABLED */
#define HAL_CORTEX_MODULE_ENABLED
/* #define HAL_CRC_MODULE_ENABLED */
/* #define HAL_CRYP_MODULE_ENABLED */
#define HAL_DAC_MODULE_ENABLED
/* #define HAL_DFSM_MODULE_ENABLED */
#define HAL_DMA_MODULE_ENABLED
/* #define HAL_FIREWALL_MODULE_ENABLED */
#define HAL_FLASH_MODULE_ENABLED
```

All four files that are contained with the target board folder define how that board is configured and how it will behave once the code is compiled and pushed to the target. Before we compile our project and deploy it, let's first look at the startup code and how we can modify it with a custom startup configuration.

Navigating the startup code

The startup code for the STM32 port can be found in `main.c`, which is located in the `micropython/ports/stm32` directory. This folder also contains the code for various peripheral modules. In order to make heads or tails of the startup code, I recommend that you open `main.c` and locate the `stm32_main` function. `stm32_main` contains the initialization sequence for MicroPython.

In addition to `stm32_main.c`, the `main.c` module also contains several additional functions that are used to support the system startup. The support code in `main.c` includes additional initialization for items such as the following:

- A flash error state code
- A filesystem reset code, such as creating default `main.py` and `boot.py` files
- Filesystem initialization
- SD card initialization

The initialization sequence is not complicated, but it does contain quite a few steps. When I encounter a code base like this, one of the first things I do is open up the software package I use for software architecture development and draw out the sequence. Drawing out the initialization in a flowchart helps me to visualize what the code is doing. I can then reference this diagram when I need to. Since the startup sequence is long, we will look at a series of diagrams that show generally how MicroPython starts up. As you walk through the sequence and examine the code, you'll notice that I have left out some details that I don't believe to be important to our discussions in this book:

1. The initialization starts by setting up the processor cache and prefetch buffers. The higher-end STM32 devices include cache and several other features designed to improve execution efficiency. Once the cache is set up, the initialization follows a sequence very similar to what an embedded software engineer would expect in any system. First, a system tick is set up. MicroPython leverages the STM32 HAL APIs that require a system tick to keep track of time.

2. Next, the GPIO clocks are initialized. Every peripheral has a clock that can be turned on or off based on whether the peripheral is being used. By default, these clocks are turned off in order to maximize energy efficiency. It just means that before we initialize a peripheral, we must turn each one on. After the GPIO clocks are initialized, there is an option to call a function named `MICRO_BOARD_EARLY_INIT`.

   `MICRO_BOARD_EARLY_INIT` is an interesting optional function. It gives us, the developer, the ability to execute custom code to initialize our board and the items connected to it. We can configure whether this function is executed or not by defining `MICRO_BOARD_EARLY_INIT` in our `mpconfigboard.h` file and then defining the function in our own custom module.

We will discuss this function in much more detail in the next section when we create our own custom initializations for our development board. The following diagram shows the initialization sequence up to this point:

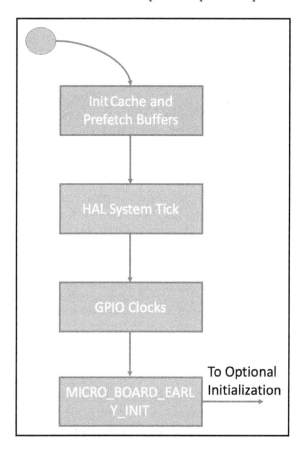

3. At this point in the initialization sequence, we enter a sequence where there are several optional initializations. For example, if a developer wants to, they can enable a startup RAM test that validates RAM to ensure memory integrity. They can also initialize thread support and the LWIP networking stack. If there is a user switch on the board, the switch is also initialized. The reason the switch is initialized so early on is because holding the switch can force the system to restore default settings or enter other modes. More information about this can be found in the MicroPython documentation online (refer to the *Further reading* section). The exact sequence is shown in the following diagram:

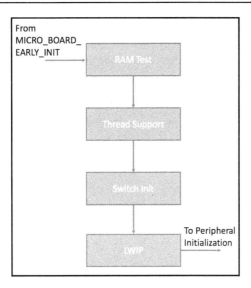

This sequence is configurable and optional for the initialization process, which is based on the MicroPython kernel configuration files that the developer can customize.

4. Once the optional features have been initialized, the kernel will then set up commonly used peripherals. These include **UART**, **SPI**, **I2C, SD Card**, and general memory management. This is shown in the following diagram:

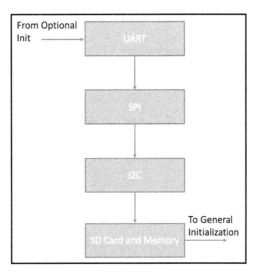

5. Once the peripherals are set up, the next sequence initializes MicroPython. This is done by first setting the LED status, configuring the garbage collection, and then setting up advanced peripherals, such as CAN and USB. The following diagram shows the first steps in initializing the MicroPython kernel:

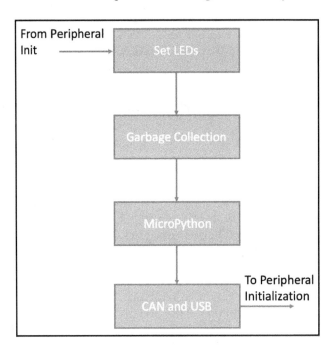

Finally, at this point, MicroPython is configured and our microcontroller is set up. The only thing left to do is to mount the filesystem that will be used by the application and initialize any external devices that might be connected. These could be accelerometers, network controllers, servo motors, or anything else. Once these are set up, the current directory in the filesystem will be checked for the `boot.py` script and it will be executed. `boot.py` normally just points to `main.py` after configuring some basic USB settings for the device. These settings are beyond the scope of our current discussion, but more information about them can be found in the MicroPython documentation.

If `boot.py` finds that there is no `main.py`, or perhaps it's just a short or blank script, then the REPL will be loaded and we can interact with the system through the REPL. This final sequence, that is, the last steps in the initialization sequence that results in running an onboard script or entering the REPL, is shown in the following diagram:

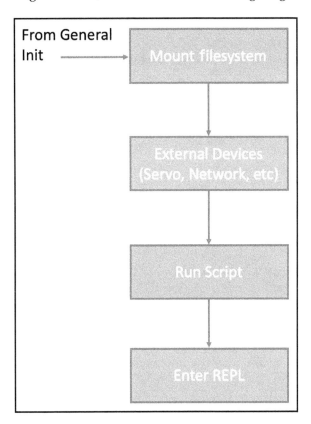

If you dig a little bit deeper into the startup code, you'll also notice that there are additional steps that are followed if a developer soft-resets the system through the REPL using *Ctrl + D*. For now, we are not going to worry about this additional code but it's something I do recommend you take a look at and understand.

In the next section, we will examine how we can customize the kernels' startup code by creating our own `MICRO_BOARD_EARLY_INIT` function that configures our onboard GPIO to settings that match our application.

Modifying the default GPIO initialization

There are times when a developer may want to customize the startup state of the GPIO pins. For example, there may be a secondary power regulatory on the board that will power up circuitry that needs to be placed in its initial state (whether that's on or off). There could be a device connected to a pin that will drive it and we want to make sure that it is configured as an input. Whatever the case may be, we can customize the kernel with custom initialization code that will set our pin states early in the boot-up process.

The steps for customizing our startup code are pretty simple and are listed as follows:

1. Update the `mpconfigboard.h` board module with the `MICROPY_BOARD_EARLY_INIT` definition and the function name that will be called.
2. Create a module to contain the code.
3. Define the function that will be executed.
4. Add the custom startup code.

Let's look at each step in detail:

1. First, we need to open `mpconfigboard.h` and create a macro that defines the function we want to execute early in the boot process. This is done by navigating to our board file directory (`B_L475E_IOT01A`) and then adding the following line of code:

```
void MyCustom_board_early_init(void);
#define MICROPY_BOARD_EARLY_INIT    MyCustom_board_early_init
```

Remember that the MicroPython kernel is written in C so we are going to be writing C code for this customization. The preceding line of code is defining the `MICROPY_BOARD_EARLY_INIT` macro, which will replace all its occurrences with a call to `MyCustom_board_early_init`. The substitution will occur in `main.c` in the `stm32_main` function that we looked at earlier in this chapter. We also need to make sure that we provide the declaration for our function. Public declarations are placed within a header file, so we can just create the declaration before our macro.

2. Next, we need to create the `MyCustom_board_early_init` function. The best place to create this function is in its own custom module that we add to the `B_L475E_IOT01A` board folder. By using this folder, we can keep all the customized code in one location and prevent accidentally changing any core MicroPython kernel code. My personal preference is to create a module named `board_init.c`.

3. Next, we want to add in the minimum amount of code we will need to get the kernel to compile successfully. This can be done by adding the following `include` files:

```
#include STM32_HAL_H
#include <stdio.h>
#include <stdint.h>
```

4. We can then add our definition for `MyCustom_board_early_init` using the following lines of C code:

```
void MyCustom_board_early_init(void)
{
    // Place your custom init code here!
}
```

5. Finally, we get to add our custom code! For `B_L475E_IOT01A`, we are most likely going to want to adjust the default settings on the Arduino header's digital pins. There are 16 pins that we could configure, `D0-D15`, in addition to the six analog pins that we could convert to digital pins if we desired. Let's look at what it would take to initialize a pin for input, output, and analog.

Before we do anything, we need to make sure that we enable the correct clocks to the GPIO port so that we can use the pin. In order to do this, we are going to have to examine the `B_L475E_IOT01A` schematic, which can be found at the STMicroelectronics website. What you will find is that the digital pins are scattered across several GPIO ports, which requires us to create our own reference table to easily use the pins. The table that maps the Arduino header designation to the microcontroller pin is as follows:

Arduino header designation	Microcontroller port designation	Arduino header function
D0	PA1	GPIO/UART4 RX
D1	PA0	GPIO/UART4_TX
D2	PD14	GPIO/INT0_EXTI14
D3	PB0	GPIO/PWM/INT1_EXTI0
D4	PA3	GPIO
D5	PB4	GPIO/PWM

D6	PB1	GPIO/PWM
D7	PA4	GPIO
D8	PB2	GPIO
D9	PA15	GPIO/PWM
D10	PA10	GPIO/SPI1_SS/PWM
D11	PA7	GPIO/SPI1_MOSI/PWM
D12	PA6	GPIO/SPI1_MISO
D13	PA5	GPIO/SPI1_SCK/LED1
D14	PB9	GPIO/I2C1_SDA
D15	PB8	GPIO/I2C1_SCL

As you can see from the preceding table, there are three GPIO ports that are used on the development board:

- GPIO A
- GPIO B
- GPIO D

Before we add any custom code, we need to make sure that we enable the clocks for these ports. The C code that developers need to add to their `MyCustom_board_early_init` function is as follows:

```
__GPIOA_CLK_ENABLE();
__GPIOB_CLK_ENABLE();
__GPIOD_CLK_ENABLE();
```

The MicroPython kernel uses the STM32 HAL, which already defines low-level access functions, so we don't need to write low-level code ourselves. We can easily leverage the STM32 HAL to initialize our system and then we can wait for the MicroPython kernel to boot and do any of the heavy lifting in our Python scripts. Before we access these functions, let's create a few helper variables and initialize them so that we can easily configure our pins:

1. First, we'll create an initialization structure for the GPIO outputs, which configures the typical parameters for a GPIO pin, as in the following snippet:

```
GPIO_InitTypeDef GPIO_InitOutput;
GPIO_InitOutput.Speed = GPIO_SPEED_HIGH;
GPIO_InitOutput.Mode = GPIO_MODE_OUTPUT_PP;
GPIO_InitOutput.Pull = GPIO_PULLUP;
```

2. Next, we will create a similar structure for the input pins, as in the following snippet:

```
GPIO_InitTypeDef GPIO_InitInput;
GPIO_InitInput.Speed = GPIO_SPEED_HIGH;
GPIO_InitInput.Mode = GPIO_MODE_INPUT;
GPIO_InitInput.Pull = GPIO_NOPULL;
```

3. Finally, we will create a configuration variable for analog, as follows:

```
GPIO_InitTypeDef GPIO_InitAnalog;
GPIO_InitAnalog.Speed = GPIO_SPEED_HIGH;
GPIO_InitAnalog.Mode = GPIO_MODE_ANALOG;
GPIO_InitAnalog.Pull = GPIO_NOPULL;
```

As you can see from this pattern, we could easily set up configuration structures for I2C, SPI, PWM, and other peripherals if we wanted to. If that is something you are interested in, you can try it out, but it is beyond the scope of our discussion.

Each pin is configured separately based on the desired function. In order to save space, we will just configure a couple of pins as an example and then you can customize your own initialization as you see fit. Let's start by initializing our ports, as follows:

- D0 – High
- D1 – Low
- D2 – High
- D3 – Low

By default, the board initializes the pins as High, so we should be able to easily see this pattern on a logic analyzer's output.

The code to set up the pin is now pretty simple:

1. First, we will write the output state to the pin before setting it as an output. This is a common practice to prevent any temporary transient behavior on the output pin during configuration. Once we set the pin, we then configure it as an output. The STM32 HAL code to set up the D0 and D1 Arduino headers is shown in the following code. It is necessary to set and configure the D0 and D1 pins as outputs:

```
// Set Arduino-D0 High (PA1) then configure the pin
HAL_GPIO_WritePin(GPIOA, GPIO_PIN_1, GPIO_PIN_SET);
GPIO_InitOutput.Pin = GPIO_PIN_1;
HAL_GPIO_Init(GPIOA, &GPIO_InitOutput);
```

```
// Set Arduino-D1 High (PA0) then configure the pin
HAL_GPIO_WritePin(GPIOA, GPIO_PIN_0, GPIO_PIN_RESET);
GPIO_InitOutput.Pin = GPIO_PIN_0;
HAL_GPIO_Init(GPIOA, &GPIO_InitOutput);
```

The STM32 HAL code necessary to set up and configure the D2 and D3 pins as outputs is as follows:

```
// Set Arduino-D2 High (PD14) then configure the pin
HAL_GPIO_WritePin(GPIOD, GPIO_PIN_14, GPIO_PIN_SET);
GPIO_InitOutput.Pin = GPIO_PIN_14;
HAL_GPIO_Init(GPIOD, &GPIO_InitOutput);

// Set Arduino-D3 High (PB0) then configure the pin
HAL_GPIO_WritePin(GPIOB, GPIO_PIN_0, GPIO_PIN_RESET);
GPIO_InitOutput.Pin = GPIO_PIN_0;
HAL_GPIO_Init(GPIOB, &GPIO_InitOutput);
```

2. We can now select another digital pin to configure as an input. Let's choose D7 since this is a pin that is dedicated as GPIO only. We can configure the pin as a digital input, as in the following code:

```
GPIO_InitInput.Pin = GPIO_PIN_4;
HAL_GPIO_Init(GPIOA, &GPIO_InitInput);
```

3. Finally, we can set up a pin as analog as well, such as A0. The STM32 HAL code necessary to configure the A0 pin as an analog input is as follows:

```
GPIO_InitAnalog.Pin = GPIO_PIN_0;
HAL_GPIO_Init(GPIOC, &GPIO_InitAnalog);
```

Keep in mind that we don't necessarily have to customize the kernel code. We can configure these pins from within a Python script once the MicroPython kernel has loaded. As I mentioned before, there are times when configuring the pins as fast as possible is critical and that is why we would want to customize the kernel this way.

There are also times when we may want to decrease the amount of code that exists on the MicroPython filesystem and want to increase execution efficiency. We can do these things by compiling modules into bytecode and then either including them in the MicroPython filesystem or directly building them into the kernel. Let's now examine how we can add Python modules to the MicroPython kernel.

Adding MicroPython modules to the kernel

MicroPython has a feature that allows a developer to compile their own libraries and then include them within the MicroPython kernel. These modules are often called **frozen modules** because they are compiled into bytecode. There are several advantages to compiling a module into a frozen module, including the following:

- The Python module cannot be modified without flashing the kernel.
- The module is compiled into bytecode, which keeps the source code away from prying eyes.
- Updating the application scripts is faster because there are fewer modules to update.
- If something goes wrong with the filesystem and it gets set back to default, the compiled modules will still be present and can be called as part of the default script to get the system back into a safe state.
- You can put the compiled module into zero wait RAM if it has speed-critical functionality, which will ensure it executes as efficiently as possible.
- The compiled module can now also be stored and executed from flash, which will free up RAM for the Python compiler and scripts that are stored on the filesystem.

Let's look at how we can use the MPY cross compiler to compile the `PCA8574.py`, `button_RGB`, and `LED_RGB` modules that we created in `Chapter 3`, *Writing a MicroPython Driver for an I/O Expander*.

The compilation process

When you first downloaded the MicroPython code, you may have noticed that in the main directory there is a mpy-cross folder. This folder contains the MicroPython cross compiler. Before running the cross compiler on our own code, we need to first rebuild it. The process to do this is straightforward:

1. First, navigate to the micropython main directory. Executing ls in the Terminal should reveal a directory structure similar to that shown in the following screenshot:

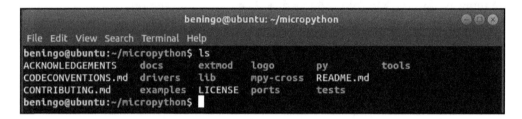

2. Next, you'll want to enter the following command into the Terminal and press the *Enter* key:

   ```
   make -C mpy-cross
   ```

3. The mpy-cross tool should now be compiled and we are almost ready to cross-compile our first module. Before we do that, we want to make sure that all of our frozen modules are stored within a single folder related to the board that we are working on. In this case, we want to navigate to the ports/stm32/boards/B_L475E_IOT01A folder and create a scripts folder. This folder will hold all of our frozen modules. Since the directory structure is deep, I recommend also creating a scripts folder in mpy-cross. We will use this folder to compile our module and then move it to the scripts folder in our board folder. I have found that this is the least error-prone way to do it, but you can use whichever method you are most comfortable with.

4. Finally, copy the PCA8574.py, button_RGB, and LED_RGB modules into the scripts folder within mpy-cross. We are now ready to cross-compile our modules.

In the Terminal, enter the `mpy-cross` directory and then execute the following Terminal commands:

```
./mpy-cross scripts/button_rgb.py
./mpy-cross scripts/LED_RGB.py
./mpy-cross scripts/PCA8574.py
```

If you examine the `scripts` directory, you will find that each of the files now also has a file with the same name, but with the extension `.mpy`. An example of this is shown in the following screenshot:

After cross-compiling the Python modules, a developer will find a matching `.mpy` file in their `scripts` directory, which is the bytecode for their module.

The `.mpy` files are the compiled bytecode modules and they can now be copied to the MicroPython filesystem. If they are referenced in the application, the precompiled bytecode will execute. Keep in mind that if you are going to compile a lot of modules, the `mpy-cross` compiler can only handle one file at a time. It may be more useful to develop a script that will pull the filenames of the Python scripts in the directory and then invoke `mpy-cross`. This will save a lot of Terminal work.

It's important to note that we only want to use `mpy-cross` if we plan to manually deploy the generated `.mpy` files to our device's filesystem. If we want them to be deployed into the kernel, we can include them in our kernel build and the make file will automatically compile our Python scripts. We just need to make sure that we point the kernel to where our scripts are.

We have now successfully made our desired changes to the kernel. Let's look at how we can deploy the new kernel with our frozen modules to the development board.

Deploying the custom kernel to a board

There are two steps that we need to follow in order to deploy our custom kernel to our development board. First, we need to compile our new kernel. Second, we need to take the output files and program them into the flash memory on our development board. Let's start by looking at how we can compile our kernel.

The compiled output files

Compiling the kernel requires us to execute just a couple of commands that will run the make file on our MicroPython port. Before attempting to invoke the make file, let's first return to the `ports/stm32/` folder in the Terminal. I recommend that you clean any previously compiled versions of the kernel by executing the following command:

```
make clean BOARD=B_L475E_IOT01A
```

Once this has been done, we would normally just execute the following statement in order to compile our kernel:

```
make BOARD=B_L475E_IOT01A
```

In this case, using this command will not include the modules that we want to include in the kernel. We must tell the compiler to include these modules in the kernel and tell it where they are located. We can do that by executing the following:

```
make BOARD= B_L475E_IOT01A FROZEN_MPY_DIR=boards/ B_L475E_IOT01A /scripts
```

The compilation may take several minutes, depending on the machine that you are compiling the kernel on. Once it is complete, you should see a final output, as in the following screenshot:

```
CC usbdev/class/src/usbd_msc_bot.c
CC usbdev/class/src/usbd_msc_scsi.c
CC usbdev/class/src/usbd_msc_data.c
CC build-B_L475E_IOT01A/pins_B_L475E_IOT01A.c
LINK build-B_L475E_IOT01A/firmware.elf
   text    data     bss     dec     hex filename
 322608     104   27772  350484   55914 build-B_L475E_IOT01A/firmware.elf
GEN build-B_L475E_IOT01A/firmware.dfu
GEN build-B_L475E_IOT01A/firmware.hex
beningo@ubuntu:~/micropython/ports/stm32$
```

Take a moment to look back through the output messages and see whether you can find our `.mpy` modules. This is a good way to verify that they were included in the kernel build. You can see in the following screenshot that the entries will start with MPY and then include the path and the filename of our modules.

You'll notice in the screenshot that if you want to include Python modules in the kernel, you do not need to precompile them with `mpy-cross`. Instead, you can let the MicroPython make file cross-compile them for you, which can save a lot of manual work:

```
MPY boards/B_L475E_IOT01A/scripts/PCA8574.py
MPY boards/B_L475E_IOT01A/scripts/button_rgb.py
MPY boards/B_L475E_IOT01A/scripts/LED_RGB.py
GEN build-B_L475E_IOT01A/frozen_mpy.c
CC build-B_L475E_IOT01A/frozen_mpy.c
```

We are now ready to deploy our custom kernel to our development board.

Programming the board

If you look back, you'll notice that two different types of files are generated by the build process. First, we have a `.dfu` file. The `.dfu` file is a **Device Firmware Update** (**DFU**) file format, which is supported by the USB standard. We can use Linux-based `dfu-util` or the STMicroelectronics `DfuSe` tool to program these files into flash. Alternatively, there is a hex file output as well. We can use the STMicroelectronics ST utility to program the board as well.

My personal preference is to use `dfu-util`. I've found this to be the simplest approach because it does not require the use of an external flash programmer. The DFU update mechanism is built into the STM32 microcontrollers by pulling the boot pin high while the microcontroller starts up. This then loads the STM32 bootloader, which can communicate with `dfu-util` to perform the firmware update.

If you look at the schematic for `B_L475E_IOT01A`, you will notice that the development board has a **solder bridge** (**SB**) that can be used to select boot from flash or bootloader mode. The solder bridges that we are interested in are **SB9** and **SB13**, shown in the following circuit diagram:

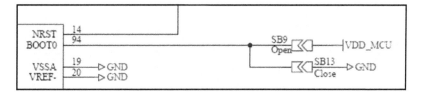

(image source: STMicroelectronics)

The `B_L475E_IOT01A` schematic shows that the **BOOT0** pin can be controlled using solder bridges that are built into the development board.

The problem with the way these solder bridges work is that if you want to boot from flash, you need to solder a bridge across **SB13**. If you want the DFU to run, you need to unsolder **SB13** and solder **SB9**. Obviously, this is not convenient during development or production. The best solution for allowing us to easily switch between modes is to add a switch that will allow us to choose which mode we want the processor to boot into. A generic circuit diagram that can be used to add a switch to our board is shown in the following diagram:

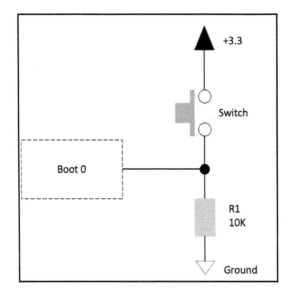

The preceding diagram shows a simple switch circuit that can be used to control whether the development board boots to flash or in bootloader mode.

The process to add a switch to the development board requires five steps. These are as follows:

1. Desolder **SB13**.
2. Solder a 10K 0603 resistor onto **SB13**.
3. Solder leads onto the switch using a 30-gauge wire-wrapping wire.
4. Solder the first lead to the **VDD_MCU** lead of **SB9**.
5. Solder the second lead to the **BOOT0** side of **SB9**.

We now have a switch that can control which mode the microcontroller boots into.

The board is now ready to be programmed. When I first programmed B_L475E_IOT01A, it appeared that the DFU utility did not perform a complete chip erase on the board. Since B_L475E_IOT01A comes with some pre-installed applications, it's useful to download the st-link utility and perform a chip erase of the development board. This will provide a clean environment to load the new MicroPython kernel into. I don't want to go into detail about how to use the st-link utility, but the steps you'll need to follow are as follows:

1. Download the st-link utility.
2. Install the utility.
3. Run it.
4. Plug in B_L475E_IOT01A using the st-link USB connector.
5. Select **Program | Chip Erase**.

You will now have a completely erased microcontroller.

Now, from your Linux Terminal, install dfu-util using the following command:

```
sudo apt-get install dfu-util
```

Flip the switch that you installed on B_L475E_IOT01A and then press the reset button on the development board so that it enumerates as an STM32 bootloader. This is the DFU-capable mode. Use the following command to program the device:

```
dfu-util -a 0 0483:df11 -D build-B_L475E_IOT01A/firmware.dfu
```

Congratulations! The custom MicroPython kernel is now on the board and ready to test.

Testing the updated kernel

Once you have programmed B_L475E_IOT01A, flip the switch back to normal boot and then press the reset button on the development board. You should see the familiar pyb drive mount on the filesystem and have access to the MicroPython REPL. In order to test that our libraries are included and everything is working as expected, we are going to do two things. First, we are going to wire in the RobotDyn I/O expander and the RGB pushbutton so that we can run our application from Chapter 3, *Writing a MicroPython Driver for an I/O Expander*, on our new kernel and board. Second, we are going to use a logic analyzer to look at the initialized pins to make sure that they are behaving the way we set them to.

The schematic diagram to connect the RobotDyn I/O expander and the RGB pushbutton is going to change slightly from the one we had in Chapter 3, *Writing a MicroPython Driver for an I/O Expander*. The reason for this is that we have a different board with different pin assignments. The changes are quite minor and are easily made using the schematic diagram, as follows:

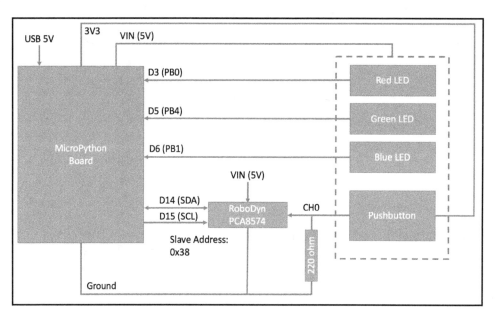

You will notice that for the PWM channels, I've listed the Arduino connector name and also the physical microcontroller pin port. The reason I have done this is that while we will be tempted, in our software, to use the Arduino pin designation, the kernel is using the microcontroller pin. So, in our updated code, we wouldn't use D3 to access the **D3** pin, but instead PB0. If you want to change this, you can go back into the kernel and in the B_L475E_IOT01A boards folder, change the pin designations in the pins file and then recompile and deploy the kernel.

In Chapter 1, *Down the Rabbit Hole with MicroPython*, I mentioned how easy it can be to port a Python application between different hardware platforms. We are about to see a perfect example of this. We first developed an application in Chapter 3, *Writing a MicroPython Driver for an I/O Expander*, for the pyboard that controlled the RGB LEDs and the I/O expander. With the new development board, we can copy our original main.py script to the filesystem of the new board. Note that we don't need to include the supporting libraries because they are built into the kernel.

We now have three changes to the code that we need to make:

1. We need to update which pins are used for the PWM.
2. We need to update which timers are used to generate the PWM.
3. We need to update which timer channels are used to generate the PWM.

As you can see, this requires us to make the following changes:

```
Line 57: PinList = [Pin('PB0'), Pin('PB4'), Pin('PB1')]
Line 60: TimerList = [3,3,3]
Line 66: TimerChList = [3,4,1]
```

That's it! We just moved our entire application to a new MicroPython development board and the only changes we had to make were in those three lines of code! We can now connect a logic analyzer to the **D0-D3**, **D14**, **D15**, and **D9** Arduino pins and run our application the same way we have in previous chapters. When we do that and acquire a trace, we will find that the results are as follows:

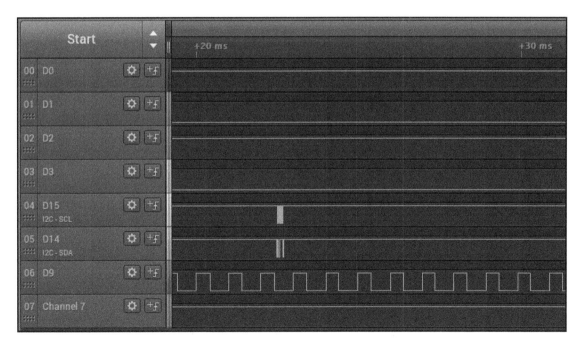

Deploying the custom kernel that adjusts the default I/O states can be seen in this screenshot. The pattern generated was HIGH, LOW, HIGH, LOW, I2C SCL, I2C, SDA, and then a PWM signal.

As you can see, our custom initialized GPIO is set as expected. We can see the I2C messages being sent to the RobotDyn board and we can see that our red LED is on and that there is a PWM signal driving the LED behavior, just as before.

Summary

As we saw in this chapter, developers are able to go into the MicroPython kernel and customize it for their applications. These customizations can be as simple as adjusting the names of the pins on the development board or adjusting the startup states of the GPIO pins, or as complex as communicating with an external device. We also saw that we can save space and increase the execution efficiency of our applications by converting modules into frozen modules, which are then built into the MicroPython kernel. If we need to update those modules, we can also cross-compile them using `mpy-cross` and deploy a precompiled bytecode version of the module onto our filesystem.

Now that we have a solid foundation on how to develop MicroPython applications and how we can customize the kernel, in the next chapter, we will examine how we can create our own custom debugging tools, which will allow us to visualize data in our system.

Questions

1. In which folder in the kernel can you find all the MicroPython supported architectures?
2. Which microcontroller architecture has the most supported development boards?
3. Which three types of files can be found in a development board folder?
4. What are a few features that make `STM32L475E_IOT01A` interesting for MicroPython?
5. Which board kernel file can be modified to change the pin designation that is used to control a pin in a MicroPython script?

6. What function must be defined in order to customize the startup code initialization?
7. What steps should be followed to customize the startup code?
8. Which compiler tool is used to generate `.mpy` files and convert Python scripts to frozen modules?
9. What are the advantages of using a frozen module?
10. What command is used to compile the kernel with frozen modules?

Further reading

1. MicroPython on microcontrollers: `http://docs.micropython.org/en/v1.9.3/unix/reference/constrained.html`
2. General documentation for MicroPython: `https://docs.micropython.org/en/latest/`

6
A Custom Debugging Tool to Visualize Sensor Data

The greatest challenge that every embedded software developer faces is troubleshooting their embedded system. When I speak at conferences such as *Embedded World*, the *Embedded Systems Conference*, and *Arm TechCon*, or when I've polled registrants and attendees to my courses and newsletter (*Embedded Bytes*), on average, developers spend 40% of their time debugging their software. If the average project length is 12 months, that's as much as a year being spent on failure work!

The ability to debug and visualize what an embedded system is doing can help to decrease the amount of time we spend debugging by providing developers with critical system information and a way to easily see what the software is doing. In this chapter, we will build a tool in Python that allows us to visualize what our MicroPython-based embedded system is doing. We will create a test system that generates a stream of sensor data that is then received on a host machine to visualize the system behavior.

The following topics will be covered in this chapter:

- Debugging and visualization embedded systems
- Visualizer requirements
- Visualizer design
- Visualizer construction
- Running the visualizer

Technical requirements

The example code for this chapter can be found at the following GitHub location: `https://github.com/PacktPublishing/MicroPython-Projects/tree/master/Chapter06`.

In order to run the examples, you will want to have the following hardware and software available:

- A MicroPython supported development board
- A UART to USB converter
- A host machine running Python 3.x
- A terminal application (such as PuTTy, RealTerm, Terminal, and many others)
- A text editor such as Sublime Text

Debugging and visualizing embedded systems

A picture is worth a thousand lines of code. As developers, we live in a world of 1s and 0s, registers, peripherals, and scripts that are all interacting with each other and the world around them. Understanding what our software is doing, or the sensors that are connected to it, can dramatically help us develop the system faster but also help us see what the system is doing and better understand how our software is executing.

If you do a search on Google for serial communication plotting, you'll find over a million pages that cover tools such as Mbed's Serial Port Plotter, MegunoLink, ArduinoPlot, and so on. Some of these tools are free, while some require a license that costs less than $50. However, you will find that despite so many options, there really isn't one tool that gives you the flexibility and scalability that is required if you are going to be developing an embedded system.

While we could just select the best fitting plotting software and call it good, there are so many more advantages to us creating our own visualization tool, such as the following:

- The ability to customize the user interface
- Send as much data as we want to as many plots as we want
- Filter the data that we do receive
- Save data if we so choose to a file for later analysis
- Create buttons to send commands and control the system

These are just a few thoughts on the advantages, not to mention that we can easily adapt the tool for our own purposes. For example, we might decide that we don't just want to see sensor data but have tasks send a message when they start and stop executing. This would allow us to create our own custom trace software that we could use to debug the software that we write.

Now, let's define what the requirements are for our custom debugging tool that will allow us to visualize sensor data.

Visualizer requirements

The main purpose of this project is to develop the base code that can be used to receive data coming from a MicroPython board over a serial port and parse that data so that we can then graph it in real time. There are two main areas that we need to consider the requirements for: hardware and software.

Hardware requirements

The visualizer that we are going to be designing is going to be strictly a software development project. There are no hardware requirements for the project. However, there are a few general recommendations.

First, you can use any MicroPython board that you are interested in. While you can select any board, the example project will be written assuming that you are going to use the STM32L475 IoT Discovery board, so you may need to make a few minor modifications to the script to make sure you use the right hardware ports for your board.

Second, this project will send sensor data to the visualizer through the standard UART interface. We are going to assume that the sensors we are monitoring are transmitting humidity and temperature data, so the sample rates are going to be slow. This will allow us to set the baud rate at 115200, which is pretty fast for handling sensors that will be monitored at rates exceeding 10 Hz. Additional sensors could be added to the system at faster baud rates as well. A developer would just have to make sure that they are able to successfully transmit all the data to the host. Since 115200 is a relatively slow baud rate with modern hardware, a developer may also want to consider increasing the baud rate to 1,000,000 bits per second.

Third, keep in mind that there is more than one way to send serial data to the visualizer. If a developer wanted to, they could modify `boot.py` so that the MicroPython board shows up as a **virtual communication port** (**VCP**). This can be done by uncommenting the following line in `boot.py`:

```
pyb.usb_mode('VCP+MSC') # act as a serial and a storage device
```

The only advantage to using the VCP is that you would not need a UART to USB converter to provide the visualizer with serial data to plot.

Finally, since we want our visualizer to be able to handle generic sensor data, we can either select a sensor module that collects humidity and temperature data, parse it, and send that to the visualizer, or we can create test data that does not require any external sensor to be connected to the device.

Software requirements

The software requirements for this project are as follows:

- The visualizer will be written in Python 3.x.
- The visualizer will receive sensor data on the host machine through a selectable communication port.
- The sensor data will be displayed in real time as new sensor data becomes available.
- The visualizer will be scalable and reusable so that it can be used in future development projects (which occur throughout the rest of this book).

These requirements demonstrate the features that need to be implemented and leave the implementation details up to the developer to use their best judgment.

Visualizer design

At this stage in the project, we've discovered what the requirements for the project are. We are now going to develop a hardware and software architecture. The best way to picture an architecture is through a map that is general enough to provide directions on where we need to head but does not provide enough details regarding how to restrict how we get there. The architecture should be flexible so that we can deal with any changing requirements on the fly.

For our purposes, we will use this section to explore the high-level architecture and then develop the detailed design that we can construct the project in the next section

The visualizer hardware architecture

As we mentioned earlier, there are two ways that we can design the hardware interface for the visualizer. First, we can use a live sensor such as a temperature and humidity sensor such as an AM2302, DHT11, or DHT22. These sensors typically just have VCC, ground, and data out. There is a complete tutorial on these sensors that can be found on the Adafruit website at `https://learn.adafruit.com/dht/connecting-to-a-dhtxx-sensor`.

In a configuration where we set up the STM32L475 IoT Discovery board, we can connect the live sensor to the development board and the visualizer using the setup shown in the following diagram:

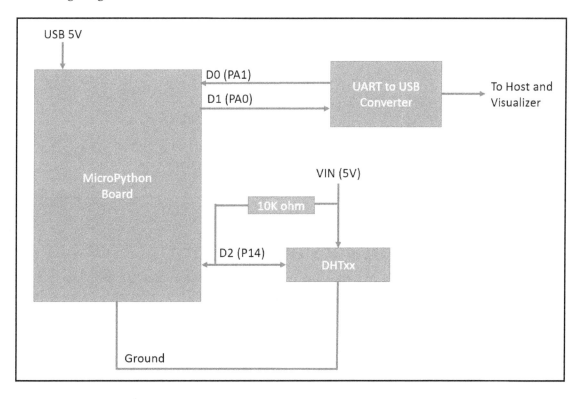

As we can see, this is an example setup of how the MicroPython board and a sensor can be connected to the host computer running the visualizer.

One of the major disadvantages of using this setup initially is that we have several unknowns in the system. We have integrated a sensor that we need to validate and make sure our code works for, and then we must develop the code to communicate with the visualizer. The sensor we select may also not vary much, so it may be hard for us to effectively prove out the visualizer.

This brings us to the second option, which is to not use a live sensor at this point and, instead, generate known values to send to the visualizer that will allow us to validate that our visualizer works so that we can add our sensors to the system. There are several advantages to doing this, such as the following:

- Less code to write initially
- No need to troubleshoot sensor code
- A simpler hardware setup

For this project, we are going to use a simplified hardware configuration that can be used to develop the visualizer, as shown in the following diagram:

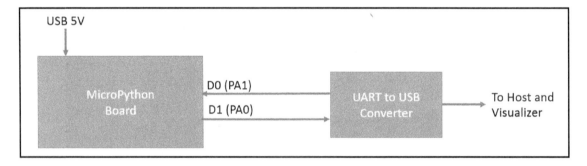

The visualizer software architecture

Looking back at the software requirements for this project, we can identify that there are several key functions that the visualizer will need to perform. These functions include the following:

- Opening and closing the desired communication port
- Setting up and displaying data on a chart
- Receiving and parsing data coming from the communication port
- Plotting the data on the chart

We can represent all these features in a very simple software flowchart. The flowchart can be seen in the following diagram:

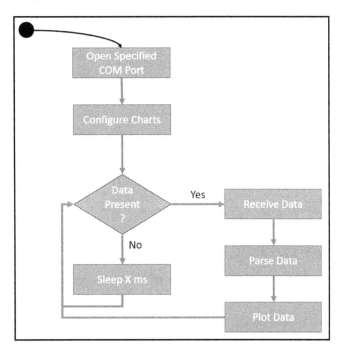

As you can see from the flowchart, when we run the script, we will specify which communication port to expect the data to be coming in on. We will then configure what library is being used to display a chart and get that set up and ready to run. At that point, we just need to wait for data to be received.

When data is received, we pull that data out of the receive buffer and then parse it to determine which of our charts the data should be plotted on. Finally, the data is plotted and we wait for more data to be received. If there is no data plot, then we can simply sleep the application or if we want to be sophisticated, we could set up notifications stating that data is present. At this point, we are now ready to start constructing the visualizer.

Constructing the visualizer

The visualizer is going to leverage existing libraries in order to minimize the effort that is required to receive and plot data. There are two libraries that are particularly interesting for this project: pySerial and Matplotlib.

pySerial is a Python module that encapsulates all the features and functions that are needed to interact with a serial port. `pySerial` can run on multiple operating systems, such as Windows, Mac OS X, and Linux, to name a few. It includes a module called `serial` that provides useful features for interacting with the serial port, such as the following:

- Open
- Close
- Send
- Receive

Matplotlib is a Python library that provides the functionality for 2D data plotting, which can be used interactively or can be used for publication-quality figures. The number and types of charts that can be created are quite extensive. For our purposes, we will just use a good old scatter plot.

Installing the project libraries

Before we start writing the code, let's make sure that we have our host machine up to date on all its software libraries:

1. First, make sure that you are using the latest version of Python 3. For me, that is Python 3.7, but Python 3.x should work without any issues.
2. Next, make sure that your `pip` installation is up to date by opening a Terminal or command console and typing the following:

   ```
   python -m pip install –upgrade pip
   ```

3. Follow the prompts to update `pip` to the latest version. It may take a few minutes to upgrade, depending on your internet connection and how old your `pip` is.
4. Once the `pip` update is complete, we will need to install pySerial and Matplotlib. To install pySerial, use the updated `pip` by typing the following command into the Terminal:

   ```
   pip install pySerial
   ```

5. Again, follow the prompts until the installation is complete. Then, run the following in the Terminal to install Matplotlib:

   ```
   pip install Matplotlib
   ```

The host computer is now ready for us to start writing the visualizer, but first, we need to write a MicroPython application that will send sensor data to the host for plotting over a serial port.

Setting up a serial data stream in MicroPython

As we saw in the hardware architecture for this project, we are going to be using a serial port on the MicroPython device to send a stream of known data to the visualizer to plot. Once we've tested and debugged both sets of code, we can update our MicroPython device to send real sensor data. For now, we just need to send known values that we can use for testing:

1. Before we do anything, we need to make sure that we import the **Universal Asynchronous Receiver/Transmitter** (**UART**) module from `pyb` and set the emergency exception buffer size. Just like we did in previous projects, this can be done using the following code:

```
import micropython                          # For emergency exception
buffer
from pyb import UART
# Buffer for interrupt error messages
micropython.alloc_emergency_exception_buf(100)
```

2. Next, we need to determine which UART we selected to communicate with the serial to UART converter. This can be done by reviewing the hardware architecture and board schematics. For the STM32F475 IoT board, the D0 and D1 pins, which are the UART transmit and receive pins, correspond to UART4. To initialize these pins as a UART functionality and to set the baud rate to `115200`, the following lines of Python code can be written:

```
# Create a uart object, uart4, and setup the serial parameters
uart4 = UART(4, 115200)
uart4.init(115200, bits=8, parity=None, stop=1)
```

3. Next, we want to create a few variables that will be used to track the sample time and the data that will be sent to the visualizer. In this case, we want to keep track of the following variables:
    - `Time`
    - `Temperature`
    - `Humidity`

These variables can be declared as floating-point variables, as follows:

```
# Create variables to store time, temperature and humidity
Time = 0.0
Temperature = -20.0
Humidity = 34.5
```

4. The main loop for the code has a few steps that it needs to perform, which include the following:
   1. Update the time
   2. Update the temperature
   3. Update the humidity
   4. Create the sensor string data to send
   5. Send the latest sensor data

The test loop should run at a frequency of 1 Hz, which means that the main program loop will look as follows:

```
while True:
    # Update Time
    # Update Sensors
    # Create string data
    # Send sensor data
    pyb.delay(1000)
```

5. The code necessary to update the time is nothing more than incrementing the time variable by one. However, the temperature and humidity data are going to be a little more complicated. After all, we don't want to just send any old thing. For the temperature data, we'll start incrementing the temperature throughout each loop by 1 degree until it reaches +20, where it will then turn around and return to -20. The code to pull this off is as follows:

```
# Update Temperature
if TempDir == 1:
    Temperature = Temperature + 1
    if Temperature >= 20:
        TempDir = 0
else:
    Temperature = Temperature - 1
    if Temperature <= -20:
        TempDir = 1
```

6. For the humidity, we do something very similar, except that our variable names and the boundary conditions for the humidity will be 25 on the low end and 35 on the high end. The code necessary to generate this behavior is as follows:

```
#Update Humidity
if HumidDir == 1:
  Humidity = Humidity + 0.5
  if Humidity >= 35:
    HumidDir = 0
else:
  Humidity = Humidity - 0.5
  if Humidity <= 25:
    HumidDir = 1
```

7. There are many different formats that we could use to send the sensor data to the visualizer application. The simplest is to send the data with the following format:

```
Chart for the chart, time stamp, sensor data
```

8. If we wanted to be super robust, we could also wrap this data in a packet format with sync characters, opcode, data packet size, and a checksum. For the most part, this would be overkill for a simple data visualizer that is used for debugging. We can prepare the data and send it as a string by converting the floating-point values into strings and concatenating them together, as follows:

```
# Create string data
TemperatureDataString = '1,' + str(Time) + ',' + str(Temperature)
+'\n'
HumidityDataString = '2,' + str(Time) + ',' + str(Humidity) +'\n'
```

9. The strings are then easy to transmit through the uart4 serial object by writing the following:

```
# Send sensor data
print(TemperatureDataString)
uart4.write(TemperatureDataString)
print(HumidityDataString)
uart4.write(HumidityDataString)
```

Notice that right before we transmit each packet, we print what we are sending to the Terminal. This makes it so much easier to see what the application is doing and will provide useful information in case things don't go as expected. At this point, if you were to run the Python code and connect to the terminal, you would see a sequence of strings being printed, which looks similar to what's being shown in the following screenshot:

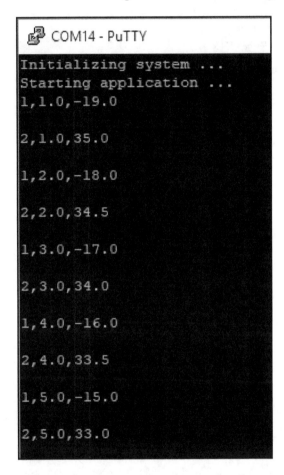

Here, we are seeing the Terminal output for the MicroPython code, which is simulating sensor data and transmitting it to the visualizer application.

We are now ready to collect this sensor data from the host serial port (COM port) and plot it in real time.

Opening a COM port using command-line arguments

On the host machine, create a new Python script using your favorite text editor. I recommend naming the script `VisualizerTool.py`. You could also name it something like `RTPlotter.py` or anything else that you think provides a good description for the module. Now, follow these steps:

1. Our first step to building the visualizer is to integrate the pySerial library and provide command-line options so that we can select which port the data will be coming in on. In order to do this, we need to import the pySerial and `args` modules into the script using the following code:

   ```
   import serial
   import argparse
   ```

2. We also want to be able to cleanly exit the script if a developer does not provide a communication port to connect to. To do this, we want to include the `sys` module using the following code:

   ```
   import sys
   ```

3. Next, we can create a serial object named `ser` that will be used to interact with the serial port. During the object instantiation, we do not want to set up any of the parameters or open a port quite yet. We want to create the object and then once the user passes in the communication port, we can initialize and open the port. The code to create the serial port object is as follows:

   ```
   ser = serial.Serial()
   ```

4. The easiest way to get the communication port from the command line is to use the `parser` argument module. We can create `parser` in a function named `main` that will then be called when the script is executed. The first step in this process is to create a function called `main` that instantiates an argument parsing object, as shown in the following code:

   ```
   def main()
     parser = argparse.ArgumentParser()
   ```

5. Next, we want to add a new argument to the object. The argument that we are interested in is a port argument. This will be a string that holds the port to connect to. The port will be entered using text such as COM5, ttyUSB0, and so on. We can add a new argument using the `add_argument` method, which allows us to create the argument name and provide a description, as shown here:

```
parser.add_argument("--port", help="The communication port to
connect
  to the target")
```

6. When the script runs, we can parse the arguments that are passed into the script by creating a new variable named `args` and using the `parse_args` method, as shown here:

```
args = parser.parse_args()
```

7. There may be times where we want to add multiple arguments that are passed into the script, so it's a good idea to test the `args` variable for the arguments that we are interested in using. For example, we can test `args.port` to see if a port has been passed in and if so, we can proceed to set up the communication port, as shown in the following code:

```
if args.port:
    ser.port = args.port
    ser.baudrate = 115200
    ser.parity = serial.PARITY_NONE
    ser.stopbits = serial.STOPBITS_ONE
    ser.bytesize = serial.EIGHTBITS
    try:
      ser.open()
      print(args.port + " Opened Successfully!")
    except Exception as e: print(e)
else:
  print("A communication port was not provided using --port")
  sys.exit()
```

As you can see from this setup code, we test the port and if it is present, we configure the port and set the baud rate to `115200`, along with the port settings. We could pass these settings in on the command line or even create a configuration file that we read into the script when it starts. For our purposes, we'll *assume* the baud rate settings and just pass in the communication port to keep things simple. Remember, it's always better to build out a robust and strong foundation and then add features as time goes on.

Since we are not validating whether the port being provided to the script is valid, we wrap our `ser.open()` method in a `try/except` case that will either open the port successfully or cause an error, which we will print to the Terminal. This will help us, or a would-be user, figure out what we did wrong when we tried to execute the script. Finally, if we did not pass a `port` argument into the script, we provide a polite message stating that we need to use the `–port` argument in order to use the script and then gracefully exit the application.

8. After the `main` function, we also want to use some scripting to test if a `main` function exists within our script and if so, we want to make sure that the `main` function is called. This can be done using the following code:

```
if __name__ == "__main__":
        main()
```

9. At this point, we should be able to run the script and open the port that we pass into the script. The script will run silently if successful and then just return to the Terminal. If you want to explicitly see that the port is opening successfully, you could add a `print` statement after `ser.open()`, as follows:

```
print(args.port + " Opened Succesfully!")
```

Now that the communication port interface has been successfully tested, we are ready to integrate Matplotlib and create a few scatter plots.

Creating a user interface with Matplotlib

Matplotlib has several different charts, styles, and options that we could use to graph our data in real time, but the ones that we are going to use are the `pyplot` and the animation features. `pyplot` allows us to create the standard *xy* dataset plot, while the `animation` module allows us to periodically update the plot with new data that is coming into the application. In order to use these modules, we need to add them to our application using the following imports:

```
import matplotlib.pyplot as plt
import matplotlib.animation as animation
```

Next, we want to write the code that will display each dataset, temperature, and humidity on separate figures. In order to do this, we are going to use the following process:

1. Instantiate a new plot figure.
2. Add a subtitle to the figure.
3. Create a subplot that will contain the x,y data.
4. Label the x axis.
5. Label the y axis.
6. Create a figure manager.
7. Set the figure location on the monitor.

For each of these steps, only a single line of Python code is required to accomplish the task. The code required to create the temperature figure is as follows:

```python
fig = plt.figure()
fig.suptitle("Temperature", fontsize =16)
ax1 = fig.add_subplot(1,1,1)
ax1.set_xlabel('Time (s)')
ax1.set_ylabel('Temperature (Degrees C)')
Figure1Manager = plt.get_current_fig_manager()
Figure1Manager.window.wm_geometry("+250+250")
```

As you can see, we instantiate the `fig` object using `plt.figure()` and then provide it with its subtitle name by using the `suptitle` method. We then add a subplot to the figure using `add_subplot`. The three ones that are passed into this function specify the number of rows and columns that the graph will have, along with the index of where it will be displayed. We want the largest graph possible in our window, so we select all the ones.

The most interesting piece of code might be that for the window manager geometry. We can directly tell the figure where we want it to be rendered on the screen. In this case, I selected that I wanted the figure to be drawn +250 pixels down and +250 pixels to the right. This allows me to space out the drawn figures so that there is a nice look and feel to it once the second figure is drawn.

The second figure for the humidity is created using the following code:

```python
# Setup Figure 2 for humidity plotting
fig2 = plt.figure()
fig2.suptitle("Humidity", fontsize =16)
ax2 = fig2.add_subplot(1,1,1)
ax2.set_xlabel('Time (s)')
ax2.set_ylabel('Relative Humidity (%)')
Figure2Manager = plt.get_current_fig_manager()
Figure2Manager.window.wm_geometry("+900+250")
```

As you can see, it's done almost identically to the first figure, except we have created new objects to manage the second figure, updated the axis names, and changed the window manager geometry to +900+250. At this point, if you were to run the script and include a call to the plt.show() method, you would see the following plots. As shown here, it's confirmed that the code to generate the temperature and humidity figures is working:

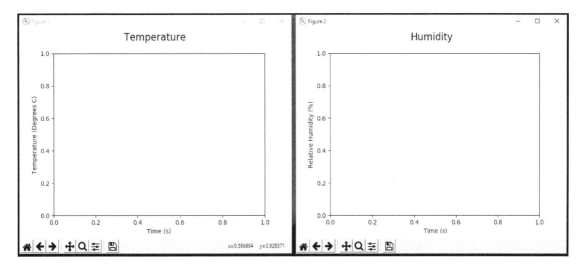

As shown in the preceding screenshot, the drawn figures have our title, axis names, and a toolbar at the bottom. This toolbar includes the ability to move the dataset around by zooming in and out, configuring the subplot settings, and even saving the data.

Now that we have the graphs for our visualizer, let's look at how we can close the loop by creating an animation that periodically processes the incoming serial data and then plots it on the figures.

Plotting the incoming data stream

We now have all the pieces that we need in order to display our sensor data in real time; a figure to plot the data on and a serial data stream to retrieve the data from. The only thing missing now is the code necessary to connect these two pieces. We are going to use the animations feature of Matplotlib in order to this.

The animation feature essentially allows us to create a separate thread that will run on the host for each figure that we want to update. We select the figure that will be updated, the function that will be called, and the interval that we want the plot to be updated at. I've found that on my host machine, updating any faster than a few times per second causes a fair amount of lag if I want to resize or interact with the display. For that reason, I recommend updating at 1 or 2 Hz. To make this value configurable, I would create a variable within our script, as follows:

```
INTERVAL_UPDATE_MS = 500
```

In order to update the figures and show them, we want to add the following three lines of code in our `main` function, after the code that successfully opens the serial port:

```
ani = animation.FuncAnimation(fig, animate, interval=INTERVAL_UPDATE_MS)
ani2 = animation.FuncAnimation(fig2, animate, interval=INTERVAL_UPDATE_MS)
plt.show()
```

As you can see, this code creates two animations that will manage our two figures at the update interval that we select. You'll also notice that the function is expecting a function named `animate`. This function will tie together the incoming serial data and allow us to update the plot. There are several things that we will want the `animate` function to accomplish, such as the following:

- Detect if there is new data present
- Parse the incoming serial data
- Store the data in the appropriate data buffer
- Update the plots

Before we can create the `animate` function, we want to create two sets of lists that hold the *x* and *y* data for the two figures. There are several different ways that we can do this in Python, but we are going to use lists, as shown in the following code:

```
# Stores the x,y data for the temperature figure (1)
Fig1DataX = []
Fig1DataY = []
# Stores the x,y data for the humidity figure (2)
Fig2DataX = []
Fig2DataY = []
```

We are using lists in this way because it's easy to just append new data to them once the serial stream has been received. Now that we have the lists that will store our data, let's receive the data stream and plot it.

Let's start by creating an outline of our `animate` function. We can do this by creating the function and then writing the pseudocode using comments. For example, our animation function at this point should look something like the following:

```
def animate(i):
    # Check to see if there is data waiting to be processed.
    # If data is present, process it, otherwise, refresh the figures
        # While there is data present, read in the data one character at a
time
        # If a newline character is reached, parse the string and store the
data
    # Refresh the plots
```

We can implement the `animate` function one layer at a time, starting with the outmost layer:

1. The first thing that we need to do is create a variable that will store the received characters. We can do this by creating an `InputString` variable at the top of the `animate` function, as follows:

   ```
   InputString = ""
   ```

2. Next, we want to check to see if any characters are present and if there are, for now, we will just print out a message stating that we received a character and then we will update the plots. The resulting code will look something like the following:

   ```
   if(ser.inWaiting() > 0):
       print("Received a character!")

   ax1.clear()
   ax1.plot(Fig1DataX, Fig1DataY)
   ax1.set_xlabel('Time (s)')
   ax1.set_ylabel('Temperature (Degrees C)')
   ax2.clear()
   ax2.plot(Fig2DataX, Fig2DataY)
   ax2.set_xlabel('Time (s)')
   ax2.set_ylabel('Relative Humidity (%)')
   ```

Notice that in this code, we are updating each figure on its own using the following process:

1. Clear the current contents.
2. Plot the x,y data.
3. Set the axis labels again.

When we clear the existing data from the plot, it also resets our axis labels, so we need to redraw them. Currently, we are also using the clear command because we are refreshing all the points on the plot. For a first place implementation, this was the easiest way to get the chart up and running without losing any of the data. In the future, you may decide to just add the new incoming data and keep a separate variable for all the incoming data. We've placed no limits on how large the lists can grow, so at some point, it would make sense to add code that will limit how large they get and clear them out once some maximum number of samples has been received.

We can now move to the next layer in the animate function, which is to start reading in the data. We can replace our print statement with a while loop that will execute until there are no characters in the serial receive buffer. While there is data, we will simply read in a single character into a variable named SerData. The code for this is as follows:

```
while(ser.inWaiting() > 0):
   SerData = ser.read(1)
```

At this point, we want to write some logic that will look at the character that has been received and if it is a newline character, process the InputString variable and if it is not a newline character, we will simply concatenate the new character to the existing InputString. When we do this, we want to make sure that we use the right character encoding by using the decode method with utf-8 specified. The code for this is as follows:

```
if "\n" in SerData.decode("utf-8"):
   # Parse the InputString
else:
   InputString = InputString + SerData.decode("utf-8")
```

This brings us to the core of the parsing in the final layer of the code. As you may recall, the data packets that are coming from the MicroPython device are in the following format:

PlotNumber, X-Data, Y-Data

We used a comma delimited format so that we could use the split() Python function to split the string when it encountered a comma. We can then check the first element in the new data list to see if it is a 1 for a temperature plot or a 2 for a humidity plot. Once we determine which it is, we convert the string data into a floating-point number and store it in the appropriate data list. Our InputString is then reset and we should have a fully functional visualizer. This final layer of code for parsing the string can be seen in the following code:

```
SplitStrData = InputString.split(',')
print(SplitStrData)
if(int(SplitStrData[0]) == 1):
```

```
    Fig1DataX.append(float(SplitStrData[1]))
    Fig1DataY.append(float(SplitStrData[2]))
  elif(int(SplitStrData[0]) == 2):
    Fig2DataX.append(float(SplitStrData[1]))
    Fig2DataY.append(float(SplitStrData[2]))
  InputString = ""
  SplitStrData = None
```

We are now ready to test and run our visualizer tool.

Running the visualizer

Now, we are ready to test the visualizer, which will require several steps. These steps include doing the following:

1. Starting the MicroPython application
2. Identifying the COM port the data is received on the host
3. Starting the visualizer on the host

First, set up and run the MicroPython script. When you connect to your MicroPython Terminal, you should see that the Terminal is displaying information similar to what can be seen in the following screenshot. As we can see, the transmission of sensor data packets over UART is successful:

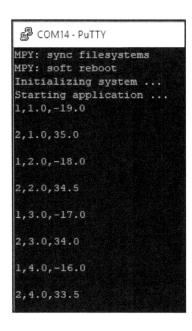

Next, we can identify which communication port the USB to serial adapter is using. The format for the serial port will vary, depending on the operating system that you are using, along with how you found the COM port. I am using a Microsoft Windows machine, and my USB to serial adapter is currently COM5.

This brings us to the final step, which is to execute our visualizer script. This can be done by running the script with the –`port` option, as follows:

```
python RTPlotter.py -port COM5
```

If everything went according to plan, you should now see two figures on your monitor and a few times each second, the figures should be updating with fresh sensor values. If you let the system run for a few minutes, you should see that a pattern emerges in the data, similar to the one shown in the following image. This shows that executing the visualizer with the script-generated sensor data is successful:

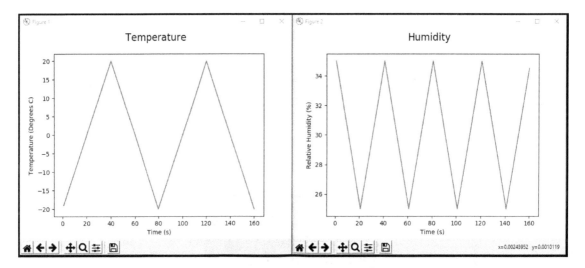

Congratulations! At this point, you now have a working visualizer that you have been able to verify receives sensor data from the MicroPython board successfully. I would recommend that you play with the interface and come to understand how you can zoom in, zoom out, and save the data.

We are now ready to discuss what next steps you might take with this project in order to further hone your skills.

Going further with visualizer enhancements

Now that we have a functional visualizer, there are so many enhancements that we can make to improve the functionality and the usefulness of our new tool. While these enhancements are beyond the scope of this book, I think it's still a good idea to discuss them in order to give you ideas regarding where you can take this project from here. Let's examine a few ideas regarding new features and code enhancements you can make to this project.

The visualizer, while functional, is not the most scalable piece of code. As you may recall, we hardcoded the two different charts that appear when we run the visualizer. While this is useful for testing, it would be great to create a configuration file that would contain the following information:

- Chart name
- X axis label
- Y axis label
- Refresh rate
- Chart screen location

The configuration file could list each piece of information for all the charts that will be included in the visualizer when it is executed. The visualizer would start up, read the file, and then use a simple loop to instantiate all the charts. By doing this, the visualizer would become much more scalable and would require that only the configuration file be modified for any project. With the addition of a configuration file, the Terminal interface arguments could also be modified so that a developer can pass along the name of the configuration file that they want to use during that execution cycle.

The next enhancement that could be made to the visualizer is to improve the robustness of the communications between the MicroPython board and the host computer. Right now, the data stream is simple and does not include any checksums to validate the data. We've written our code to assume that there will never be a problem, but if the noise gets injected into the serial lines, there is no way to detect that the data has become corrupted. This can be resolved by adding a simple and fast checksum algorithm such as Fletcher 16 to the data.

Another idea that would be useful to implement in the visualizer is the ability to save the received data to a file. There may be times where we will want to save the incoming data and then open it in a spreadsheet to apply a filter or further analyze the data. While the chart will let you save a PNG image, having the raw data that was received would also be quite useful, and it doesn't take much to add this feature. Again, a developer could add a Terminal argument that, when used, would save the incoming data to the file for later processing.

The visualizer we created was designed to plot data from our device, but it could also be modified to allow two-way communication. The serial interface could be updated to allow a serial message to be sent to the MicroPython device, which could then turn on an LED, run a motor, or any number of potential activities. This opens the door for us to integrate the test harness example that we looked at earlier into the visualizer so that you have one comprehensive piece of software that can display what is happening on the MicroPython device but also direct how it will behave and function.

Summary

In this chapter, we explored how we can use the UART and on-board a MicroPython board to transmit a stream of data that provides us developers with insights into how our system is behaving. We created a stream of known data that represented temperature and humidity data to verify that a host-based visualizer application was able to parse the data stream and then plot the data in real time. With this communication loop closed, we now have the ability to plot important information such as sensor values, but we can also transmit trace data from our MicroPython application and then plot it to get a better understanding of how our applications are behaving and use this information to troubleshoot our applications.

In the next chapter, we are going to look at how we can integrate motion and gesture detection sensors and interact with them using MicroPython to control a robot.

Questions

1. What files are used to modify what USB classes are supported on startup by the MicroPython board?
2. What are some reasons we would use generated data in our development rather than a live sensor?
3. At what chart refresh rate does the user interface start to become sluggish?
4. What are some reasons for using the MicroPython UART for communication over using the USB?
5. What Python function is used to convert a floating-point number into a string?
6. What module is used to create command-line arguments?
7. What are some new features that could be added to the visualizer to enhance its capabilities?

Further reading

1. pySerial documentation (https://pythonhosted.org/pyserial/)
2. Matplotlib documentation (https://matplotlib.org/)

Device Control Using Gestures 7

Knobs, buttons, levers, and touch screens have dominated the controls world by being the primary way that a user interacts with an embedded device. These tactile interfaces aren't the only way to interact with a device. In recent years, new sensors and technologies have created opportunities to create tactile-less interfaces that rely on hand movements and gestures. These gesture-based controls can be a far more intuitive and natural way to interact with a device.

In this chapter, we will examine how to integrate a gesture controller into an embedded device that allows us to control it using gestures.

The following topics will be covered in this chapter:

- An introduction to gesture controllers
- Gesture controller requirements
- Gesture controller hardware and software design
- Constructing a gesture controller
- Testing gesture controller applications

Technical requirements

The example code for this chapter can be found at `https://github.com/PacktPublishing/MicroPython-Projects/tree/master/Chapter07`.

In order to run the examples, you will need to have the following hardware and software:

- A MicroPython supported development board
- An Adafruit ADPS9960 breakout board
- A prototyping breadboard
- Wire jumpers
- Four LEDs with appropriately sized resistors
- A terminal application (PuTTy, RealTerm, Terminal, or one of many others)
- A text editor, such as Sublime Text

Introducing gesture controllers

Gesture controllers provide developers with the ability to create unique interfaces to their embedded product that allows the user to interact with their device in a hands-free way.

Gesture technology can vary quite dramatically in its capabilities and the technology that drives it. For example, a low-end system can take advantage of an **infrared light-emitting diode** (**IR LED**) and a photodiode with a cost of less than $10, whereas a higher-end system, such as Leap or the discontinued Microsoft Kinect, might cost several hundred dollars. High-end solutions often use several cameras, including an IR camera, to capture motion and then break it down into a gesture.

For most readers, integrating Leap, or another gesture controller that is typically USB-based, is going to be outside your price range and will also require quite a bit of development time. These higher-end solutions provide **software development kits** (**SDKs**) for Windows, macOS, and Linux, which means considerable work would need to be done to port the SDK so that it can be used with MicroPython. In this project, we are going to use a simple, low-cost integrated gesture controller that is based on an IR LED and a photodiode. All the electronics are integrated into a single package and provided by Avago as the APDS-9960 breakout board.

The APDS-9960 is a digital proximity, ambient light, and RGB gesture sensor. For our purposes, we are interested in the digital proximity and gesture sensor aspects. We want to use the sensor to detect when someone waves their hand across the sensor so that we can detect the following gestures:

- Forward
- Backward
- Left
- Right

These are the typical gestures that we might want to use to control a robot or other device, or perhaps even a coffee maker or stove. We could also add additional gestures, such as up, down, or something far more complex and customized. The APDS-9960, which is a gesture controller, does not provide us with the gesture answer. Instead, it provides a series of counts for its photodiodes that we, as the developer, then need to analyze and interpret to determine what gesture was presented to the sensor. We will explore how the gesture controller works once we get into the hardware design, but first, we should discuss what our requirements are.

Gesture controller requirements

The main purpose of this project is to build a cost-effective gesture controller that we can integrate into an embedded device and use to control the device. Our device should be able to control relays, send a message out on Wi-Fi or Bluetooth, or carry out many other possibilities. With this project, we want to set up the building blocks that will make our detected gesture turn an LED on for five seconds and then turn it off. The LED that lights up will correspond to the gesture that was detected, which will also be printed to the terminal. Let's now look at our hardware and software requirements.

Hardware requirements

The hardware requirements for our gesture controller are much stricter than in our previous projects. While in the past we kept the system requirements pretty loose, in this project we are going to specify the exact hardware components that will be used in the project. We normally want to keep the requirements loose to allow an engineer to select the parts that they think best fit the application. However, in the real world, we don't always have that luxury! Sometimes, there are monetary requirements that force a developer to use a specific part, such as a customer preference, or even a relationship with a company that makes using a specific part a necessary requirement.

For the gesture controller, our hardware requirements are as follows:

- The gesture controller will be based on the Avago APDS-9960 breakout board.
- The system will have four LEDs, each one representing one of the four defined gestures that will be detected by the system: forward, backward, left, and right.

From a hardware viewpoint, we don't have too many requirements, but they are quite specific to the hardware that we will be using. The reason for this is that for our example, I want to ensure you are using the same hardware as I am in case there are differences in the results.

Software requirements

The general behavior for the gesture controller software can be summed up in just a few simple requirements. In these requirements, we are just specifying the system-level software requirements. As we design our controller, we'll see that there are a lot of best practices we can implement that could be considered software requirements. The software requirements we are interested in listing at this point include the following:

1. The gesture controller should be able to detect the following gestures:
   - Forward
   - Backward
   - Left
   - Right
2. When a gesture is detected, the gesture will be printed in the terminal. If a gesture type cannot be determined, unknown will be printed in the terminal.
3. When a gesture is detected, an LED corresponding to the detected gesture will be turned on for five seconds to signify the detection of a gesture.

If we were designing a battery-operated device, we might also add in requirements for optimizing the gesture controller power profile. After all, the energy consumption of the device will depend on how hard we drive the LEDs. We are going to leave those types of exercises up to you to play with once the controller is working.

Hardware and software design

The requirements for this project give us a very concrete direction concerning the hardware and software, but at the same time, there is quite a bit of wiggle room as to how exactly we implement our architecture. In this section, we are going to develop the hardware and software architecture that we will use to build our gesture controller.

The gesture hardware architecture

There are just three major components that we need to be concerned about within the hardware architecture:

- The MicroPython development boards
- The APDS-9960
- The LEDs

Just as in the previous projects, we can power the MicroPython board through a USB connector, at least during development. As we saw in the last lab, if you are using the STM32 IoT Discovery node with the Arduino prototyping board, there are +5V and +3V output headers. The development boards for the APDS-9960 from Adafruit and SparkFun can take 3V, so they can be powered directly from the MicroPython board. In most cases, it also makes sense to power the LEDs through +3V and then use a **General Purpose Input/Output** (**GPIO**) pin to control the state or brightness through a **pulse width modulation** (**PWM**) or just an on or off switch

There are two communication interfaces that we need to concern ourselves with. The first is the communication interface between the MicroPython board and the APDS-9960. The APDS-9660 uses **inter-integrated circuit** (**I2C**), so that will be the interface that is used. The last interface is just the USB console interface, the **REPL** (short for **Read-Eval-Print Loop**), that we will use to display the gesture that was detected.

The following figure summarizes the hardware architecture for the gesture controller:

The detailed hardware design

As we look at the hardware architecture, we can see that there are several areas that we can further define in our detailed hardware design. These include the following:

- Selecting the APDS-9960 development board
- Assigning I/O pins to interface to the APDS-9960 and the LEDs

There are several different development boards that are available for the APDS-9960. For the most part, they are all relatively comparable. They offer an on-chip regulator so that the development board can accept +5V and often also include a +3V out pin so that other devices can also be powered off that regulator. The two development boards that I like the most are from Adafruit and SparkFun. Either one can work for this project, but I chose the board from Adafruit because it was around half the price of the other. The development board also exposes an interrupt pin that notifies developers when there is gesture data available to be processed. The software developer can either poll the chip or wait for the interrupt pin to query the data, but for simplicity, we will just poll it.

The I/O pin assignments for this project can be assigned pretty generically, except for the interrupt pin. The interrupt pin needs to be connected to **D2**, which is the interrupt pin that is exposed on the Arduino shield connector. Other than that assignment, the pins can be assigned sequentially to the LEDs, as in this diagram of the entire hardware design:

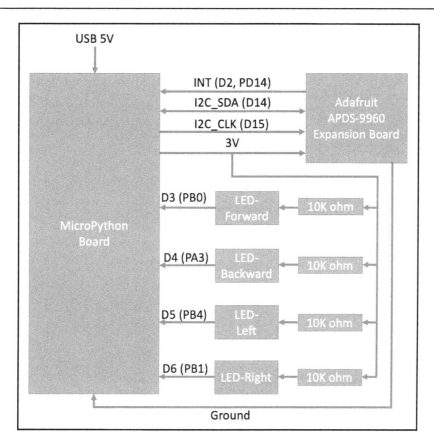

Let's now look at the software architecture for this application.

The software architecture

The application code for our gesture controller is going to be simple. The application needs to first instantiate a gesture object and tell it which I2C bus the APDS-9960 is located on. Once the gesture controller object has been created, we simply make a call to the object's gesture status method to determine whether a gesture is present or not. If one is present, then we get the gesture that was detected, which then updates the LEDs based on the detected gesture. When we receive a new gesture, we want that gesture to stay on the LEDs for several seconds before it disappears.

After we receive a new valid gesture, we will signal to the application that we want to latch the LEDs. The actual mechanism used to control the latch will not be shown here because we want the developer to decide for themselves what the most efficient means is when they build the application. The flow diagram for the gesture controller application can be seen here:

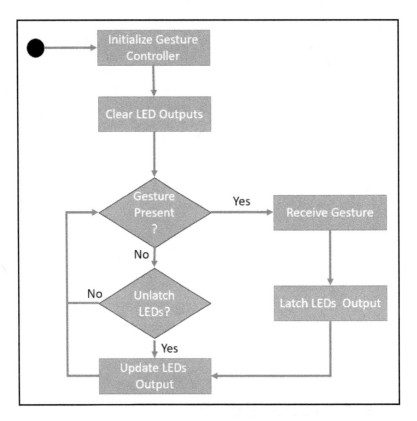

Now that we have a general feel for how we want the application to execute, let's take a closer look at the class we would like to implement for the APDS-9960. The APDS-9960 has quite a few capabilities associated with it, such as the following:

- Ambient light and RGB color sensing
- Proximity sensing
- Gesture detection

While we could create a class that implements all of these features and allows the user to specify which capabilities they will be using, we want to keep our class simple. So, for simplicity's sake, we will create a class that only focuses on getting the gesture piece to function.

For our gesture class to operate, there are two main methods that we need to make sure that we have implemented. First, we need the constructor for our class to initialize the APDS-9960. Initialization should include configuring all the APDS-9960 registers as required for the application. We can do this by creating a separate configuration module that contains all the registered settings for our class. We can also just hardcode it into our application as well. That would make it less scalable but it would get the system initialized to a known and working state first.

Next, we need a method that will allow us to get the results from any gestures that have been made. This function could simply be called `GestureGet`. The `GestureGet` method would not only return the detected gesture but also pull the data from the chip, process it, and then determine what data was received. Basically, it would do everything needed to interact with the gesture controller in a single method. This method will allow the gesture-controller user to easily access the high-level gesture function from the APDS-9960. Here is an example class diagram for the APDS-9960's gesture capabilities:

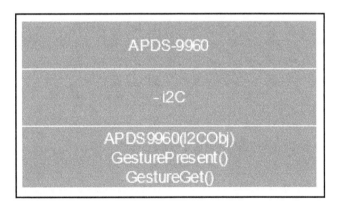

At this point, we've described the high-level architecture interactions between the application code and the `APDS-9960` class. As I mentioned earlier, this looks nice and simple. The real devil, though, is in the details, which we will explore in the next section.

Constructing the gesture controller

We are going to look at building the gesture controller in several different chunks. First, we are going to explore the theory behind how the APDS-9960 works. Once we understand how it works, we will then develop the APDS-9960 driver that is shown in the class diagram in the *The software architecture* section. Finally, we will write our high-level application that uses the class. At that point, we will be ready to test the controller. Let's get started!

The APDS-9960 theory of operation

The APDS-9960 has four directional photodiodes, which are used to detect the reflected infrared light that is generated by integrated IR LEDs. The reflected light can be used to sense motion, such as distance, direction, and even velocity. The APDS-9960 is broken up into several different states that provide capabilities, such as proximity detection, a gesture engine, and color detection. The features that are most relevant to a gesture controller are the proximity and gesture states, which can be used to first sense a hand and then provide relevant data to determine which gesture motion was given to the system.

The most important state included in the APDS-9960 is the gesture engine. The gesture engine is quite flexible and can be triggered either manually or automatically. Automatic triggering is performed by initializing the proximity engine and setting a trigger level that, once exceeded, kicks off the gesture engine. Developers are able to fine-tune the gesture controller by utilizing features such as the following:

- Ambient light subtraction
- Cross-talk cancellation
- Amplifying gain and LED output
- Energy management
- Gesture conversion delay

Each application and environment may require minor modifications to these settings in order to fine-tune the APDS-9960 to sense gestures. You can get a feel for the overall hardware capabilities of the APDS-9960 by reviewing the following block diagram:

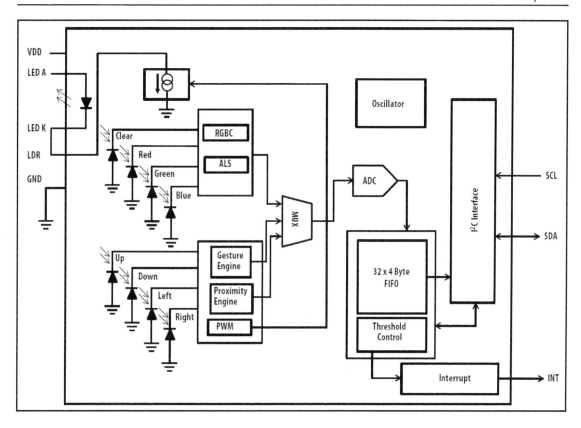

Interfacing to the APDS-9960 only requires three signal lines. Two signals are used by the I2C for bidirectional communication to set up the APDS-9960 registers and then to read the result registers. The third signal, which is optional, is an interrupt signal that notifies the connected microcontroller that there is gesture data ready to be analyzed. The data is stored as four 8-bit signals that correspond to how much IR energy was reflected and detected by the photodiodes. The data is stored in a **first in first out** (**FIFO**) queue, which can store at most 32 readings.

The photodiodes are arranged so that the readings correspond to up, down, left, and right. While you may believe that these correspond to the gesture, they are really just the arrangement of the photodiodes in the APDS-9960. In order to tease a gesture result out of the device, numerous readings need to be acquired and then analyzed based on the readings in all four photodiodes over time.

When the APDS-9960 is first powered up, it enters a low-power sleep mode. It's up to the developer to configure the registers and then power up the device. The I2C can wake the device but it will return to sleep unless the **Power ON** (**PON**) bit is set to 1.

At this point, the device enters an idle state but still doesn't run any of the analog engines until its corresponding **enable** bit is set to 1. Once the APDS-9960 is initialized, it will traverse a state machine based on the way that it is configured. The state diagram for the APDS-9960 is as follows. During each cycle, the APDS-9960 will potentially run each engine, provided that it is enabled:

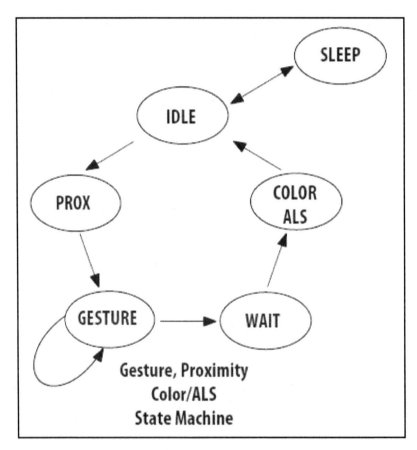

The datasheet for the APDS-9960 contains several useful diagrams that provide the register settings necessary to get the device up and running in different modes. In general, a developer will want to review the flowchart from the Avago datasheet, which can be seen in the following diagram. The flowchart demonstrates the flow of the code and settings that need to be configured in order to allow each engine to execute:

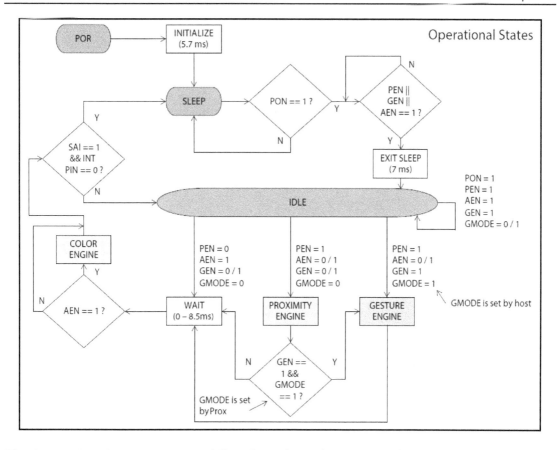

The Avago APDS-9960 operational flowchart shows how to initialize the device and what settings are necessary to get it to transition into various operational engines.

Analyzing gesture data

Since the APDS-9960 only provides the raw data for a gesture, it's up to the developer to create an algorithm that can determine what gesture movement was actually created. While we like to create software architecture up front and design how everything will work before writing any code, it's sometimes necessary to do some experiments first. These experiments are designed to help us understand the components that we are working with and to help us design an algorithm that can determine what gesture was made. These experiments, however, should not be considered as producing the production code. Developers are simply improving their understanding of the part and the resultant test code should be refactored, cleaned up, or even completely rewritten once a developer understands the component.

For our gesture controller, we are interested in detecting four different gestures: forward, backward, left, and right. In order to design an algorithm that can accurately detect these gestures, we need to acquire some data on the APDS-9960 that shows us how the component behaves. In order to do this, we can acquire a few samples for the different gestures. The following graphs show what each photodiode sees for the different gestures that we are interested in. Take a few minutes to examine these plots. The APDS-9960 diode output for a right-to-left gesture swipe is shown in the following diagram:

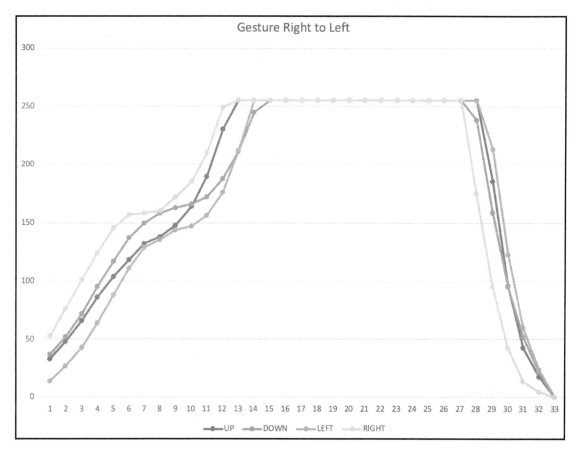

 Note: The data here is clipped at the maximum but that won't affect our algorithm.

The APDS-9960 diode output for a left-to-right gesture swipe is shown in the following diagram:

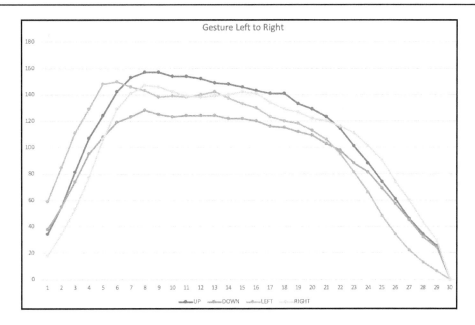

We can see the APDS-9960 diode output for a front-to-back gesture swipe in the following diagram:

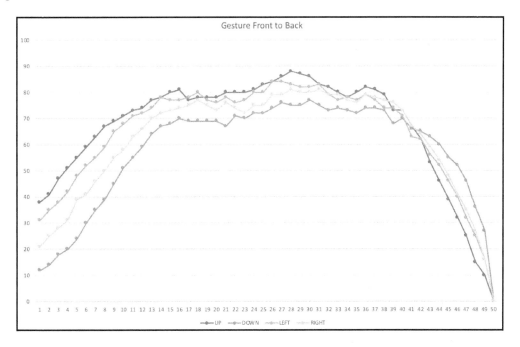

The APDS-9960 diode output for a back-to-front gesture swipe is shown in the following diagram:

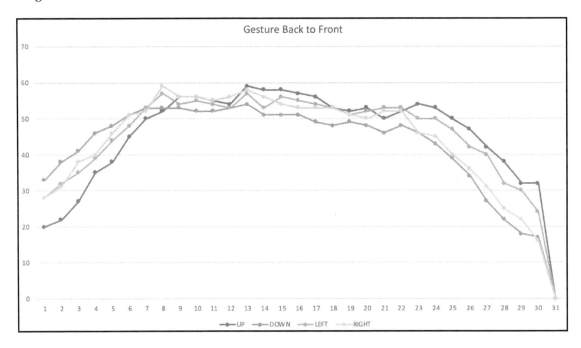

If you examine the different plots closely, you'll notice a few important points:

- The diode that is the opposite of the gesture direction will start with the greatest number of counts.
- The diode that is associated with the gesture will end with the highest number of counts.
- The diodes that are not in line with the gesture will have a small count differential compared to the diodes in line with the gesture.

As the developer, we can choose how we want the gesture controller to work. For example, we could design gestures that require a hand to be placed over the controller for some period of time and then have a directional swipe conclude the gesture. We could limit the time frame of the gesture to a few hundred milliseconds, which would enforce a complete one-side-to-the-other gesture. It's really up to us, as the developer, how a gesture is initialized and finalized. For our controller, we are going to assume that when a hand is detected, it is already making a gesture movement. This will allow us to use a timer to limit the window in which we can detect the gesture.

The APDS-9960 gesture driver

The gesture driver that we are going to write for this project isn't so much a driver as it is a dedicated application module. A driver should be a generic implementation of how to interact with the APDS-9960. We are going to write a class that does the following:

- Interacts only with the proximity and gesture engines
- Executes dedicated initialization code
- Contains all the application code to return the gesture that is sensed

The gesture application is therefore integrated into the driver functionality. If we really wanted to create an APDS-9960 driver, we'd create a class that would interact with all the analog engines in the APDS-9960, from a very generic viewpoint, and then create another class that uses the data from the APDS-9960 to generate the gestures we are interested in. If we were doing this for a production project, that would be the direction we would go in, but for a DIY project, an integrated application module will work just fine.

Before we dive into the driver module, we should spend a few minutes discussing how the driver should act. There are several important behavioral characteristics that we need to discuss:

- First, we don't want the gesture engine to run unless a hand has got to within a certain distance of the sensor. In order to do this, we can enable the proximity engine and set a proximity threshold that, once reached, will flip the internal **GMODE** bit and cause the APDS-9960 to change states to the gesture engine. Doing this will prevent us from accidentally transitioning into the gesture engine and receiving information that is not associated with a gesture.
- Next, it's possible that when we start the application, there is gesture data already in the FIFO ready to be processed. We don't want this data to interfere with any new gestures, so when we start our application, we want to make sure that we empty out this buffer before we start looking for new gestures.
- Finally, we want to make sure that the primary method returns the gesture that was detected. This will help simplify our application code.

Before we write the `APDS_9960` class, there are several constants that should be created within the `APDS_9960` module. First, the APDS-9960 always has an I2C address of `0x39`. Next, there are several different register settings and bits that need to be set correctly in order for the proximity and gesture engines to work correctly. Going into the details on how all these settings work is beyond the scope of this chapter, but the settings that we are going to be using are as follows:

```
# Register Definitions
REGISTER_ENABLE = 0x80
REGISTER_CONTROL = 0x8F
REGISTER_PDATA = 0x9C
REGISTER_GPENTH = 0xA0
REGISTER_EXTH = 0xA1
REGISTER_GCONFIG1 = 0xA2
REGISTER_GCONFIG2 = 0xA3
REGISTER_GCONFIG4 = 0xAB
REGISTER_GFLVL = 0xAE
REGISTER_GSTATUS = 0xAF
REGISTER_GFIFO_U = 0xFC
REGISTER_GFIFO_D = 0xFD
REGISTER_GFIFO_L = 0xFE
REGISTER_GFIFO_R = 0xFF
# Register Bit Definitions
REGISTER_ENABLE_BIT_PON = 0x01
REGISTER_ENABLE_BIT_PEN = 0x04
REGISTER_ENABLE_BIT_GEN = 0x40
REGISETER_BIT_PIEN = 0x20
REGISTER_BIT_LDRIVE = 0xC0
REGISTER_GCONFIG4_BIT_GMODE = 0x1
REGISTER_GSTATUS_BIT_GVALID = 0x1
REGISTER_GCONTROL_BITS_GFIFOTH = 0x0C
```

It is highly recommended that, at this time, you take the previous register settings and read through the APDS-9960 datasheet so that you can understand how these settings affect the way the chip behaves.

The APDS-9960 gesture class constructor

The first step in implementing our gesture class is to create the constructor:

1. We can start by defining the class, along with the methods we will need in the class, as follows:

```
class APDS_9960():
    GESTURE_FORWARD = 0x0
```

```
GESTURE_BACKWARD = 0x1
GESTURE_LEFT = 0x2
GESTURE_RIGHT = 0x3
def __init__(self,I2CObject, Verbose):
    print("Object Initialized!")
def Detect(self):
    print("Detecting Gesture ...")
```

As you can see from the preceding code snippet, we have defined a few variables that will be used to define what gesture was detected, along with the creation of our construction and the main method that will be used to detect a gesture.

2. Next, we want to use the I2C object that was passed into the constructor to determine whether the APDS-9960 is present or not. We can do this by using the following code:

```
self.i2c = I2CObject
self.DeviceList = self.i2c.scan()
for Device in range(len(self.DeviceList)):
        if self.DeviceList[Device] == APDS_9960_ADDRESS:
                self.APDS_9960_PRESENT = True
        else:
                print("APDS9960 not present!")
                return False
```

If the module is not detected, then we return `False` and the higher-level application can decide how to handle the error.

3. The next step is to define the operating modes and set the IR gain, the proximity, and the gesture threshold values. For benchtop testing, we set the gain to the maximum amount. We then want the gesture to start recording data once the threshold hits 40 counts in the leading photodetector and then exit when it drops below 30 counts in the trailing photodetector. This can be done by using the following code:

```
# Enable the PON, PEN, GEN
self.mode = REGISTER_ENABLE_BIT_PEN + REGISTER_ENABLE_BIT_GEN
# Set the analog engine mode
self.i2c.mem_write(self.mode, APDS_9960_ADDRESS,
REGISTER_ENABLE,timeout=1000)
# Set the IR gain to maximum
self.i2c.mem_write(0x0C, APDS_9960_ADDRESS,
REGISTER_CONTROL,timeout=1000)
# Set the proximity threshold that will enable GMODE
self.i2c.mem_write(PROXIMITY_THRESHOLD_COUNT, APDS_9960_ADDRESS,
    REGISTER_GPENTH, timeout=1000)
```

```
# Set the gesture exit threshold
self.i2c.mem_write(GESTURE_EXIT_THRESHOLD_COUNT, APDS_9960_ADDRESS,
    REGISTER_EXTH, timeout=1000)
```

4. With the mode configured, we also want to set the gain in the photodetectors to 4 with a maximum engine wait time. Since there are other settings in this register, we first want to read the current value and then modify it before writing to the register. This operation can be seen in the following code:

```
# Read the GCONFIG2 register and set the gain to 4. Also set
maximum wait time
self.registerData = self.i2c.mem_read(1, APDS_9960_ADDRESS,
REGISTER_GCONFIG2)
self.registerData = ord(self.registerData) | 0x40 | 0x0
self.i2c.mem_write(self.registerData, APDS_9960_ADDRESS,
REGISTER_GCONFIG2, timeout=1000)
```

5. When we power up our system, the APDS-9960 shouldn't have any data in the FIFO, but we can't assume that we are running from a clean power cycle. It's possible that the application crashed or perhaps some settings were changed on the fly. There could be data sitting in the FIFO that won't be associated with any new gesture or could be accidentally interpreted as a new gesture. We want to clear that data out before finishing the initialization. We can do this by reading the GestureCount register and then looping through and reading the FIFO data until there is no more data in the register. We can do this by using the following code:

```
self.GestureCount = ord(self.i2c.mem_read(1, APDS_9960_ADDRESS,
    REGISTER_GFLVL))
while self.GestureCount > 0:
    self.gestureData = self.i2c.mem_read(4, APDS_9960_ADDRESS,
        REGISTER_GFIFO_U)
    self.GestureCount = ord(self.i2c.mem_read(1, APDS_9960_ADDRESS,
        REGISTER_GFLVL))
    if self.__Verbose == True:
        print("GestureRemaining= ", self.GestureCount)
```

Notice that if we have enabled Verbose mode, we will see an output at the start of the application that shows us that any data remaining in the buffer has been cleared out.

6. Finally, we are ready to enable the APDS-9960 and create a few final variables that will be used by the `Detect()` method to detect gestures. We can do this by using the following code:

```
# Enable the PON, PEN, GEN
self.mode = REGISTER_ENABLE_BIT_PON + REGISTER_ENABLE_BIT_PEN +
REGISTER_ENABLE_BIT_GEN
# Set the analog engine mode
self.i2c.mem_write(self.mode, APDS_9960_ADDRESS,
REGISTER_ENABLE,timeout=1000)
self.GestureData = []
self.GestureDataCount = 0
self.TimeSinceLastGestureData = utime.ticks_ms()
self.TimeNow = utime.ticks_ms()
self.GestureInProgress = False

def Verbose(self, State):
    self.__Verbose = False
```

Let's now look at how we can detect whether a gesture is present in the data.

The APDS-9960 gesture class detect method

Looking back at the APDS-9960 diode output for a right-to-left gesture swipe (which we have seen previously in this chapter in the *Analyzing gesture data* section), it might make you wonder how on Earth we are going to detect a gesture. If you look at the leading edge, the opposite direction of the gesture's photodiode has a higher signal for a while but as the gesture progresses, the signal flops and, by the end, the direction of the gesture has a higher signal. If you look around on the internet, there are several different integration methods that are used to detect the leading edge, the trailing edge, and many others. We just want something simple.

For our controller, we are going to cheat but in a way that has proven to be very accurate. We are going to collect all of the gesture data and then we are going to throw away the last data point received and process the four previous data points. That's it! If a gesture generated `120` data points, we are looking at 4 of the last 5 points! You might be wondering how we know that we've reached the end of the gesture. In order to do this, we will read the system tick from MicroPython and once 100 milliseconds have elapsed with no data, we will process whatever is in the data buffer.

The first step in detecting a gesture is to either wait for an interrupt that tells us there is data present or to poll the APDS-9960. For this project, I decided that polling the device is perfectly acceptable but, if we were designing a low-power or battery-operated device, we would want to use the interrupt functionality (I'll leave that to you to try for fun!). We can determine if there is data present in the FIFO by reading the GSTATUS register's GVALID bit. If the bit is set, there is data present and we can read the data.

If there is data present, we will read how much data is there and then read all of that data into a list named GestureData. We will limit the amount of data that can be stored in the list to 255 items. The reason we want to limit how much data is there is to prevent an out-of-memory error from occurring if someone holds their hand over the sensor without making a gesture movement. With every new piece of data that we receive, we read the system tick in milliseconds and save it in TimeSinceLastGestureData. This will be used to signify when the gesture has timed out. The code segment can be written as follows:

```python
# Check to see if there is valid gesture data present
self.GesturePresent = ord((self.i2c.mem_read(1, APDS_9960_ADDRESS,
    REGISTER_GSTATUS))) & REGISTER_GSTATUS_BIT_GVALID
if self.GesturePresent == 0x1:
    self.GestureInProgress = True
    self.GestureCount = ord(self.i2c.mem_read(1,APDS_9960_ADDRESS,
        REGISTER_GFLVL))
    while self.GestureCount > 0:
        self.GestureData.append(self.i2c.mem_read(4,
            APDS_9960_ADDRESS, REGISTER_GFIFO_U))
        self.GestureDataCount+=1
        self.GestureCount = ord(self.i2c.mem_read
            (1,APDS_9960_ADDRESS, REGISTER_GFLVL))
        if(self.GestureDataCount > GESTURE_DATA_LIST_SIZE_MAX):
            self.GestureDataClear()
    if (self.GestureDataCount > 0) and (self.__Verbose == True):
        print("GestureData=", self.GestureData[self.
            GestureDataCount-1][0],self.GestureData
            [self.GestureDataCount-1][1],
            self.GestureData[self.GestureDataCount-1]
            [2],self.GestureData[self.GestureDataCount-1][3])
        self.TimeSinceLastGestureData = utime.ticks_ms()
else:
    if self.GestureInProgress == False:
        self.TimeSinceLastGestureData = utime.ticks_ms()
```

At this point, all the developer needs to do is determine whether it is time to process the received data. This is done by reading the current time on the microcontroller and then subtracting `TimeSinceLastGestureData`. If the result is greater than 100 milliseconds, or whatever is set in `GESTURE_PROCESS_TIMEOUT`, then we call `GestureData_Process` and pass in the data list, along with how many elements are in the list. `GestureData_Process` will tell us whether there is a gesture present and if so, we will return the gesture after clearing out the received gesture data. The code for this is as follows:

```
self.TimeNow = utime.ticks_ms()
if((self.TimeNow - self.TimeSinceLastGestureData) >
GESTURE_PROCESS_TIMEOUT):
    self.GestureInProgress = False
    if self.__Verbose == True:
        print("Process Gesture Data!")
    self.Result = self.GestureData_Process(self.GestureData,
        self.GestureDataCount)
    self.GestureDataClear()
    return self.Result
```

The real magic in gesture detection occurs in `GestureData_Process`. The algorithm is super simple:

1. First, we loop through the four data points that are present before the last data point. During each iteration, we subtract the **up** photodiode from the **down** photodiode and add the result to the value stored in `Gesture_Vertical`.

2. Next, we subtract the **left** photodiode from the **right** photodiode and add the result to the value stored in `Gesture_Horizontal`. When the loop completes, we will have the count differential between the horizontal and vertical axes for our four data points. The code for this loop is as follows:

```
Gesture_Vertical = 0
Gesture_Horizontal = 0
for i in range ((GestureDataCount- 5), (GestureDataCount -1)):
    if self.__Verbose == True:
        print("GestureData=", GestureData[i][0],GestureData[i]
            [1],GestureData[i][2],GestureData[i][3])
    Gesture_Vertical += GestureData[i][0] - GestureData[i][1]
    Gesture_Horizontal += GestureData[i][2] - GestureData[i][3]
```

3. Next, we take the absolute values of `Gesture_Horizontal` and `Gesture_Vertical`. Whichever one has the larger value is the axis that the gesture motion was in. For example, if `Gesture_Horizontal` was larger, then we had either a left or a right gesture movement. Once we know which axis to look at, we can look at whether the count value is positive or negative. For the vertical axis, if the count value is negative, then the gesture was in a backward direction. A positive value for the vertical axis would mean that the gesture was forwards. For the horizontal axis, if the count total is negative, then the gesture was to the right. If the horizontal axis count is positive, then the gesture was to the left. The code to perform this check is as follows:

```
if(abs(Gesture_Vertical) > abs(Gesture_Horizontal)):
  if Gesture_Vertical < 0:
      Gesture = self.GESTURE_BACKWARD
  else:
      Gesture = self.GESTURE_FORWARD
else:
  if Gesture_Horizontal < 0:
      Gesture = self.GESTURE_RIGHT
  else:
      Gesture = self.GESTURE_LEFT

return Gesture
```

At this point, the user application will have a gesture that it can use for its application code. Let's now look at how our application code can use the `APDS-9960` class to detect a gesture and then control our LEDs.

The gesture controller applications

The controller application has several different activities that it needs to perform, such as the following:

1. Initialize the gesture class.
2. Initialize the LED pins.
3. Call the gesture class.
4. If a gesture is detected, notify the user through the terminal and by setting an LED as high for 5 seconds.

Let's look at these steps in detail:

1. The first step in the application is to initialize the I2C bus that will be used to communicate with the APDS-9960. In this project, we are using `I2C(1)` and the code to initialize it is as follows:

```
# Create a uart object, uart4, and setup the serial parameters
i2c = I2C(1) # create on bus 1
i2c = I2C(1, I2C.MASTER)              # create and init as a master
i2c.init(I2C.MASTER, baudrate=400000) # init as a master
```

2. Once the I2C bus is initialized, we want to initialize the LEDs that are connected to `D2` through `D5`. If you are using the STM32L475 IoT Discovery node, you may recall from `Chapter 5`, *Customizing the MicroPython Kernel Start Up Code*, that we need to use the microcontroller pin designation rather than the Arduino header designations (unless you made the kernel modifications). If you are using a different development board, you will need to review your configuration to determine which pins to initialize. My LEDs are supplied with **voltage common collector** (**VCC**) and the I/O line is used to pull them to ground when they will be turned on. The initialization code for the LEDs is as follows:

```
# Initialize the pins that will be used for LED control
LED_Forward = pyb.Pin('PD14', pyb.Pin.OUT_PP)
LED_Backward = pyb.Pin('PB0', pyb.Pin.OUT_PP)
LED_Left = pyb.Pin('PB4', pyb.Pin.OUT_PP)
LED_Right = pyb.Pin('PA3', pyb.Pin.OUT_PP)
# Set the LED's initial state to off
LED_Forward.value(1)
LED_Backward.value(1)
LED_Left.value(1)
LED_Right.value(1)
```

It's interesting to note that developers can either use the `value()` method or the `high()` method. We will use both in our application, just so that you get to experience both methods.

3. With our LEDs and I2C bus initialized, we can now create our gesture object. We can do this with the following code:

```
# Initialize the gesture driver and disable debug messages
Gesture = APDS_9960(i2c, False)
```

We are passing in our initialized `i2c` object and the `False` value because we don't want to see debugging information in the terminal. If you want to see the debugging information, which includes gesture data, then change `False` to `True`.

4. In order to detect when the application should turn off the LEDs, we need two variables: `GestureDetected` and `GestureDetectedTime`. These are initialized as in the following code:

```
GestureDetectedTime = utime.ticks_ms()
```

The `while` loop in our application will first start out by calling the `Detect()` method from the `Gesture` object. We can see this here:

```
# Main application loop
while True:
Result = Gesture.Detect()
```

If a gesture is detected, `Result` will show what it was. We can use a simple `if/elif` block to determine which gesture was detected. If there is a gesture, we will do the following:

1. Set `GestureDetected` to `True`.
2. Record the current microcontroller tick time.
3. Turn on the associated LED.
4. Print the gesture direction to the REPL.

The code to do this is as follows:

```
if Result == APDS_9960.GESTURE_LEFT:
  GestureDetected = True
  GestureDetectedTime = utime.ticks_ms()
  LED_Left.low()
  print("Gesture Left!")
elif Result == APDS_9960.GESTURE_RIGHT:
  GestureDetected = True
  GestureDetectedTime = utime.ticks_ms()
  LED_Right.low()
  print("Gesture Right!")
elif Result == APDS_9960.GESTURE_FORWARD:
  GestureDetected = True
  GestureDetectedTime = utime.ticks_ms()
  LED_Forward.low()
  print("Gesture Forward!")
elif Result == APDS_9960.GESTURE_BACKWARD:
  GestureDetected = True
  GestureDetectedTime = utime.ticks_ms()
  LED_Backward.low()
  print("Gesture Backward!")
```

The preceding code could be refactored, but I will leave that as an exercise for you to try!

The last piece of the application is to turn off the LED after 5 seconds have passed. This is just a filler example that later could control relays, a radio, or many other devices. The code to clear out the LEDs is as follows:

```
if GestureDetected is True:
  if (utime.ticks_ms() - GestureDetectedTime) > 5000:
    GestureDetected = False
    LED_Backward.high()
    LED_Forward.high()
    LED_Right.high()
    LED_Left.high()
```

At this point, we are now ready to test our gesture controller!

Testing the gesture controller

The code for this project can again be found at `https://github.com/PacktPublishing/MicroPython-Projects/tree/master/ch7`.

Download the code and then copy it to your development board. If you aren't using an STM32L475 IoT Discovery node, you may need to modify the LED pins or the I2C bus you are using, but otherwise, the application should run without any other issues.

Once the application and the APDS-9660 module are copied to your MicroPython board, in the REPL, press *Ctrl + D*. This will perform a soft reboot and start the application. You can now present the APDS-9660 with a gesture. If you swipe right, you should see `Right!` in the REPL, along with one of your LEDs turning on. If you swipe left, you'll see `Left!` and the LED associated with it will turn on. The LEDs should turn off within 5 seconds. If you find this is too long, change the `timeout` value to something such as `2000` to get a 2-second timeout.

If you present the controller with right, left, forward, and then backward gestures, you should see something very similar to the following screenshot. It is showing the gesture control application output when presented with a right gesture, a left gesture, a forward gesture, and a backward gesture:

```
COM17 - PuTTY

MPY: sync filesystems
MPY: soft reboot
Initializing system ...
Starting application ...
Gesture Right!
Gesture Left!
Gesture Forward!
Gesture Backward!
```

If you want to see the gesture data, you can press *Ctrl* + *C* and then initialize the gesture object with `True`. When you do this and then do a right swipe, you may see data similar to that in the following screenshot:

```
COM17 - PuTTY

GestureData= 10 16 18 9
GestureData= 15 26 28 20
GestureData= 22 33 32 27
GestureData= 33 39 39 33
GestureData= 38 39 43 39
GestureData= 41 37 39 39
GestureData= 45 38 41 40
GestureData= 41 34 39 39
GestureData= 41 36 40 40
GestureData= 41 35 38 40
GestureData= 36 32 28 38
GestureData= 22 20 11 27
GestureData= 12 12 5 16
GestureData= 8 7 3 12
Process Gesture Data!
GestureData= 22 20 11 27
GestureData= 18 18 9 24
GestureData= 16 15 6 19
GestureData= 12 12 5 16
Gesture Right!
```

The preceding screenshot shows the debug output for a right-swipe gesture. The data order for the photodiodes is up, down, left, and right.

Congratulations! You now have a gesture controller that you can use in your own projects!

 Note: For anything that moves, you will want to improve the robustness of the code and take into account a backup control in case the gesture controller fails or provides erroneous data.

Summary

In this chapter, we explored how to build a gesture controller using the Avago APDS-9960. We saw that the APDS-9960 is a very sophisticated device but, through a carefully crafted software architecture, we were able to abstract this complexity into a few simple calls in our application code. We also looked at how to parse incoming gesture data. You can easily expand upon our gesture controller to add additional functionality, such as light sensing and proximity detection.

In the next chapter, we will shift gears and look at how we can build an automation and control device with MicroPython and an Android-capable tablet.

Questions

1. What are the technologies that are typically used in gesture control applications?
2. What four main gestures were covered in this chapter?
3. What three analog engines are provided in the APDS-9660?
4. What is the difference between a driver and an integrated application module?
5. What method was used to determine the gesture direction?

Further reading

- The Avago APDS-9960 datasheet: https://cdn.sparkfun.com/assets/learn_tutorials/3/2/1/Avago-APDS-9960-datasheet.pdf

Automation and Control Using Android **8**

Automation and control are two of the driving forces behind the **Internet of Things** (**IoT**). The ability to control a network of devices locally or remotely and gather their sensor data can provide the ability to analyze and control your environment in a way that has never before been possible. In this chapter, we will build an automation and control sensor node using an ESP32 running MicroPython. We will also create a generic sensor node that can be controlled and queried locally from an Android application.

The following topics will be covered in this chapter:

- An introduction to automation and control
- The MicroPython controller
- Setting up an Android application
- Android application implementation
- Testing and debugging

Technical requirements

The example code for this chapter can be found at `https://github.com/PacktPublishing/`
`MicroPython-Projects`.

In order to run the examples, you will need the following hardware and software:

- An ESP32 development board running MicroPython (ESP32 WROVER-B)
- A prototyping breadboard
- Wire jumpers
- A terminal application (such as PuTTy, RealTerm, Terminal, or one of the many others)
- A text editor, such as PyCharm

The sensor node project requirements

The main purpose of this project is to build a cost-effective sensor node that can be used for local automation control. The sensor node will acquire sensor data, such as temperature and humidity readings, and provide a connectivity interface to a mobile device that can not only be used to read that data but also, perhaps more importantly, allow the end user to then control and manage the device. In order to make the project as scalable as possible for you, we will use generic sensors and controls through simple, low-cost LEDs. You can replace the LEDs with any control mechanism that you desire, such as relays, motors, or switches with additional hardware adjustments. By the end of this project, you'll have an Android-controlled, connected sensor node that can be easily scaled for nearly any application.

Let's now look at our hardware requirements.

Hardware requirements

For this project, we are going to get outside our normal MicroPython comfort zone by working with the ESP32 module. The ESP32 module is a low-cost Wi-Fi/Bluetooth combination module that is very cost effective. The onboard module, the ESP32-WROVER-B, typically sells for less than $5! What's even better is that it is capable of running MicroPython, so we can easily develop connected applications without having to break our personal budgets.

For the sensor node, we can define several simple requirements that will allow us to test out our automation and control capabilities, which we can then scale in hardware later for more complex applications. Our hardware requirements for this project will be as follows:

- The sensor node will use ESP32-DevKitC to provide Wi-Fi and general processing capabilities.
- The system will have two LEDs that will represent the output control mechanisms for the connected sensor node. (These outputs could later be connected to relay boards, transistors, or other output mechanisms, such as motors, with additional protection circuitry added.)

These simple requirements will allow us to rapidly prototype a connected sensor node that we can use for automation and control. Let's now look at our software requirements.

Software requirements

There are several key requirements for software that will be necessary in order to successfully build a scalable sensor node system. These requirements include the following:

- The ESP32-DevKitC hardware should run MicroPython. (This will require flashing the development board with the latest MicroPython firmware for ESP32.)
- The system should enable the WebREPL client with a security password to wirelessly update the onboard firmware.
- The system should act as a Wi-Fi access point to allow mobile devices to connect directly to the sensor node.
- An Android mobile device application will be used to send and receive socket communication messages with the sensor node.
- The socket communication messages should include messages to do the following:
  - Control two outputs on the ESP32 that can simulate control and automation
  - Receive sensor data from the sensor node

You can do so much with a connected sensor node, but we are limited by the size of this book and time. A few additional ideas for you to consider include the following:

- The ESP32 will act in station mode and connect to the local Wi-Fi network.
- The Bluetooth radio will be used for local communication and configuration.
- Sensor data will be posted to an online server at an address to be determined.

I'll leave the additional requirements up to you to consider. In this chapter, we will just focus on the basics to allow you to get familiar with the ESP32 and understand how we can get basic socket communication up and running. Let's now design our hardware and software systems.

Hardware and software design

In this section, we are going to explore how we can rapidly prototype our sensor node to explore how we can perform automation and control using an Android device. Before we dive in and start building our project, it's always a good idea to spend just a few minutes thinking through the hardware and software architecture.

The hardware architecture

For this project, there are essentially three major components that we need in order to execute our idea:

- An ESP32-DevKitC board
- Several LEDs
- A few pushbuttons

Once the idea has been proven, we can replace the LEDs with circuits to directly control objects and the switches with contact monitors. We can also add various sensors to the I2C and SPI buses, depending on what our end automation and control application happens to be. In the lab, we are going to start with a simple hardware setup, which can be seen in the following diagram:

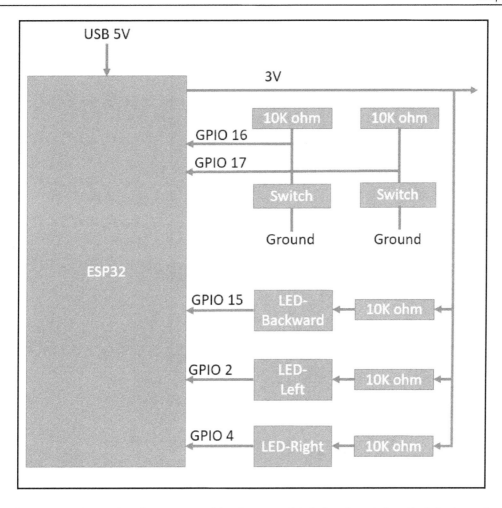

Since this project is so simple to start with, there are high-level and detailed designs that are identical to this case. We can now dive into our software architecture, which will be a bit more complicated.

The software architecture

The sensor node software is going to be broken up into two main tasks: a system status task and a socket receive task. The system status task will periodically sample sensors and then package that data into a message that will be transmitted to a socket server. That socket server will be running on an Android device.

The following flowchart describes general behavior for the system status task:

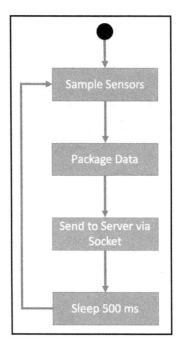

The **receive** task is responsible for acquiring string data from the socket server and then processing that data. The general flow for this task can be seen in the following diagram:

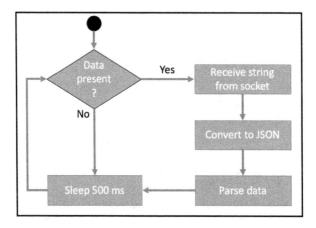

Now that we understand what these two tasks need to do, let's start to build the system.

Building a sensor node

We are now ready to start building our Android-controlled sensor node using the ESP32. In this section, we are going to build the sensor node. This will require us to do the following:

1. Install MicroPython on the ESP32.
2. Set up the sensor node as a Wi-Fi access point.
3. Install `uasyncio`.
4. Set up an Anaconda environment.
5. Write your application code.

There's a fair amount of work to do, so let's get started!

Installing MicroPython on the ESP32

The first step to getting our project underway is to install MicroPython on the ESP32 development. We saw in `Chapter 5`, *Customizing the MicroPython Kernel Start Up Code*, how we can get into the MicroPython kernel, customize it, and then rebuild the kernel. To install MicroPython on the ESP32, we don't have to go through all those steps. Instead, we can use a shortcut by downloading the latest stable build from the MicroPython website, at `https:/ /micropython.org/download#esp32`.

You will notice that there are several different versions available:

- A generic version with support for BLE, LAN, and PPP
- A generic-SPIRAM version with support for BLE, LAN, and PPP
- A generic version with support for BLE but not LAN or PPP
- A generic-SPIRAM version with support for BLE but not LAN or PPP

The version that you select will be completely dependent on the development board end application that you want to develop. For example, if the development board that you selected supports an external 4 MB PSRAM, which is included in the module, then you can select one of the SPIRAM images in order to gain access to this additional RAM. Assuming this is the case and the application only needs support for Bluetooth, then a developer would select the **Generic-SPIRAM with support for BLE but not LAN or PPP** image. In this project, we are going to use the **Generic-SPIRAM with support for BLE, LAN, and PPP** image, so please feel free to download the latest image this time.

Setting up the ESP32 flash utilities

In order to download the ESP32 MicroPython image to the ESP32 development board, we need to download the Espressif ESP32 flash utility tool. This tool can be downloaded from GitHub at `https://github.com/espressif/esptool`.

Alternatively, you can download and install `esptool` from your computer terminal with `pip`, using the following command:

```
pip install esptool
```

This tool is what we will use to program MicroPython into our development board.

Programming the ESP32 with MicroPython

Once you have downloaded your ESP32 image and installed `esptool`, it is time to flash the development board with the MicroPython kernel. With a brand new development board, we must first erase the existing firmware. Once the firmware is erased, we can then program a new image onto the device and, after a reset, we should see the familiar MicroPython REPL appear in the terminal. Let's get started:

1. Plug the ESP32 development board into the computer.
2. Open a terminal or Command Prompt.
3. Navigate to your Python installation.
4. Type the following command to erase your ESP32 firmware. Note that you will need to identify which serial port the board has enumerated on:

```
esptool.py –chip esp32 –port COM3 erase_flash
```

If this is successful, you should find that the terminal shows an output similar to the one in the following screenshot:

```
C:\Python37>esptool.py --chip esp32 --port COM3 erase_flash
esptool.py v2.8
Serial port COM3
Connecting....
Chip is ESP32D0WDQ5 (revision 1)
Features: WiFi, BT, Dual Core, 240MHz, VRef calibration in efuse, Coding Scheme None
Crystal is 40MHz
MAC: 4c:11:ae:6b:2d:54
Uploading stub...
Running stub...
Stub running...
Erasing flash (this may take a while)...
Chip erase completed successfully in 8.9s
Hard resetting via RTS pin...
```

5. Make sure that your new ESP32 image's path is readily available. You may want to copy the image and place it in your Python folder temporarily.

6. Enter the following command to program MicroPython onto the ESP32:

```
esptool.py --chip esp32 --port COM3 --baud 460800 write_flash -z
0x1000 esp32spiram-idf3-20191220-v1.12.bin
```

Note that you will need to update the image name to the latest version that you downloaded and update the port that your development board is connected to. The update operation may take a few minutes and will look something like the following during the entire process:

```
C:\Python37>esptool.py --chip esp32 --port COM3 --baud 460800 write_flash -z 0x1000 esp32spiram-idf3-20191220-v1.12.bin
esptool.py v2.8
Serial port COM3
Connecting....
Chip is ESP32D0WDQ5 (revision 1)
Features: WiFi, BT, Dual Core, 240MHz, VRef calibration in efuse, Coding Scheme None
Crystal is 40MHz
MAC: 4c:11:ae:6b:2d:54
Uploading stub...
Running stub...
Stub running...
Changing baud rate to 460800
Changed.
Configuring flash size...
Auto-detected Flash size: 4MB
Compressed 1327936 bytes to 816930...
Wrote 1327936 bytes (816930 compressed) at 0x00001000 in 19.1 seconds (effective 555.5 kbit/s)...
Hash of data verified.

Leaving...
Hard resetting via RTS pin...
```

7. Once the firmware has been programmed, press the *reset* button on your development board to ensure that you get a clean bootup.

8. Open a terminal and set the baud rate to `115200`.

9. Press *Ctrl + D*. You should now see the ESP32 perform a soft reboot and load the MicroPython REPL as follows:

```
COM3 - PuTTY                                              —    □    ✕

MPY: soft reboot
MicroPython v1.12 on 2019-12-20; ESP32 module (spiram) with ESP32
Type "help()" for more information.
>>> ▯
```

Congratulations! You now have MicroPython running on the ESP32!

Testing MicroPython with LEDs

MicroPython is now installed on our ESP32 module, but before we start to set up Wi-Fi and build a more complex application, it's always a good idea to start with something simple and then build up the complexity. In the software world, we often print `Hello World` as a sanity check, but in the hardware world, blinking an LED is a great test.

For a quick test, connect an LED with a 220-ohm series resistor to pin 2 of the ESP32 Devkit-C connect. I connect the resistor to the 3.3 volts pin and the LED anode and then the LED cathode directly to pin 2. When I say pin 2 in this case, I mean the pin that is labeled with the number 2 on the board solder mask. This doesn't represent the physical pin 2 but the I/O pin 2.

Once you have the LED connected, open your serial prompt so that you are in the MicroPython REPL. Create the following function in the REPL:

```
def toggle(p):
    p.value(not p.value())
```

Make sure that you press *Enter* enough times to get back to the main prompt. Now, let's define a pin that is connected to our LED:

```
import machine
pin = machine.Pin(2, machine.Pin.OUT)
```

Finally, we can create a simple loop that will call the pin every 500 milliseconds using the following code:

```
import time
while True:
            toggle(pin)
            time.sleep_ms(500)
```

Once you have pressed *Enter* several times, the function will be complete and you will observe that the LED is blinking at the desired frequency. Now that we have verified that MicroPython is fully functional and that we can interface it's hardware successfully, use *Ctrl + C* to stop the application from executing. Let's now set up our Wi-Fi access.

Setting up WebREPL

The ESP32 MicroPython firmware behaves a little bit different from the firmware for the STM32 processors. When the ESP32 development board is plugged into a computer, it enumerates and provides the familiar serial REPL that we have all come to know and love. However, the board does not enumerate as a mass storage device. This leaves us developers with two options for loading our Python scripts:

- Use the raw REPL mode
- Use WebREPL

In this section, I'm going to show you how we can go about setting up WebREPL.

WebREPL is exactly what it sounds like—an HTML-based web page that allows a developer to interact with the ESP32 MicroPython kernel. WebREPL allows a developer to connect to the ESP32 Wi-Fi and then, through the web page files, they can be transferred onto or off the filesystem.

By default, WebREPL is disabled. In order to enable it, perform the following steps:

1. Connect to the ESP32 serial REPL in a terminal.
2. Type the following and then press *Enter*:

   ```
   import webrepl_setup
   ```

3. At the prompt, press *E* and then *Enter*.
4. Enter a password of between *4–9* characters.
5. Reboot the system by pressing *Y* and then *Enter*.

This entire sequence and the results that will be printed in the terminal can be seen in the following screenshot:

```
MicroPython v1.12 on 2019-12-20; ESP32 module (spiram) with ESP32
Type "help()" for more information.
>>> import webrepl_setup
WebREPL daemon auto-start status: disabled

Would you like to (E)nable or (D)isable it running on boot?
(Empty line to quit)
> E
To enable WebREPL, you must set password for it
New password (4-9 chars): Python
Confirm password: Python
Changes will be activated after reboot
Would you like to reboot now? (y/n) y
ets Jun  8 2016 00:22:57
```

Once the ESP32 restarts, you might expect the Wi-Fi radio to be enabled by default and that you would be able to connect to its SSID. Unfortunately, you would be mistaken. In order to enable the Wi-Fi radio, we will need to issue a few commands through the serial REPL and then update the `boot.py` script so that Wi-Fi is enabled by default.

In the serial REPL, type the following commands to enable the Wi-Fi radio:

```
import network
ap_if = network.WLAN(network.AP_IF)
ap_if.active(True)
```

You'll find that the Wi-Fi radio is now enabled. You should now see the ESP32 broadcasting on an SSID, such as ESP_6B2D55. The SSID can be broken down into two parts: ESP and XXXXXX. The ESP part shows that this is an ESP module, while the remaining six characters are part of the device's MAC address. This means that your SSID for the device will remain the same from one boot to the next, but if you configure multiple modules, they will each have their own unique default SSID.

Once WebREPL is enabled, there are two options for using it to connect to the ESP32:

1. A developer can navigate to `http://micropython.org/webrepl` in their web browser and then, after the page loads, they can connect to their ESP32.
2. WebREPL can be downloaded from `https://github.com/micropython/webrepl` and run directly from the local computer.

Running WebREPL will result in an interface similar to the one shown in the following screenshot:

There are several important features to notice about WebREPL:

- First, WebREPL does not support HTTPS, so all connections must be done through HTTP.
- Second, the default IP address for the ESP32 is `192.168.4.1`. The port that we connect through is `8266`, which is representative of the original MicroPython port to the ESP8266 processors.
- Finally, in order to establish a connection, you'll need to remember what your WebREPL password is.

Once a developer connects through WebREPL, they can interact with the MicroPython device exactly how they would if they had connected through a serial interface. The only difference is that on the right-hand side of the web page, there are options to send a file to the ESP32 filesystem and an option to get a file. As I mentioned earlier, we want to update our filesystem so that the Wi-Fi radio is automatically enabled. To do this, we will modify the `boot.py` script using the following procedure:

1. After connecting through WebREPL, type `boot.py` in the **Get a file** box.
2. Press the **Get from device** button.
3. Open the `boot.py` file that was just downloaded in a text editor of your choice. You'll find that `boot.py` has just two lines of code:

   ```
   import webrepl
   webrepl.start()
   ```

4. Update the `boot.py` script to appear as follows:

   ```
   import webrepl
   import network
   ap_if = network.WLAN(network.AP_IF)
   ap_if.active(True)
   ```

5. In WebREPL, click the **Choose a file** button in the **Send a file** section.
6. Navigate to the modified `boot.py` file and select it.
7. Click the **Send to device** button to upload the new boot script.

The Wi-Fi radio access point will now be enabled by default when the ESP32 powers up.

Simplifying application development with Anaconda

WebREPL is a really cool tool that can be useful for working with an interactive web page to move files to and from the ESP32 over Wi-Fi. For a seasoned developer, developing software with WebREPL can seem quite tedious. For that reason, in this section, I'm going to discuss an alternative way for you to push the application code to the ESP32. We are going to do that using an **Anaconda prompt**.

Anaconda is a free package and environment manager that contains a Python distribution that includes thousands of open source packages. It provides an Anaconda prompt that can be used across any major PC platform and that allows a developer to create their own Python virtual machines. Most importantly for us, it provides a convenient way to download ampy, which is an Adafruit package specifically designed to interface with the ESP32 for MicroPython development.

In order to set up Anaconda, perform the following steps:

1. Visit `https://www.anaconda.com/distribution/`, click **Download**, and select your platform.
2. Once downloaded, install Anaconda.
3. When the download is complete, open the Anaconda prompt.

From within the prompt, set up your environment by issuing the following commands:

1. `conda create -n ESP32-uPython python =3.7`
2. `conda activate ESP32-uPython`
3. `pip3 install ampy-adafruit`

Successfully installing ampy will result in a terminal output that looks something like the following:

```
Anaconda Prompt (Anaconda3)                                          —   □   ×

(ampy) C:\ESP32>pip3 install adafruit-ampy
Collecting adafruit-ampy
  Using cached adafruit_ampy-1.0.7-py2.py3-none-any.whl (16 kB)
Requirement already satisfied: pyserial in c:\python37\lib\site-packages (from adafruit-ampy) (3.4)
Requirement already satisfied: click in c:\python37\lib\site-packages (from adafruit-ampy) (7.0)
Requirement already satisfied: python-dotenv in c:\python37\lib\site-packages (from adafruit-ampy) (0.10.3)
Installing collected packages: adafruit-ampy
Successfully installed adafruit-ampy-1.0.7

(ampy) C:\ESP32>
```

You now have an Anaconda Python virtual machine set up that we can use to transfer files to and from the ESP32. Let's quickly write a simple script to practice sending and getting scripts:

1. From within the prompt, use the following command to pull the default `main.py` script (obviously changing `COM3` to the port that your device is on):

   ```
   ampy –port COM3 --baud 115200 get main.py main.py
   ```

2. Yes, `main.py` is written twice in order to tell the prompt that we want to download the file. Once you have downloaded `main.py`, open it in your favorite text editor. Write a simple toggle application similar to the one shown here:

   ```
   import machine
   import time
   pin = machine.Pin(2, machine.Pin.OUT)
   def toggle(p):
               p.value(not p.value())
   while True:
               toggle(pin)
               time.sleep_ms(500)
   ```

3. Save the script and then use the following command to upload the new script:

   ```
   ampy --port COM3 --baud 115200 put main.py
   ```

4. Make sure that you connect an LED to the GPIO 2. Unplug the ESP32 and then plug it back in. You should now see your LED blinking at a rate of 500 milliseconds! You now have a simpler way to interact with the ESP32 and push your scripts to it.

 Note: Once you close out of Anaconda, your ampy virtual machine will be closed. When you open Anaconda again, you will be in the base environment. To restart your ampy environment, type `activate ampy`. This will get you back to where you can use the terminal to load your code.

Installing uasyncio

As you may recall from earlier chapters, uasyncio is a cooperative scheduling module that is very useful for creating concurrent tasks. By default, the MicroPython port for the ESP32 does not have the `uasyncio` library built into the MicroPython kernel. It's up to us to install it ourselves.

Now, there are several ways that we can go about installing it, which are documented at `https://github.com/peterhinch/micropython-async/blob/master/TUTORIAL.md`. I highly recommend that you review the tutorial there. In case you are in a hurry, I'll provide the basic steps on how to install `uasyncio` on the ESP32 here:

1. Download uasyncio from `https://github.com/micropython/micropython-lib`. You can do this by either downloading the `.zip` file or by cloning the repository using the following command:

   ```
   git clone https://github.com/micropython/micropython-lib.git
   ```

2. Navigate to the folder that you are working out of in Anaconda and create a directory named `uasyncio`.

3. Within the `micropython-lib` download, copy the following files to the new `usyncio` folder:

   - `uasyncio/uasyncio/__init__.py`
   - `uasyncio.core/uasyncio/core.py`
   - `uasyncio.synchro/uasyncio/synchro.py`
   - `asyncio.queues/uasyncio/queues.py`

4. In the Anaconda prompt, issue the following command to install the `uasyncio` directory:

   ```
   ampy --port COM3 --baud 115200 put asyncio
   ```

The preceding command will copy the `asyncio` directory and all of its contents to the ESP32.

Writing the sensor node application

Now that our environment is all set up, it's time for us to start writing our application. We are going to look at each individual piece of the application and develop them one at a time.

Imports and supporting objects

We are going to start our application by first importing the libraries and modules that we need for our application. First, we are going to use `machine` to access the GPIO ports. `machine` is a generic MicroPython library that will allow us to easily port our code to any MicroPython-based device. Next, we are going to use the socket library for all of our socket communications. We will use `asyncio` to schedule our application tasks. Finally, we will use **ujson** to create and parse JSON messages. The import section of our script will appear as follows:

```
import machine
import socket
import uasyncio as asyncio
import ujson
```

LEDs and local control

We are using LEDs to simulate the control of physical mechanisms that we may want to control with our sensor node. In order to control the LEDs, we need to assign several GPIO pins to the LEDs and create a few simple functions to command them, such as `gpio_on` and `gpio_off`. We can create a few LED objects using the following code:

```
LED1 = machine.Pin(2, machine.Pin.OUT)
LED2 = machine.Pin(0, machine.Pin.OUT)
LED3 = machine.Pin(4, machine.Pin.OUT)
```

As you can see, we use `machine` to generically assign the specific pins that we will be using and to set the output mode. With the pins assigned, we can then write a few helper functions to control the LEDs, such as the following:

```
def gpio_toggle(p):
    p.value(not p.value())
def gpio_on(p):
    p.value(0)
def gpio_off(p):
    p.value(1)
```

With these functions in place, we are now ready to start building out our socket application.

socket_connect()

We are going to create a function that allows us to connect to a socket server. The function definition is as follows:

```
def socket_connect(address, port):
    s.settimeout(1.0)
    addr_info = socket.getaddrinfo(address, port)
    addr = addr_info[0][-1]
    try:
        print("Attempting to connect to socket server ...")
        s.connect(addr)
        print("Connection successful!")
    except Exception as e:
        print(e)
```

As you can see, we pass in an IP address and port number for where the socket server is located. We then use `socket.getaddrinfo` to create the `addr_info` object that can be passed into the socket connect method. We wrap the connection attempt in `try/except` just in case we run into a connection issue, such as the server not existing.

There are two primary tasks that we need to develop: a `receive` task and a `system status` task. Let's develop those now, along with any supporting application classes and functions.

socket_receive()

The `receive` function will retrieve data that is sent to the sensor node from the socket server. There are several different methods that can be used to pull data from the socket, but the one that we are going to use is `recv`. The `recv` method allows us to specify how many bytes of data we want to pull from the socket before processing it. This is more of a maximum number than a minimum. The data in the socket is received as a string. We want to take that string and convert it into a JSON dictionary that can then be parsed. We do this by using the `ujson.loads` method.

There is something important to understand about our `socket_receive` function. The function is going to be running as a task through uasyncio. This means that after a short time, the `recv` method will time out and the task will then run and yield the CPU if there is no data to process. In this example, I've set the time for the task to run every `0.5` seconds, but it can be changed based on the application's needs. It also means that when the `recv` method times out, we will receive a connection timeout exception!

We want to make sure that in our error handler, we don't print out this message constantly, so a few extra lines of code are necessary to process the exception. In general, our `socket_receive` code would look something like the following:

```
def socket_receive():
    while True:
        try:
            receive_string = s.recv(500)
            rxjsonobj = ujson.loads(receive_string)
            parse_command(rxjsonobj)
        except Exception as e:
            if errno.ETIMEDOUT:
                pass
            else:
                print(e)
        await asyncio.sleep(0.5)
```

You'll notice from looking at the preceding code that we haven't yet defined the `parse_command` function. Before we define the `parse_command` function, let's first define the sensor node class that describes our example hardware and holds our object data.

The IotDevice class

The `IotDevice` class will contain the specific behavior for our sensor node. This class will contain the methods necessary to sample our sensors, control external devices, and so on. For our example, the `IotDevice` class will perform several functions, including the following:

- Manage the state of the LEDs (which represent the external devices to control)
- Manage sensor variables, such as temperature and humidity
- Hold the IoT device's ID
- Include methods for sampling and controlling the IoT device

The first step is to create the `IotDevice` class and build the constructor. An example of what this might look like can be seen in the following code:

```
class IotDevice:
    def __init__(self):
        self.LED1 = "Off"
        self.LED2 = "Off"
        self.LED3 = "Off"
        self.Temperature = 21.1
        self.Humidity = 63.4
        self.ID = "14-3826"
```

We can then create a method that would manage sampling the onboard sensors. Now, we don't have any sensors in our example so we will use the temperature and humidity variables we created in our constructor and just create a pattern for it to generate, such as incrementing every time the sample method is called. An example sample method can be seen here:

```
def sample(self):
    self.Temperature = self.Temperature + 0.1
    if self.Temperature >= 30.0:
        self.Temperature = 15
    self.Humidity = self.Humidity + 0.5
    if self.Humidity >= 100:
        self.Humidity = 25.0
```

If you are following along, a great extension to this code would be to integrate a real temperature and humidity sensor that could then be sampled to provide real value. I'll leave that as an exercise for you to try out.

Let's now look at how we can implement our command parsing function.

Command parsing

The command parsing function is going to parse the incoming socket data, which will be in JSON, to determine what command the system is receiving. The commands that we will look at supporting right now are as follows:

- LED1
- LED2
- LED3

These commands can have only two possible values:

- On
- Off

Now, if you recall, the `receive` function takes the received string and then reconstructs it into a JSON-formatted dictionary. Our parsing function needs to search the dictionary to see whether there are references to our command words in the message and, if there are, we can reference the value using the command as a key. For example, our `parse_command` function might look something like the following:

```
def parse_command(message):
    if "LED1" in message:
```

```
        if message["LED1"] == "On":
            gpio_on(LED1)
            Device.LED1 = "On"
            print("LED 1 On")
        else:
            gpio_off(LED1)
            Device.LED1 = "Off"
            print("LED 1 Off")
    if "LED2" in message:
        if message["LED2"] == "On":
            gpio_on(LED2)
            Device.LED2 = "On"
            print("LED 2 On")
        else:
            gpio_off(LED2)
            Device.LED2 = "Off"
            print("LED 2 Off")
    if "LED3" in message:
        if message["LED3"] == "On":
            gpio_on(LED3)
            Device.LED3 = "On"
            print("LED 3 On")
        else:
            gpio_off(LED3)
            Device.LED3 = "Off"
            print("LED 3 Off")
```

In this example, we use separate `if` statements to check whether the command is in the message by using statements such as the following:

```
if "LED1" in message:
```

If there is a reference to that command in the dictionary, we use the `LED1` command as a key to the dictionary to then get an `On` or `Off` value by using the following code line:

```
if message["LED1"] == "On":
```

At this point, we can decide what we want our application to do when we receive that command and value.

 Note: There are improvements that can be made; for example, the `parse` command and GPIO functionality could be built into our `IotDevice` class, but I've left them separate in this example so that they can be easily removed when you add your own custom code.

Extending the command parser is as easy as adding additional `if` statements to the function to check for other command and status values.

The system status task

We are now able to receive and parse commands, but we also need to be able to send status information back to the server. In order to do this, we are going to create a system status task that will call the `IotDevice` object's sample method and then package the data up and send it in JSON format to the socket server. This `system_status` task will be added to the `asyncio` task list when we write the main application code. The task code can be seen as follows:

```
def system_status():
    while True:
        # Sample Sensors or get the latest result
        Device.sample()
        data = {}
        data['id'] = Device.ID
        data['temperature'] = Device.Temperature
        data['humidity'] = Device.Humidity
        data['led1'] = Device.LED1
        data['led2'] = Device.LED2
        data['led3'] = Device.LED3
        socket_send(data)
        await asyncio.sleep(0.5)
```

There are two things that you'll notice:

- First, we are sending update information to the server every 500 milliseconds. This is probably faster than is necessary, but again can be easily adjusted for the application needs.
- You will also notice that we pass the data into a function named `socket_send`.

Let's now look at the `socket_send` function in a little more detail.

socket_send()

The `socket_send` function needs to take the packaged data and then convert it into a JSON string. This can be done using the `ujson.dumps` function. This function takes the received JSON data and then literally dumps it into a string that can then be transmitted. The function looks like the following:

```
def socket_send(Data):
    mystring = ujson.dumps(Data)
    try:
        s.write(mystring + "\r\n")
    except Exception as e:
```

```
if errno.ECONNRESET:
    socket_connect()
print(e)
```

You can see that once we create the string, we can access the `s` object, which is our socket connection, and then call the `write` method. If there is an error sending, then we just print it into the REPL. With this in place, we have everything we need to finally pull together the main application.

The main application

The main application has several tasks that it needs to complete, such as the following:

1. Instantiate the `IotDevice` object.
2. Initialize the LEDs to `Off`.
3. Create the socket connection.
4. Initialize the scheduler.

Let's look at the code for each of these:

1. First, instantiate the `IotDevice` object and initialize the LEDs, as follows:

   ```
   Device = IotDevice()
   gpio_off(LED1)
   gpio_off(LED2)
   gpio_off(LED3)
   ```

2. Next, we want to create the socket object and then connect to the socket server. We are going to use a socket server that is hosted on an Android device for our example, but it could easily be hosted on the web somewhere and we could then set up a relay for the socket server, an Android device, and our sensor node. The options are limitless, but we will use Android with the socket server for now.

   The socket server address that we will use will depend on the application. I'll talk more about this in the *Testing the sensor node* section. For now, we will use the `1024` port and the `192.168.4.2` address. The code to create the socket and connect to the server is as follows:

   ```
   s = socket.socket()
   socket_connect("192.168.4.2", 1024)
   ```

3. Finally, we need to initialize the cooperative scheduler. There are two tasks that we want to create: one for the system status and the other for receiving data from the socket. The code looks like the following:

```
loop = asyncio.get_event_loop()

loop.create_task(system_status())
loop.create_task(socket_receive())
loop.run_forever()
```

Don't forget that each task has to have a `while` loop in it.

We now have everything in place and are ready to test our sensor node using an Android socket server. In the next section, I will describe how to set up the server on Android and then establish two-way communication with our sensor node.

Testing the sensor node

The code for this project can again be found at `https://github.com/PacktPublishing/MicroPython-Projects/ch8`. Download the code and then copy it to your development board using the procedure that we discussed in the *Simplifying application development with Anaconda* section.

The Android socket server

There are several different pre-built socket applications that are written for use on Android. The application that I used to test the sensor node was called **Simple TCP Socket Tester**, but other applications could also be used. The socket tester is particularly interesting because it allows the Android tablet to act either as a socket server or a socket client. This provides us with the flexibility to use the same application, regardless of whether we have our ESP32 act as a client or a server.

Take a few moments now to go to the Google Play Store app and install Simple TCP Socket Tester.

Once you have downloaded the application, open it and you will find a screen that looks like the following:

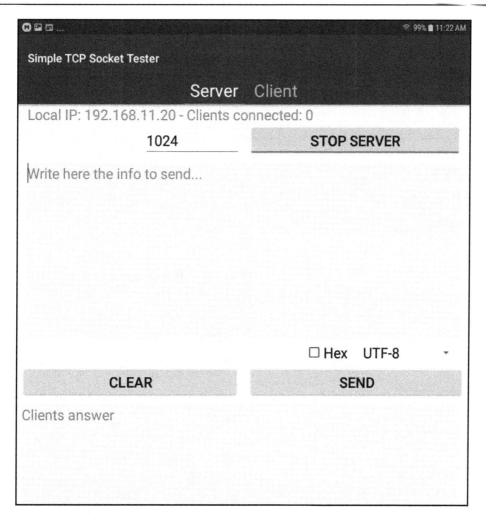

Notice that there are two areas at the top, one for the server and one for the client. The IP address that it is assigned will be based on the IP address of the Android device. We have a button to start and stop the server, along with the ability to specify the port that will be used.

Below the server configuration, we have a textbox to send string messages from the socket server to the client that is connected, and then below that, we have a textbox that shows the client messages. Just like most applications, we are able to clear these boxes out as well.

In order to successfully communicate with the sensor node, we need to complete the following steps:

1. Power up the sensor node with the application running.
2. Connect your Android device to the sensor node's Wi-Fi. The SSID will start with **ESP_** followed by six characters from the MAC address, as shown:

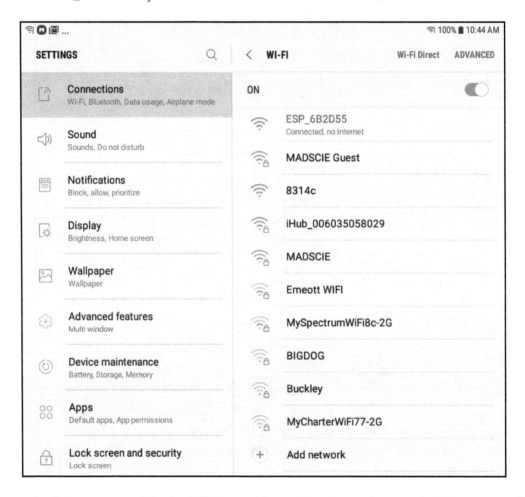

3. Once connected, in the REPL, stop the application and restart it. This ensures that the application can successfully connect to the server.

4. In the Android application, observe that the number of clients has gone from **0** to **1**. You might also see that the IP address has changed since you are now on a different network.

5. You should also see that messages are now coming in from the sensor node displaying the sensor sample data, as shown here:

```
{"led3": "Off", "led1": "Off", "humidity": 66.9, "led2": "Off", "id":
"14-3826", "temperature": 21.8}
```

Now that we have a connection and see a stream of data from the device, let's look at what messages we can send to the device to control the LEDs.

Commanding the sensor node

The command parser that we created earlier has several commands that you will recognize:

- LED1
- LED2
- LED3

We need to send these commands to the sensor node in a JSON formatted string. For example, we can send a message to turn on LED1 by sending the following code line:

```
{"LED1": "On"}
```

We can also turn the same LED off by sending the following code line:

```
{"LED1": "Off"}
```

We are not limited to controlling a single LED at once. For example, we can construct a JSON message that allows us to command all the LEDs at once. If I wanted to turn on LED1 and LED3 while turning LED2 off, I could construct a JSON message that looks like the following:

```
{"LED1": "On", "LED2": "Off", "LED3": "On"}
```

The final test for our sensor node is to try this in our socket test application.

Testing the commands

Testing our control of the LEDs just requires us to construct a JSON message, such as those that we created in the previous section. The steps to perform the test can be found here:

1. Verify that the TCP Socket Tester application is connected by verifying that it has 1 connected client and that you can see data packets streaming to the server from the sensor node.

2. In the **Write here the info to send...** section of the application, type in the following JSON message:

   ```
   {"LED1": "On", "LED2": "Off", "LED3": "On"}
   ```

3. Press the **SEND** button. You will find that your LEDs have now turned on!

4. Now, update the message to the following:

   ```
   {"LED1": "Off", "LED2": "On", "LED3": "Off"}
   ```

5. Press the **SEND** button. You'll see that the LED states have switched.

The Android application messages might look something like the following:

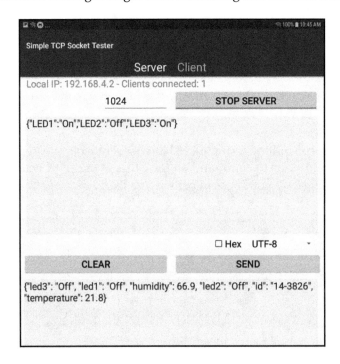

Congratulations! You now have a functional sensor node that can communicate with a socket server. The possibilities for where you can go from here are endless!

Summary

In this chapter, we explored how we can build an Android controlled sensor node using the ESP32 and an Android-based socket server. We learned how to deploy MicroPython on the ESP32 and how to install the `asyncio` module. We also examined how to write a script that would allow us to connect to a socket server and transmit and receive data from it.

The example we used simply sent fake sensor data in JSON format to the server and accepted data from the server in JSON format. The received messages were then parsed and used to control the LEDs, which can now be swapped out for more interesting control schemes, such as motors, and relays.

In the next chapter, we will design and build a basic object detection mechanism using machine learning and MicroPython.

Questions

1. What library do we use to create tasks within MicroPython?
2. What MicroPython image do we use when flashing the ESP32?
3. What tool is used to flash the ESP32 with MicroPython?
4. Which MicroPython module can be used to generically control I/O across any MicroPython port?
5. What methods can be used to push scripts to the ESP32?

Further reading

- https://docs.anaconda.com/anaconda/user-guide/getting-started/
- https://docs.micropython.org/en/latest/library/usocket.html

9
Building an Object Detection Application Using Machine Learning

The ability to recognize objects is becoming a critical skill for embedded systems. Whether the system needs to recognize an object on an assembly line or recognize a person or objects in its path, environmental awareness is becoming an important feature for many systems. Hand coding a recognition algorithm using traditional coding techniques is extremely difficult and challenging. Using machine learning and leveraging the CIFAR-10 classes, to build object recognition into a system, is nearly as simple as writing a *Hello World!* application.

In this project, we will explore machine learning and the embedded libraries that allow us to perform object detection on a microcontroller-based device.

The following topics will be covered in this chapter:

- An introduction to machine learning
- Object detection requirements
- Object detection design and theory
- Implementing and testing object detection

Technical requirements

The example code for this chapter can be found at the following GitHub location:

`https://github.com/PacktPublishing/MicroPython-Projects`

In order to run the examples, you will want to have the following hardware and software available:

- An OpenMV camera module
- OpenMV IDE
- A breadboard
- Wire jumpers

Introducing machine learning

Traditionally, embedded software developers had eight core pillars or skills that they needed to master in order to successfully design and build an embedded product. These included the following:

- Architecture design
- Code analysis
- Defect management/debugging
- Documentation
- Language skills
- Processes and standards
- Testing
- Tools

An important and emerging area of interest for many developers, and a tool that has the potential to be a game-changer in embedded software development, is **machine learning**.

According to the great scholar that is Wikipedia:

"Machine learning is a field of computer science that often uses statistical techniques to give computers the ability to 'learn' with data, without being explicitly programmed."

It's important to note that in this definition, the machine is not actually learning, but is instead using an algorithm to statistically determine a result based on the input that it is provided with. Many machine learning algorithms use a collection of neurons that may contain multiple inputs and outputs that are set up in layers to decompose the problem. Each input to a neuron has a weight associated with it and each neuron has an activation bias associated with it that determines whether the neuron's output *fires*.

The output layer neurons often output a single value that provides the statistical chance that the output is a particular value. For example, the output from a neuron that represents the number 0 may have an output of 0.97, which means there is a 97% chance that the image provided to it is a numerical 0. A simple example of how a perceptron neuron works can be seen in the following diagram:

In the preceding diagram, the perceptron neuron is only allowed to have input values of zero or one and output **0** or **1**. It contains three inputs that have weights associated with them, such as **4**, **-2** and **1**, respectively. The neuron has an activation bias equal to three. The output can only be a zero or a one in this case and is determined by summing the dot product of the input value with its associated weight. If the sum of the dot product plus the activation bias is greater than **0**, then the neuron *fires* and the output would be a **1**.

As you might imagine, a perceptron was one of the first neurons employed in machine learning due to its simplicity. There are problems with using perceptrons though. For example, a very tiny change in the inputs can result in a complete change of the output. The output behaves as a step function since it can only be zero or one. This is why there are often other neuron types used, such as the sigmoid, that allow values between zero and one. This has the effect of smoothing the output so that minor changes in the input don't result in major changes to the output.

If you are new to machine learning and the last few paragraphs just flew over your head, please don't be alarmed. You won't need an in-depth understanding of the mathematical constructs that go into a machine learning algorithm to complete this chapter's project. However, if you are interested in attaining a rudimentary understanding of what is happening behind the scenes, I recommend that you watch the following YouTube videos, which provide great background on what neurons are and how they are built up to create a network that can be used for machine learning:

- `https://www.youtube.com/watch?v=aircAruvnKkt=28s` (~20 minutes)
- `https://www.youtube.com/watch?v=IHZwWFHWa-w` (~20 minutes)
- `https://www.youtube.com/watch?v=Ilg3gGewQ5U` (~14 minutes)
- `https://www.youtube.com/watch?v=tIeHLnjs5U8t=106s` (~10 minutes)

The need for intelligent systems

Machine learning provides developers with the ability to design a completely new class of system, intelligent systems. Intelligent systems are growing in importance because they enable developers to do the following:

- Solve problems that are not easy for a human to code for
- Scale system behaviors and results based on new data and situations
- Perform tasks that are easy for a human but traditionally difficult for computers
- Decrease system costs in certain applications
- And because it's cool and cutting edge

Machine learning can be applied to a wide range of applications:

- Image recognition
- Speech and audio processing
- Language processing
- Robotics
- Bioinformatics
- Chemistry
- Video games
- Search

The applications can be quite varied depending upon the processing power that is available to an application. For example, examine the following diagram:

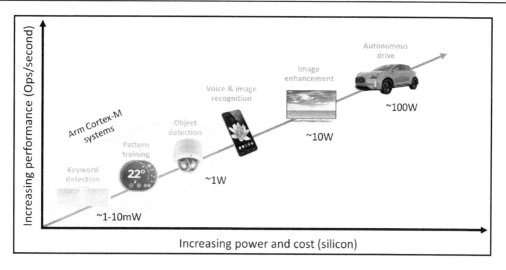

As you can see, at the low end of the power spectrum, microcontrollers based on the Arm Cortex-M processors can be used in real-time systems in applications such as keyword detection, pattern training, and object detection. These applications are often associated with IoT-based applications. As the energy profile for the processor increases, additional application domains start to become possible, including autonomous vehicles at the high end.

From a microcontroller perspective, there is a wide range of processors that can be used for machine learning. These can generally be categorized into small, medium, or large microcontroller systems, as can be seen in the following diagram:

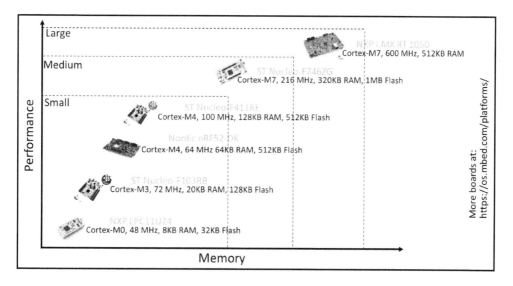

The project that we will be experimenting with within this chapter will utilize an OpenMV camera module that is based on an STM32 microcontroller, which falls into the medium category. In general, with today's technology, at a minimum, a developer would want to use a medium system to run any machine learning inferences. It is possible to do this on a small system, something that is becoming easier as technology advances, but if you are new to machine learning, then I highly recommended starting with a system that has more processing power.

For microcontroller-based embedded systems, the most common application to date is for speech recognition and image recognition. For speech recognition, a common application is to use a small microcontroller to recognize a trigger word that then wakes up an application processor. The application processor has much more processing power and can then perform full speech recognition or interact with a user or the cloud much more efficiently. Image recognition is being used in all sorts of applications, ranging from object detection to facial recognition. This chapter will focus on object detection.

Machine learning from the cloud to the edge

Machine learning is a technology that has traditionally resided in the cloud and has powered everything from search engines to your recommended playlist on your favorite streaming service. Running a machine learning inference often required a lot of processing power, especially to train the algorithm. Machine learning, therefore, has mostly lived in the cloud and has been completely off the radar to embedded system developers until just recently.

Machine learning started to find its uses for IoT edge devices, but the processing wasn't being done on the edge device. The first machine learning applications used the edge device as a sensor node to collect the information that was needed, the processing was done in the cloud, and then the result was transmitted back down to the edge device. While this saved the need to have a heavy-duty processor at the edge, machine learning is beginning to shift from the cloud to the edge for several reasons, including the following:

- **Bandwidth**: As more devices are connected to the IoT, it becomes unrealistic to have trillions of devices constantly connecting back to the cloud and transferring large amounts of data. There is limited bandwidth that can be used through the internet and, more importantly, that bandwidth costs money. The less bandwidth that is used the better, and this is helping to drive machine learning from the cloud to the edge.

- **Power**: Power is an important factor because when a data packet is sent to the cloud, devices may have to stay awake in order to receive the processed response. This means that the device will be unable to go into a low-power state and will use more energy. While this may not be an issue for a device that is connected to the power grid, many IoT devices are battery-operated devices, and the longer a Wi-Fi module is powered up, the faster that battery will be drained. Processing as much as possible at the edge can therefore potentially improve the energy usage for the device.
- **Cost**: The cost to run a machine learning algorithm in the cloud can also get expensive. Cloud-based machine learning has a monthly cost associated with it. Developers have to pay for access to the following:
  - The cloud
  - The bandwidth they use
  - The specific machine learning features they use
  - The number of devices connecting to that service, and so on.

Moving to the edge won't necessarily remove all these costs, but it can help to potentially decrease them dramatically.

- **Latency**: This is an important issue to consider when using cloud-based machine learning. Every time an edge device has to send data to the cloud and wait for a response, there is going to be a non-deterministic latency associated with that transaction. Network communications are inherently inconsistent, which means that running a real-time edge node that meets its deadlines can be nearly impossible. Again, the more that can be done at the edge, the lower the latency and the response times.
- **Reliability**: The reliability for an edge device can also be improved by removing its reliance on the cloud. If the cloud were to go down, the connection was to be severed, or even the cloud APIs were updated, the edge device's reliability could easily be compromised. The fewer device resource dependencies there are, the better it is for the system and the less complicated it will be to design and test.
- **Security**: Finally, the security for a system can be improved by keeping the system as self-contained as possible. Pushing extra data up to the cloud and processing it there increases the attack surface for a would-be hacker. For IoT devices, security is a critical component in system design.

As you can see, the need to move machine learning from the cloud to the edge is quite important to embedded system developers. Now that we understand this importance, let's define some requirements for our own machine learning project.

Object detection requirements

The main purpose of this project is to build an embedded system that can detect objects. Object detection can be applied to a wide range of applications, from robotics through IoT devices such as person recognition for a smart doorbell. For this project, we are going to have two primary goals:

- First, we want to be able to detect general objects that we could apply to a rover like a robot that is looking for objects in its path that would require it to change course.
- Second, we want to create a second project that is able to recognize whether a person is present.

Hardware requirements

There are several different approaches that we could take for object detection that would cost anywhere from a nice meal for two up to several thousand dollars. Since we don't want to break the bank in order to build this project, the one hardware requirement that we are going to have is to use the OpenMV camera module.

According to the OpenMV website:

> *"The OpenMV project is about creating low-cost, extensible, Python-powered, machine vision modules and aims at becoming the 'Arduino of Machine Vision'."*

The OpenMV Cam H7 module is based on an Arm Cortex-M7 processor, the STM32H743VI, running at 480 MHz with 1 MB of RAM and 2 MB of flash. The OpenMV Cam H7 comes with an OV7725 camera module capable of taking 640 x 480 8-bit grayscale images, or 640 x 480 16-bit RGB565 images at 60 FPS when the resolution is above 320 x 240, and 120 FPS when the resolution is below this. The camera sensor comes with a 2.8 mm lens, but there are other options available. The module itself comes in a small package that you can see as follows:

The OpenMV Cam H7 is particularly well suited for our object detection project for several reasons, including the following:

- The hardware form factor.
- The hardware module cost is well under USD 100.
- The OpenMV software framework is written in MicroPython.
- The OpenMV software framework includes machine learning libraries that will dramatically simplify our project.

For this project, all our hardware needs will be handled by the OpenMV module.

Software requirements

For this project, we are actually going to create two different projects. We will break up our requirements for each project separately.

First, we have standard object detection. For this project, our software requirements are as follows:

- Use the CIFAR10 classes to detect common objects.
- When an object is detected, use the OpenMV Cam H7 GPIO to turn on an LED.

Second, we have person detection. For this project, our software requirement is as follows:

- When a person is detected, use the OpenMV Cam H7 GPIO to turn on an LED.

We could list the specific frameworks that we want to use, such as the CMSIS-NN, but again, as we develop requirements, we don't necessarily want to design the system for the developer or constrain their ability to solve the problem unless it is absolutely necessary. For this project, we could also add a number of interesting requirements, such as writing a recognition log to an SD card, communicating a data packet back to a master processor, or something more complex. I'm going to leave those interesting additions to you though once you understand how to detect an object.

Let's now dig into the design for our system and discuss the software theory on how we can recognize objects.

Object detection design and theory

The detailed theory on how to detect objects in an image and all the machine learning details that go into it is well beyond the scope of this book. However, understanding the general theory about how to successfully perform object detection on a microcontroller device is exactly what we are interested in doing. In this section, we are going to explore the major components that are required in order to perform machine learning on a microcontroller and how those components come together to create an object detection application.

The five main components that we are going to need in order to detect objects can be seen in the following diagram:

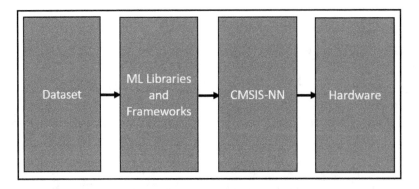

Let's explore each of these components in more detail and see how they interact with one another to achieve our goal.

The CIFAR-10 and CIFAR-100 datasets

Machine learning can only get so far without having a dataset to train the model. You may recall from earlier in the chapter that we discussed how a neural network is a collection of neurons and connections between those neurons. The connection weights and the activation bias can't be set properly without using some form of training to set their values. Setting those weights and values is really the **learning** aspect for the model.

If you were to go out on the internet, you would discover that there are tons of different datasets that are available online that can be used to train a machine learning model. If you are interested in training a model to detect whether someone is smiling, you can use the *Smiles* dataset at `https://github.com/hromi/SMILEsmileD/tree/master/SMILEs`.

You could also use the *Labeled Faces in the Wild* dataset, which can be found at `http://vis-www.cs.umass.edu/lfw/`.

No matter which dataset you decide best fits your application, there are a couple of key points that should be remembered when you consider your dataset for training your machine learning model. These include the following:

- Use 80% of your dataset for training.
- Use 20% for testing and verifying the model.
- The datasets should be labeled data.
- Your dataset should, at a minimum, contain 5,000 labeled examples per category.

The types and sizes of the datasets that are publicly available have been growing at an exponential rate. Following is an interesting diagram that has been recreated from the book *Deep Learning*, by Ian Goodfellow, Yoshua Bengio, and Aaron Courville[1]:

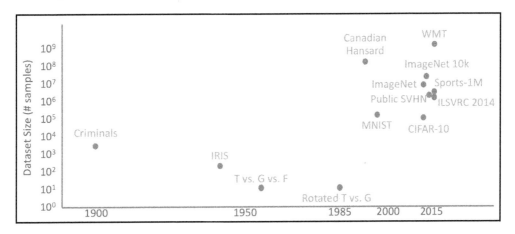

There are several things that should be noted about the preceding diagram. First, the plot lists the databases that are most popular with machine learning researchers. Second, as you can see, the size of the datasets in modern times has grown dramatically as compared to the earlier datasets.

A very popular dataset that is used among many machine learning researchers is the CIFAR-10 dataset. CIFAR-10 is a collection of 60,000 images from the following 10 image classes:

- Airplanes
- Cars
- Birds
- Cats
- Deer
- Dogs
- Frogs
- Horses
- Ships
- Trucks

Each image is a 32-pixel x 32-pixel color image. The CIFAR-10 dataset provides developers with a way to quickly try out different models and determine which ones are the best at recognizing the objects the most efficiently.

There are plenty of other datasets as well. For example, the CIFAR-100 dataset expands on CIFAR-10 by including 100 classes that contain 600 images for each class. There is also ImageNet, which contains more than 14 million images in over 20,000 categories.

For our purposes, we will keep things simple and use the CIFAR-10 dataset for our project.

Machine learning modeling languages

There are several different libraries and frameworks that developers can use to create a model for their dataset. A quick overview of the different tools can be seen in the following diagram:

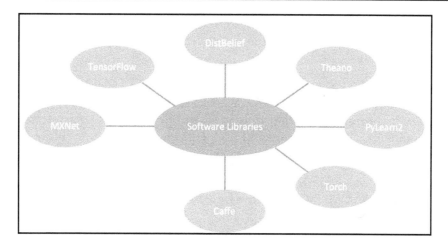

For developers working with embedded systems, it's fairly common for either TensorFlow or Caffe to be used to convert their dataset into a machine learning model.

TensorFlow is a software library developed by Google that is used for machine learning applications that use neural networks. The library was open sourced in 2015 under the Apache 2.0 license.

Caffe is a deep learning framework that is written in C++ and was developed for applications involving image classification. The framework was developed at the University of California, Berkeley, and released under a BSD license.

These libraries and frameworks allow a developer to train a machine learning model that could then be used for object detection. The problem with these tools is that they are too big to run on a microcontroller. Even a model generated from these libraries would require too much computational horsepower to be useful on a microcontroller. In order to use them effectively on a microcontroller, we require an additional tool that can convert the model into something that can run on a microcontroller. In order to do this, we use Arm-NN.

TFLu

TFLu is TensorFlow Lite for Microcontrollers. According to the tensorflow.org website:

> *TensorFlow Lite for Microcontrollers is an experimental port of TensorFlow Lite designed to run machine learning models on microcontrollers and other devices with only kilobytes of memory.*

Running a machine learning framework directly on a Cortex-M processor is impractical.

The computing resources necessary to run such frameworks are too intense for a resource-constrained device. However, it is possible to run a trained model, the inference, on a microcontroller.

On a microcontroller, the inference needs to run bare-metal in order to efficiently use the limited resources of the processor. While a microcontroller with a megabyte of RAM and flash may not seem resource-constrained to an embedded developer, for a framework that can leverage terabytes of storage space and high-end, cloud-based computing resources, a microcontroller offers nearly no resources in comparison.

TFLu helps to translate the trained model to code that can run on Cortex-M processors. It leverages API calls from CMSIS-NN, which we will discuss in more detail shortly. This can be seen quite clearly in the following diagram:

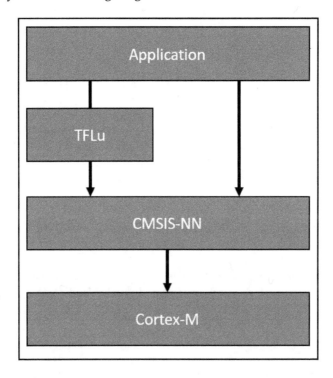

You can learn a bit more about TFLu at https://www.tensorflow.org/lite/microcontrollers. Let's now take a look at how CMSIS-NN comes into play.

CMSIS-NN

CMSIS-NN is a software framework that is optimized for the low-level **neural network** (**NN**) functions on Arm Cortex-M microcontrollers. CMSIS-NN is often called by TFLu in order to interact directly with the microcontroller hardware, but developers can make calls directly to CMSIS-NN from their application code if necessary. CMSIS-NN can be summed up as a collection of neural network functions that includes important features such as the following:

- A minimal memory footprint
- Optimizations specific to neural networks, such as data layout and offline weight ordering
- Improved performance using Cortex-M SIMD instructions

The following diagram provides the reader with an overview of what they can expect to find in CMSIS-NN. A more detailed discussion about the framework is beyond the scope of this book:

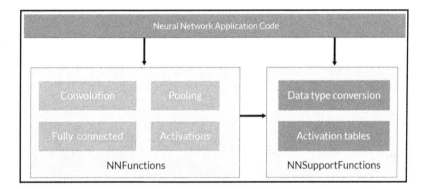

The hardware

The hardware that we will be working with within this chapter has already been described back in the section on hardware requirements. However, I think it is important to note here that the OpenMV camera does provide examples of how to use machine learning to detect objects. In fact, since the OpenMV camera uses an Arm Cortex-M processor, the very software frameworks we have just been talking about are used by OpenMV to provide machine learning capabilities!

We are now at the point where we have enough background information on what we are trying to do that we can dive in and start to implement object detection.

Implementing and testing object detection on the OpenMV camera

There are several different ways that we can implement object detection using the OpenMV camera. In this section, we are going to use two different methods:

- First, we are going to use a pretrained **convolutional neural network** (**CNN**) that was trained by OpenMV using the CIFAR-10 dataset. We will load the example and then provide it with several images to see how the network behaves and to become familiar with OpenMV operations.
- Second, we will move beyond the pretrained network and train a network of our own that we will then deploy to the OpenMV camera. By the time you have completed this section, you will be able to train a network to detect whatever object it is that you are interested in detecting and be able to start building your own control application.

Getting familiar with OpenMV IDE

Before we start playing with the pretrained CIFAR-10 network, let's first discuss how to set up and configure our OpenMV camera using OpenMV IDE. Begin by opening OpenMV IDE. You'll notice that the IDE is broken up into four main areas:

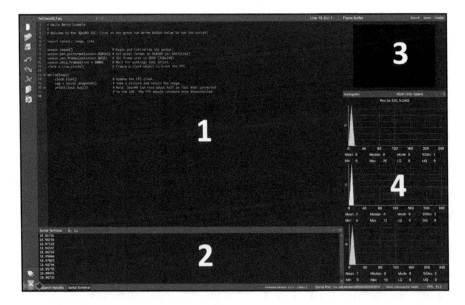

The main areas that are marked in the preceding screenshot are as follows:

1. The code editor
2. A terminal window
3. An image preview
4. An image histogram

On the lower left-hand side of the screen, you'll also notice that there are two buttons:

- One for connecting to the OpenMV camera
- One for running the current OpenMV script

By default, the OpenMV IDE loads with the hello_world.py script ready to run. This script continuously takes images from the camera and displays the **frames per second** (**FPS**) that it is able to achieve. (Note that the maximum achievable FPS is much higher if the camera is not connected to a PC). The script is shown in full as follows (script source: OpenMV IDE hello_world.py):

```
# Hello World Example
# Welcome to the OpenMV IDE! Click on the green run arrow button below
# to run the script!

import sensor, image, time

sensor.reset()                      # Reset and initialize the sensor.
sensor.set_pixformat(sensor.RGB565) # Set pixel format to RGB565
                                    # (or GRAYSCALE)
sensor.set_framesize(sensor.QVGA)   # Set frame size to QVGA (320x240)
sensor.skip_frames(time = 2000)     # Wait for settings take effect.
clock = time.clock()                # Create a clock object to track the
FPS.

while(True):
    clock.tick()                    # Update the FPS clock.
    img = sensor.snapshot()         # Take a picture and return the image.
    print(clock.fps())              # Note: OpenMV Cam runs about half
                                    # as fast when connected
                                    # to the IDE. The FPS should increase
                                    # once disconnected.
```

Let's take a moment to run this script and make sure that we are able to successfully connect to the OpenMV camera. (Note, if your camera is brand new, you should review the OpenMV getting started documentation for how to focus the camera). You can perform the following steps:

1. Connect the OpenMV camera to your computer.
2. In the lower-left corner, click the icon that looks like a plug-in order to connect the camera.
3. If this is your first time using the camera, OpenMV IDE may tell you that the firmware is outdated. Allow the IDE to update the firmware before continuing. (This may take a few minutes.)
4. Click on the green arrow execute button.

At this point, you should see a read-out in the terminal that displays the calculated FPS, as shown in the following screenshot:

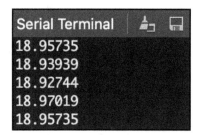

You should also see that the histogram and the image preview window changes as you move the camera around to point at different objects in your environment. Now that the camera is up and running and we have some basic experience with it, let's try playing with the pretrained CIFAR-10 network.

Implementing a pretrained CIFAR-10 network

First, if you were just running the `hello_world.py` script, go ahead and stop the script from executing by pressing the stop button in the lower left-hand corner of the OpenMV IDE. This will get you back to square one and ensure that nothing interferes with our ability to load the CIFAR-10 example.

Next, before we can execute the example code, we need to save the CIFAR-10 trained network interface on the OpenMV camera. This will provide the camera with the trained network and we will need to reference it in our application script. Perform the following steps to load and save the CIFAR-10 network file:

1. From the top menu, click **Tools | Machine Learning | CNN Network Library**.
2. In the pop-up window, navigate to **CMSIS-NN | cifar10**.
3. Click the **cifar10.network** file and select **Open**.
4. Another window will pop up. This window will ask where to save the selected file. Navigate to the **OpenMV mass storage device drive** that appeared when you connected the camera. Click **Save**.

Now that the network file is saved to the camera filesystem, we can load the example script by clicking **File | Examples | 25-Machine-Learning -| py**.

You may have noticed that there were several additional `nn_cifar10` scripts. These scripts provide examples of how to reduce the area that the network is evaluating. For example, one example will search a smaller area of the image in the center versus examining the entire image. For our purposes, we will just use the whole window classification, but I encourage you to try the others as well. The example script for `nn_cifar10_search_whole_window.py` can be seen as follows:

```
# CIFAR-10 Search Whole Window Example
#
# CIFAR is a convolutional neural network designed to classify its field of
# view into several different object types and works on RGB video data.
#
# In this example, we slide the LeNet detector window over the image and
# get a list of activations where there might be an object. Note that using
# a CNN with a sliding window is extremely compute expensive, so for an
# exhaustive search do not expect the CNN to be real-time.
import sensor, image, time, os, nn
sensor.reset()                              # Reset and initialize the sensor.
sensor.set_pixformat(sensor.RGB565)         # Set pixel format to RGB565
sensor.set_framesize(sensor.QVGA)           # Set frame size to QVGA (320x240)
sensor.set_windowing((128, 128))            # Set 128x128 window.
sensor.skip_frames(time=750)                # Don't let autogain run very long.
sensor.set_auto_gain(False)                 # Turn off autogain.
sensor.set_auto_exposure(False)             # Turn off whitebalance.
# Load the cifar10 network (You can get the network from OpenMV IDE).
net = nn.load('/cifar10.network')
# Faster, smaller and less accurate.
# net = nn.load('/cifar10_fast.network')
labels = ['airplane', 'automobile', 'bird', 'cat', 'deer', 'dog', 'frog',
    'horse', 'ship', 'truck']
```

```
clock = time.clock()
while(True):
    clock.tick()
    img = sensor.snapshot()
    # net.search() will search an roi in the image for the network
    # (or the whole image if the roi is not specified). At each location to
    # look in the image if one of the classifier outputs is larger than
    # threshold the location and label will be stored in an object list and
    # returned. At each scale the detection window is moved around in the
    # ROI
    # using x_overlap (0-1) and y_overlap (0-1) as a guide.
    # If you set the overlap to 0.5 then each detection window will overlap
    # the previous one by 50%. Note the computational workload goes WAY up
    # the more overlap. Finally, for mult-scale matching after sliding the
    # network around in the x/y dimensions the detection window will shrink
    # by scale_mul (0-1)down to min_scale (0-1). For example, if scale_mul
    # is 0.5 the detection window will shrink by 50%.
    # Note that at a lower scale there's even more area to search if
    # x_overlap and y_overlap are small... contrast_threshold skips running
    # the CNN in areas that are flat.
    for obj in net.search(img, threshold=0.6, min_scale=0.5, scale_mul=0.5,
        x_overlap=0.5, y_overlap=0.5, contrast_threshold=0.5):
        print("Detected %s - Confidence %f%%"% (labels[obj.index()],\
        obj.value()))
        img.draw_rectangle(obj.rect(), color=(255, 0, 0))
        print(clock.fps())
```

Take a few minutes to read through the comments in the script. The comments provide all the information you need to understand what is happening in the script and how it is trying to detect an object in the image. Once you have read through the comments, perform the following steps to run and test the network:

1. Click the **Run** button in the lower left-hand corner of the IDE.
2. Using a mobile device, use your favorite search engine to find and present the following images to the camera:
   - Airplanes
   - Cars
   - Birds
   - Cats
   - Deer
   - Dogs
   - Frogs
   - Horses

- Ships
- Trucks

3. While you present the images, take note of the classification result and the confidence level that you are achieving.

How did that exercise go for you? When I ran this example myself, I found that the pretrained network was able to achieve around 70% accuracy. That was under ideal conditions. In fact, I often found that it was achieving a mid-60% confidence level. An example Terminal output for my confidence levels can be seen in the following screenshot:

```
Serial Terminal
Detected airplane - Confidence 0.711765%
1.893939
Detected airplane - Confidence 0.715686%
1.893939
Detected airplane - Confidence 0.704902%
1.893939
Detected airplane - Confidence 0.701961%
1.893939
Detected airplane - Confidence 0.700000%
1.893939
Detected airplane - Confidence 0.695098%
1.893939
```

Depending on the image that I showed it, I also found that I received quite a few false classifications. For example, I provided the camera with a picture of a cat and, 7 times out of 10, it was a cat, while on the other three occasions, it was classified as a ship!

Now, this is certainly not optimal, but for getting a machine learning object detection inference up and running in just a few minutes, it really isn't that bad. Let's now take a look at an example where we train the model ourselves and run it on the OpenMV camera.

Person detection with a TensorFlow model

We can't detect an object without first training a model. Training a model requires significant resources in order to perform the calculations to set the weights and neural biases. This is usually done using backpropagation, but it depends on the techniques that are being used. The problem that is encountered by many embedded engineers looking to use machine learning is that once they train their model, they need to convert that model to something that can run within a resource constrained environment.

Working from within an embedded environment often limits the number of neural layers that can be included in a model. Models that are generated using popular tools such as Caffe or TensorFlow also generate their models in floating point. As you know, floating-point calculations are notoriously slow and cumbersome within a microcontroller environment. For this reason, once a model is trained, it needs to be quantized and optimized in order to move to fixed point mathematics and reduce the model size. This is often done using scripts that are provided by Arm to convert a model for use with TFLu and CMSIS-NN. Thankfully, we don't have to develop those scripts ourselves.

A very useful blog that you can read through on the process can be found at `https://community.arm.com/innovation/b/blog/posts/low-power-deep-learning-on-openmv-cam`.

What's great about this blog is that it even explains how you can convert a Caffe model specifically for use on the OpenMV module! All the steps are necessary to train and deploy a model using Caffe.

You may be wondering though, what about TensorFlow? TensorFlow is too resource-heavy to be used with a microcontroller directly; instead, TensorFlow Lite (TF Lite) could be used. TF Lite is an open source deep learning framework for on-device inferences. TF Lite for MCUs is an experimental port of TensorFlow Lite that is designed to run inferences on microcontrollers with only a few kilobytes of memory! For readers who are interested, you can find the port at `https://github.com/tensorflow/tensorflow/tree/master/tensorflow/lite/experimental/micro`.

The process to deploy a TF Lite model onto an embedded target is straightforward. You can see the general process in the following diagram:

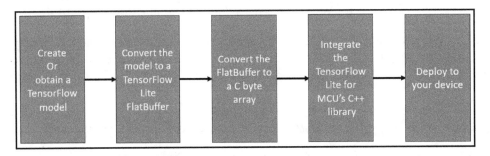

TF Lite for MCUs has also been integrated within MicroPython through the OpenMV project! You can check out the details at `http://docs.openmv.io/library/omv.tf.html`. For the most part, this integration is completely seamless for a developer and it is just useful for a developer to understand what is happening behind the scenes even though they don't have to do any of the integration themselves.

Just like before, we are going to leverage an existing model that was trained by OpenMV using TensorFlow. In this example, we are going to look at how we can detect that a person is present in the image. So, the object that we are trying to detect is a person (or at least resembles a person). Perform the following steps to prepare the system:

1. Connect your OpenMV camera to the computer.
2. Launch OpenMV IDE.
3. Load the person detection example by clicking the following: **File** | **Examples** | **25-Machine-Learning** | **tf_person_detection_search_just_center.py**.

The development window will now be filled with the example MicroPython script. Take a few minutes to read through the script. You can also find it listed as follows (script source: OpenMV `tf_person_detection_search_just_center.py`):

```
# TensorFlow Lite Person Detection Example
#
# Google's Person Detection Model detects if a person is in view.
#
# In this example we slide the detector window over the image and get a
# list
# of activations. Note that use a CNN with a sliding window is extremely
# compute
# expensive so for an exhaustive search do not expect the CNN to be real
# -time.
import sensor, image, time, os, tf
sensor.reset()                          # Reset and initialize the sensor.
sensor.set_pixformat(sensor.GRAYSCALE)  # Set pixel format to RGB565 (or
                                        # GRAYSCALE)
sensor.set_framesize(sensor.QVGA)       # Set frame size to QVGA (320x240)
sensor.set_windowing((240, 240))        # Set 240x240 window.
sensor.skip_frames(time=2000)           # Let the camera adjust.
# Load the built-in person detection network (the network is in your OpenMV
# Cam's firmware).
net = tf.load('person_detection')
labels = ['unsure', 'person', 'no_person']
clock = time.clock()
while(True):
    clock.tick()
    img = sensor.snapshot()
    # net.classify() will run the network on an roi in the image (or on the
    # whole
    # image
    # if the roi is not
    # specified). A classification score output vector will be generated
    # for each location. At each scale the
```

```
# detection window is moved around in the ROI using x_overlap (0-1) and
# y_overlap (0-1) as a guide.
# If you set the overlap to 0.5 then each detection window will overlap
# the
# previous one by 50%. Note
# the computational work load goes WAY up the more overlap. Finally,
# for
# multi-scale matching after
# sliding the network around in the x/y dimensions the detection window
# will
# shrink by scale_mul (0-1)
# down to min_scale (0-1). For example, if scale_mul is 0.5 the
# detection
# window will shrink by 50%.
# Note that at a lower scale there's even more area to search if
# x_overlap
# and y_overlap are small...
# Setting x_overlap=-1 forces the window to stay centered in the ROI in
# the x direction always. If
# y_overlap is not -1 the method will search in all vertical positions.
# Setting y_overlap=-1 forces the window to stay centered in the ROI in
# the y direction always. If
# x_overlap is not -1 the method will search in all horizontal
# positions.
# default settings just do one detection... change them to search the
# image...
for obj in net.classify(img, min_scale=0.5, scale_mul=0.5,
 x_overlap=-1, y_overlap=-1):
    print("**********\nDetections at [x=%d,y=%d,w=%d,h=%d]" %
    obj.rect())
    for i in range(len(obj.output())):
        print("%s = %f" % (labels[i], obj.output()[i]))
    img.draw_rectangle(obj.rect())
    img.draw_string(obj.x()+3, obj.y()-1, labels[obj.output().
    index(max(obj.output()))], mono_space = False)
print(clock.fps(), "fps")
```

Now that you have an idea of how the script works, let's run it! Perform the following steps:

1. Click the connect button in the lower-left corner of the OpenMV IDE.
2. Click **Run.**

3. Make sure that your serial terminal is open. If it does not display, click **Serial Terminal** in the lower-left corner.

4. Now, present a person to the camera and notice the confidence level in the terminal that there is a person present.

When I ran the example, I decided to present to it not my face, but instead my Dr. Leonard McCoy Star Trek action figure (the one played by Karl Urban). You can see that I presented the action figure to the OpenMV camera in the **person** box that is generated in the center of the view in the following screenshot:

When I presented the action figure, the image was pushed through the person detection inference that is running in the example MicroPython script. The serial terminal output can be seen in the following screenshot:

```
Serial Terminal

1.127396 fps
*********
Detections at [x=0,y=0,w=240,h=240]
unsure = 0.160784
person = 0.952941
no_person = 0.203922
*********
Detections at [x=60,y=60,w=120,h=120]
unsure = 0.172549
person = 0.952941
no_person = 0.196078
1.127396 fps
```

As you can see, the application tells us the framerate, which in this case is typically between 1–2 frames per second. You can see that it also calculates whether it thinks there is a person in the image. In this case, you can see it is ~95% sure that there is a person there. It also evaluates whether it thinks there is no person there and how unsure it is about its answers.

Using machine learning to detect objects can be that simple! If you can, find an existing model that you can leverage for application. If a model doesn't exist, then you need to train a model yourself.

Summary

In this chapter, we explored how a developer could get started with object detection applications using the OpenMV camera. We examined the machine learning technologies that drive this capability under the hood, such as CMSIS-NN. While training cannot be done on the target device, the inference can be executed on a resource-constrained processor.

Depending on the end application and the object that needs to be detected, a developer may be able to leverage existing datasets to train their model. Worst case scenario, a developer may need to acquire and classify the data themselves. With the knowledge gained in this chapter, you should now be able to train your own custom models and deploy them on the OpenMV camera. You can also leverage the existing, pretrained models and examples to develop extremely sophisticated applications.

In the next chapter, we are going to discuss where MicroPython may be headed and how it will impact the way that embedded systems are designed and built.

Questions

1. What skill areas are traditionally covered within embedded systems?
2. Why are intelligent systems now required in the industry?
3. What are the benefits of moving machine learning from the cloud to the edge?
4. What image dataset is most commonly used in machine learning algorithm development?
5. What tools are used to train and deploy a machine learning model on an embedded system?

Further reading

There are quite a few resources on machine learning and object detection that can be found throughout the internet. Many are resources that can be read, but there are also resources that can be watched on YouTube. Here are several additional resources that you will undoubtedly find useful:

- Introduction video: `https://www.youtube.com/watch?v=aircAruvnKk`
- Online book: `http://neuralnetworksanddeeplearning.com/`
- MIT course: `http://introtodeeplearning.com/`
- CMSIS-NN paper: `https://arxiv.org/abs/1801.06601`
- KWS (Keyword Spotting) paper: `https://arxiv.org/abs/1711.07128`
- OpenMV NN module documentation: `https://docs.openmv.io/library/omv.nn.html`
- Model conversion: `https://community.arm.com/innovation/b/blog/posts/low-power-deep-learning-on-openmv-cam`
- TensorFlow Lite integration in MicroPython: `http://docs.openmv.io/library/omv.tf.html`

References

Here is a list of references you can refer to:

- *Deep Learning*, Ian Goodfellow, Yoshua Bengio, and Aaron Courville, page 18.
- `https://developer.arm.com/ip-products/processors/machine-learning/arm-nn`
- `https://www.tensorflow.org/lite/microcontrollers`
- `https://www.tensorflow.org/lite/microcontrollers#developer_workflow`

The Future of MicroPython

10

Since 2013, MicroPython has been gaining popularity not just among hobbyists and Python enthusiasts, but also among professional developers who are willing to explore innovative and unconventional ways to develop embedded systems. Will MicroPython survive in the long term or is it just a short-term fad that will disappear over the next few years?

In this chapter, we will explore current trends and what the future of MicroPython might look like for professional and DIY developers. We will also examine some of the latest and greatest hardware and software for MicroPython that will help round out your MicroPython toolkit.

The following topics will be covered in this chapter:

- The advancing MicroPython
- The pyboard D-series
- Example professional projects
- Example maker projects
- How MicroPython can be used professionally
- Going further

The advancing MicroPython

The greatest advantage that MicroPython currently has going for it is that Python, in general, has become one of the most popular programming languages in the world. Whether you are working in the cloud or at the edge, with a Windows or with a Linux machine, Python can be found there. There are Python libraries for serial communication, analyzing data, creating graphical user interfaces, analyzing images, and running machine learning inferences, just to name a few. Python is widely supported and has a fantastic ecosystem surrounding it.

All the advantages that you can think of for Python can also be applied to MicroPython, in addition to several additional advantages including the following:

- Abstracting the low-level electronics
- Lowering the barrier to entry for new developers (think electrical engineers and students)

There are still many challenges that developers interested in using MicroPython still face, despite all the advantages and the advances that have been made. For example, developers who want to use MicroPython may come across the following challenges:

- The integrity of the filesystem is questionable under certain circumstances, such as after an unexpected power disruption.
- Having enough memory available for application scripts and to run the scripts.
- Developing an adequate backup and recovery mechanism for the system.
- Recovering from low-level hardware failures such as an I2C bus fault that may not be handled properly by the low-level drivers.
- Additional hardware costs for a microcontroller that can run the MicroPython kernel.
- Securing an application that uses MicroPython.

While these can be challenging for developers to overcome, they are not impossible and the continued improvements to MicroPython over the next several years will undoubtedly address them. In fact, several of these challenges are currently being dramatically improved through the pyboard D-Series module and the latest MicroPython kernel releases. Let's take a moment to explore the pyboard D-Series and some of the software capabilities that can help minimize these challenges for developers.

The pyboard D-series

While I was writing this project book, the MicroPython community was waiting in anticipation for the release of the latest flagship MicroPython development board, the pyboard D-series. (The module went into production a few months before this book was published.) Unlike its predecessors, the pyboard D-series was designed to be a module that could be used in production systems. Developers can design their end application and put all their hardware on a carrier or daughter board and then, through a mezzanine connector, add the pyboard D-series module in order to command and control their specific application hardware.

There are several advantages to the module approach for the pyboard D-series, including the following:

- Developers can design their hardware completely independently of the microcontroller.
- Over time, their product or project processing power can be upgraded or scaled by swapping out the pyboard D-series module for the latest and greatest.
- Bluetooth and Wi-Fi are included in the module, so there is no need to spend time adding these features to the carrier board.

Beyond these advantages, the pyboard D-series brought with it several new hardware capabilities and features that make MicroPython more robust and interesting for developers to use in both professional and hobby projects. Let's take a look at these new features.

The pyboard D-series hardware

First, the **pyboard D-series** (**PYBD-SFxW**) is not a single development module. There are three different versions of the module that allow developers to customize the features and capabilities that they need in their projects and can help them meet their budgets. Each module is based on an Arm Cortex-M7 microcontroller from STMicroelectronics and includes the following microcontrollers:

- STM32F722
- STM32F723
- STM32F767

The modules are designated based on the last number in the microcontroller. For example, the module that uses the STM32F722 is the PYBD-SF2W, while the STM32F767 module is the PYBD-SF6W.

These microcontrollers are all capable of running at 216 MHz, which provides a lot of processing power to run MicroPython, but they don't come clocked at their maximum speed. For example, the PYBD-SF2W has an initial clock rate of 120 MHz, while the PYBD-SF6W has a clock rate of 144 MHz. Developers have the ability to control what performance level they need from the module by adjusting the clock rate at 2 MHz increments, all the way from 48 MHz to 216 MHz. It's interesting to note that developers can even go below the 48 MHz rate, but developers will no longer be able to run the onboard Wi-Fi stack.

Changing the clock rate can be done through the `freq` method from the `machine` module. For example, we can set the clock rate to 100 MHz using the following code:

```
machine.freq(100000000)
```

The PYBD-SFxWs all come with at least 256 kB RAM, with the STM32F767 including 512 kB. Each module also includes a dedicated 2 MiB external QSPI flash module that extends the internal flash memory so that developers have more space to store their scripts. A second 2 MiB external QSPI flash module is also on the modules to store user files and data, in addition to the standard SD card slot. These devices can all be mounted on the MicroPython filesystem.

The PYBD-SFxW also includes an integrated Wi-Fi and Bluetooth 4.1 (classic and BLE) module through a Murata 1DX CYW4343 chip. The MicroPython implementation has the TCP/IP and Bluetooth stacks running on the microcontroller in order to provide developers with more flexibility to customize them. While this is great, developers working with these features will need to monitor their CPU usage because these software stacks can be demanding from a processing standpoint. It also means that they can't drop the clock rate below 48 MHz, as we previously discussed. However, these are most likely not major design constraints for most developers.

Additional features on the module that are interesting include the following:

- The ability to connect an external antenna through a selectable RF switch
- Access to I/O through a 40+40 pin mezzanine connector
- 2 I2C buses
- 4 UARTs
- 3 SPI interfaces
- 1 CAN
- 46 GPIO

There are many other features, but I would recommend visiting `http://store.micropython.org` to see them all.

The PYBD-SFxW modules are also quite small, coming in at only 23.8 x 33.5 mm! The module layout can be seen in the following image:

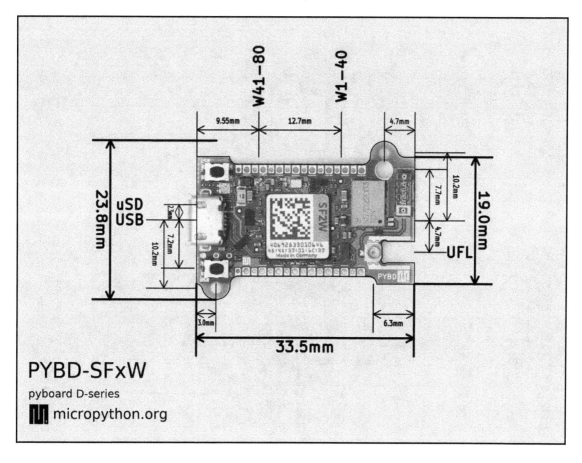

As you may have noticed, there are pins along the side of the module that provide developers with a way to access specific I/O pins. These pins are broken up into two separate categories: **X** and **Y** positions.

These are important to note because if you want to access these pins in MicroPython, you'll need to know their pin specifier. The pinouts can be seen in the following image:

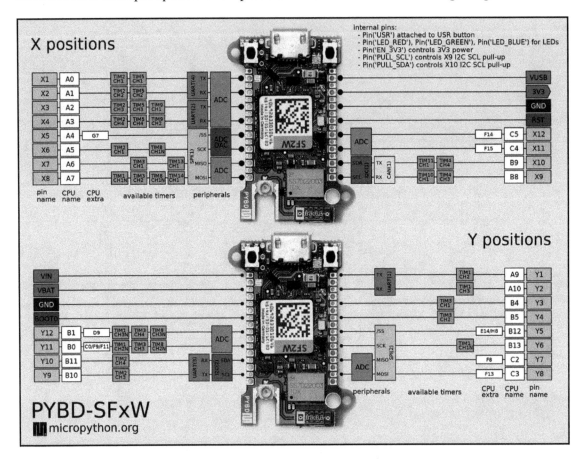

Beyond the pins that are available in the **X** and **Y** positions, there are many more GPIOs available through the WBUS connector, which is available on the bottom of the PYBD-SFxW module. The easiest way to access these pins is through an adapter board that converts the WBUS into a DIP socket that can then be placed on a breadboard. This provides us with the most effective way to start development and prototyping.

The WBUS, along with the location for many of the other parts on the PYBD-SFxW module, can be seen in the following image:

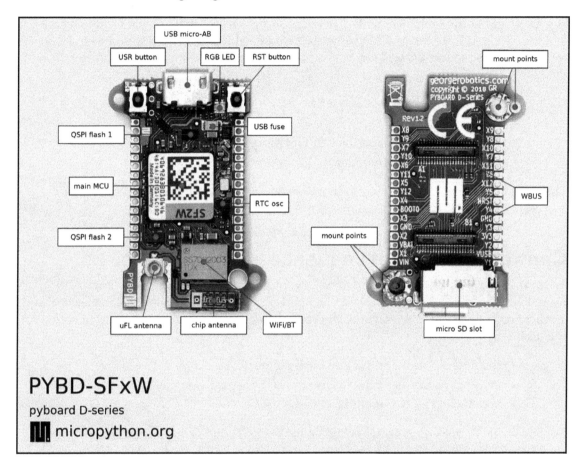

Now that we have become familiar with some of the hardware capabilities of the PYBD-SFxW module, let's look at some of the software capabilities that we can use to leverage these features.

The pyboard D-series software

Each MicroPython release brings with it new features, but also performance improvements, bug fixes, and library enhancements. There are some features that are just tried and true that have existed since the first MicroPython release, while there are also some new features. In this section, we will explore some useful software features, such as the following:

- How to control the boot sequence
- Detecting errors
- Mounting and accessing the QSPI memory
- Adjusting the clock frequency

These are features that every MicroPython developer needs to understand in order to successfully develop their application.

Controlling the boot sequence

When the MicroPython board boots, it will eventually reach a point where it needs to mount a filesystem to look for the `boot.py` and `main.py` scripts so that it can execute any application scripts. There are several different places where these scripts could be located, including the following:

- The microcontroller's internal flash memory
- An SD card that has been inserted into the SD card slot
- An attached eMMC module

So, how does MicroPython decide where to look when booting? The answer depends on the MicroPython build that you are using. For example, builds for the PYBD1.x boards always defaulted to the SD card if an SD card was inserted. If developers wanted to force MicroPython to boot from the internal flash, they would have to include the following in their SD card's `boot.py` file:

```
pyb.main(('/flash/main.py')
```

There is also the option to add a file named SKIPSD to the internal flash filesystem. During boot up, if MicroPython sees the SKIPSD file in the filesystem, even if an SD card is present, it will look at the internal flash for `boot.py` and `main.py`. Having SKIPSD is interesting because it allows developers to force the use of an internal application and if something goes wrong, the SKIPSD file could be removed and a backup copy of the application could be loaded from the SD card to safely boot the system and recover the internal filesystem.

Developers working with the new pyboard D-series will find that MicroPython works a little bit differently. Instead of defaulting to using an SD card unless the SKIPSD file is present, the kernel always boots from the internal flash and then the developer mounts the SD card and any other memory within their application. In this case, developers can mount the SD card using the following code:

```
import sys, os, pyb
if pyb.SDCard().present():
    os.mount(pyb.SDCard(), '/sd')
    sys.path[1:1] = ['/sd', '/sd/lib']
```

The preceding code checks to see whether an SD card is present. If so, it mounts the card and also adds it to the path list so that MicroPython can search it for scripts and libraries. It's important to note that while this works for detecting whether the SD card is present, this same technique cannot be used to detect whether an eMMC device is present.

With several different memory sources now available, developers need to modify their boot.py script to determine which memory source will be viewable through the USB mass storage device. For example, if a developer wanted the internal flash filesystem to be available, they would use the following line of code:

```
pyb.usb_mode('VCP+MSC', msc=(pyb.Flash(),))
```

If the developer wanted to make available the SD card, they would use the following line of code:

```
pyb.usb_mode('VCP+MSC', msc=(pyb.SDCard(),))
```

Finally, to make the eMMC available, a developer would use the following line of code:

```
pyb.usb_mode('VCP+MSC', msc=(pyb.MMCard(),))
```

As you can see, there are many different ways that a developer can configure their application to boot and configure which memory sources are available over USB. One question you may have, though, is, *what happens if something goes wrong?*

Recovering from system faults

The most common fault that will be encountered by a developer working with MicroPython is a corrupt filesystem. The filesystem can become corrupted due to a power failure that occurred before the MicroPython board was properly ejected via USB or due to a brown-out that occurred from operating the device from a battery. MicroPython uses an FAT filesystem that does not power down gracefully in situations where power is removed unexpectedly. When this happens, the filesystem can become corrupted.

The way that a developer recovers in these cases will depend on their application needs. For example, if it is a DIY project, a developer may simply boot into safe mode by following this process:

1. Connect the pyboard to USB so it powers up.
2. Hold down the USR switch, and while doing so, press and release the RST switch.
3. The LEDs will then cycle green to orange to green and orange and back again.
4. Keep holding down USR until only the orange LED is lit, and then let go of the USR switch. The orange LED should flash quickly four times, and then turn off. You are now in safe mode.

Safe mode boots MicroPython normally but skips the boot.py and main.py files. This provides the developer with access to the REPL to perform their system recovery.

It may turn out that if the filesystem was corrupted and MicroPython detected the corruption, the entire filesystem will be reset to the factory settings. This means that the following files will be completely reset:

- boot.py
- main.py
- README.txt
- pybcdc.info

While it's great that MicroPython can recover in this manner, it also means that any custom code that was created for boot.py and main.py will now be completely erased, along with any additional scripts that may have been on the filesystem. Again, for a DIY project, this may not be a big deal, but for a professional project, this could be devastating! There are a few options for recovery, though.

First, if the application is relatively simple and contains only a main.py module and a few additional modules, it's possible to include a default version of these files in the kernel that would be copied back to the filesystem if the filesystem becomes corrupted. These custom files would have to be compiled and added to the kernel, creating a custom kernel similar to how we did in Chapter 4, *Developing an Application Test Harness*. However, if we have a complex project that has dozens of files and tens of thousands of lines of code, this procedure is not going to work.

This brings us to a second recovery mechanism, which is to store a backup of our application scripts on an SD card or on eMMC memory. When the internal filesystem becomes corrupt, or vice versa, we can customize a `main.py` module that is copied back to the filesystem and then copies our application back to the filesystem. Then, once recovery is complete, the system can be restarted and boot normally. This procedure still requires us to customize the kernel `main.py` script that is created in the filesystem, but the modifications are minor compared to the first option.

Resetting the system from within a script is relatively easy and there are two options available to developers. The first option will exit the application and behave similarly to a soft reset. A soft reset will not restart the microcontroller or its peripherals. For example, if there was a timer running, the timer would continue to count. The code to perform this function can be seen as follows:

```
import sys
sys.exit()
```

What a developer really wants to do is perform a hard reset that power cycles the microcontroller and has the application launch from scratch. This can be done using the `reset` method, which is located in the `machine` module. A developer would first import `machine` and then execute the following line of code:

```
machine.reset()
```

This code can be executed from within a recovery script or it can be done from the REPL if it is readily accessible.

MicroPython in the real world

Throughout this book, we have been exploring how developers can leverage MicroPython to quickly and efficiently develop embedded systems using MicroPython. With each passing day, there are more and more examples for both DIY projects and professional products that are using MicroPython. As we move toward the conclusion of this book, I think it would be interesting to discuss how MicroPython is being used in each of these very distinct areas.

Example DIY/maker projects

DIY and maker projects are a great place to look for inspiration for your next MicroPython project, and there is no shortage of example projects out on the internet. A quick web search reveals that there are all kinds of MicroPython projects, ranging from the simple to the complex. For example, you might find projects such as the following:

- Electronic games
- Piggybanks
- Weather stations
- Irrigation systems
- Robots
- Drones

A great place to look for inspiration and to see what other developers are working on is to visit the following websites:

- Hackster.io (`https://www.hackster.io/projects/tags/micropython`)
- Hackaday.io (`https://hackaday.io/projects?tag=micropython`)

These sites have dozens of projects that makers built or are building that not only provide inspiration but also include schematics and source code that you can review to improve your own skills.

Example professional projects

Makers and hobbyists aren't the only developers leveraging MicroPython – professional developers are getting in on the action as well. One of my favorite examples of MicroPython being used by professional developers is its use in the OpenMV module. The best way to describe OpenMV is to use their own words:

> *"The OpenMV project is about creating low-cost, extensible, Python-powered, machine vision modules and aims at becoming the "Arduino of Machine Vision." Our goal is to bring machine vision algorithms closer to makers and hobbyists. We've done the difficult and time-consuming algorithm work for you, leaving more time for your creativity!"*

- https://openmv.io/

What's great about OpenMV is that the Python it uses to accomplish its mission is MicroPython! The module runs MicroPython on an STM32H7 microcontroller and all their machine vision algorithms are accessible through Python modules. Not only do developers not need to be experts in low-level microcontroller technology, but they also don't even need to be experts in machine vision! They can leverage the OpenMV libraries for objects, faces, eyes, and colors, and apply many other capabilities from within the MicroPython environment. An example of the OpenMV module can be seen as follows:

OpenMV is not the only professional team using MicroPython in their products. Another area where MicroPython is finding use is in space systems. I've worked on several applications internally at my own company and with my clients that use MicroPython in small satellite applications. For example, we have used MicroPython to create a CubeSat flight computer that can run a spacecraft and provides scalability to grow between using a microcontroller-based system and a Linux-based system. We've also developed additional CubeSat and nanosatellite subsystems such as **Electronic Power Supplies** (**EPS**) that power the spacecraft.

These applications required customizing the MicroPython kernel and also improving the robustness of several kernel modules to ensure that MicroPython would operate safely in orbit. For example, power fluctuations or an unexpected shutdown would not be allowed to corrupt the filesystem. A servicing mission for a small satellite in near-Earth orbit is just not an option and, given the costs to develop and launch a system, it's just not feasible. The MicroPython system has to run without issue or, if an issue is encountered, it needs to be able to recover on its own with minimal user interaction.

The future of MicroPython

MicroPython might look like a fad or an interesting language to play with, but it has a bright future ahead of it. Professional developers will find it interesting to rapidly prototype their systems and test their hardware without having to fully understand the low-level workings of a microcontroller. When it comes to developing a product, you want to fail fast if you are going to fail, and MicroPython provides developers with that speed and agility to quickly try out new concepts before becoming fully invested in them. DIY and maker types will find that MicroPython provides them with a far easier language to use and learn than any of the Arduino platforms that are currently quite popular.

MicroPython won't replace traditional programming languages such as C or C++ in the near future, but slowly, it will gain market share among professional developers. Developers right now might complain that the MicroPython kernel is too big or that it doesn't offer hard real-time performance or sufficient low-level error handling. As time passes by, MicroPython has become more efficient and robust, and it will continue to do so as the underlying code and third-party software, such as the STM32 HALs, become more efficient and bulletproof.

Microcontroller and memory technology is also advancing at a staggering pace, which is resulting in high-performance MCUs with megabytes of flash and RAM at extremely affordable prices. As this technology progresses, many of the efficiency and storage constraints that may be plaguing MicroPython applications will quickly disappear. MicroPython's support for external storage devices has at least temporarily solved some of these issues, in addition to providing support for eMMC. There is undoubtedly still some work to be done there, but the progress that is being made is rapid!

There are also interesting MicroPython forks that are occurring, such as CircuitPython, which are taking MicroPython in new directions for electronics education. Even if you aren't on the MicroPython bandwagon yet, it's easy to see that MicroPython has the potential to help both hobbyists and professional developers develop embedded systems and projects more efficiently. The only question remaining is how you will leverage MicroPython. The answer is only limited by your own imagination.

Going further

This chapter reviewed the major topics that have been explored in this book and set the stage for where MicroPython is going. We've also covered several other reasons and ways for developers to get more involved in MicroPython.

Thank you for coming on this journey of *MicroPython Projects*. I've tried to cover all the topics that will provide you with a foundation to create your own project with MicroPython. Engineering is always progressing, and while this book has covered core language features and processes, it was impossible to cover everything. The following are several additional resources for you to review that I hope will provide you with additional details that we weren't able to cover in this book:

- MicroPython documentation: `https://docs.micropython.org/en/latest/index.html`
- MicroPython forums: `https://forum.micropython.org/`

References

Here is a list of references you can refer to:

- Pyboard D-series: `https://pybd.io/hw/pybd_sfxw.html`
- MicroPython tutorial for pyboard: `https://docs.micropython.org/en/latest/pyboard/tutorial/reset.html`

Downloading and Running MicroPython Code

Running the script in Listing 2 on the pyboard can be accomplished in just a few easy steps:

1. Connect the pyboard to your computer.
2. Open your terminal application and connect to the pyboard (refer to the **MicroPython documentation** | **Quick reference for the pyboard** | **MicroPython tutorial for the pyboard** | **3. Getting a MicroPython REPL prompt**, for details).
3. In the terminal, press *Ctrl + C* to interrupt any currently running scripts.
4. Copy the script to the pyboard USB drive.
5. Once the red light has turned off, the pyboard flash system will be updated.
6. In the terminal, press *Ctrl + D* to perform a soft reset.

Assessments

Chapter 1

1. What Python features make it a competitive choice for use in embedded systems?
   - It's taught at many universities around the world.
   - It's easy to learn (I've seen elementary students write Python code).
   - It is object oriented.
   - It is an interpreted scripting language, which removes compilation.
   - It's supported by a robust community, including many add-on libraries, which minimizes the need to re-invent the wheel.
   - It includes error handling (something that C didn't get the memo on).
   - It's easily extensible.

2. Which three use cases does MicroPython match well with?
   - DIY projects
   - Rapid prototyping
   - Low-volume production products

3. What business ramifications should be evaluated for using MicroPython?
   - Risk tolerance for security vulnerabilities
   - Cost savings from needing fewer embedded developers
   - Impact on time-to-market
   - Overall system quality and customer reactions

4. What microcontroller architecture is supported the most by MicroPython?
   - STMicroelectronics STM32 microcontrollers

5. What decision-making tool can be used to remove human bias?
   - KT Matrix

6. What five categories make up the **Software Development Life Cycle (SDLC)**?
   - Requirements
   - Design
   - Implementation
   - Testing
   - Maintenance

7. What key combination in the REPL will produce a soft reset?
    - *Ctrl + D*

8. Which workbench resources do you need to develop a MicroPython project? Are you currently missing any?
    - Male-to-female 6" jumpers
    - Male-to-male 6" jumpers
    - Female-to-female 6" jumpers
    - A terminal application such as PuTTY or real-time
    - A high-speed micro SD card
    - Logic Analyzer
    - SPI/I2C bus tool

Chapter 2

1. What characteristics define a real-time embedded system?
    - They are event driven and do not poll inputs.
    - They are deterministic; given the same initial conditions, they produce the same outputs in the same time frame.
    - They are often resource constrained in some manner, such as the following:
        - Clock speed
        - Memory
        - Energy consumption
    - The use of a dedicated microcontroller-based processor.
    - May have a RTOS to manage system tasks.

2. What four scheduling algorithms are commonly used with MicroPython?
    - Round robin scheduling
    - Periodic scheduling using timers
    - Cooperative scheduling
    - MicroPython threads

3. What best practices should a developer follow when using callbacks in MicroPython?
   - Keep **interrupt service routines** (**ISRs**) short and fast.
   - Perform measurements to understand interrupt timing and latency.
   - Use interrupt priority settings to emulate preemption.
   - Make sure task variables are declared as volatile.
   - Avoid calling multiple functions from an ISR.
   - Disable interrupts as little as possible.

4. What process should be followed to load new code onto a MicroPython board?
   1. Connect the pyboard to your computer.
   2. Open your terminal application and connect to the pyboard (refer to the *MicroPython documention | Quick reference for the pyboard | MicroPython tutorial for the pyboard* section 3 for details).
   3. In the terminal, press *Ctrl + C* to interrupt any currently running scripts.
   4. Copy the script to the pyboard USB drive.
   5. Once the red light has turned off, the pyboard flash system will be updated.
   6. In the terminal, press *Ctrl + D* to perform a soft reset.

5. Why would a developer place `micropython.alloc_emergency_exception_buf(100)` in their application?
   - A developer would include this line of code to allocate buffer space to store exceptions where memory cannot be allocated, such as in an ISR.

6. What reasons might deter a developer from using the `_thread` library?
   - Threads are not officially supported in MicroPython. They are experimental.
   - Threads can create difficult-to-solve bugs if the developer is not familiar with multithreading best practices.
   - Threads use more resources than other techniques, such as the `asyncio` library.

7. What keywords indicate that a function is being defined as a coroutine?
   - `async/await`

Chapter 3

1. What is a high-level system diagram called?
   - A block diagram

2. What is a detailed hardware diagram called?
   - A schematic or wiring diagram

3. What three diagrams did we use in this chapter to define our software architecture?
   - An application flowchart
   - A state diagram
   - A class diagram

4. What is it called when two classes are connected together without the use of the inheritance mechanism?
   - Composition

5. What information should be included in a test case?
   - The test case number.
   - The test case objective (why are we doing the test?)
   - Conditions that need to occur before the test is performed.
   - Input that needs to be applied to the system during testing (push a button).
   - Expected results (what should we see happen?)
   - Who did the testing? (yes, who can we blame if we discover a problem in the future?)
   - When was the test performed?
   - The software version number that the test is to be performed on.

6. How can a developer create a constant in Python?
   - There are no constants in Python so it's the same as defining a variable. A developer just needs to make sure they don't modify the constant value!

7. What line of code should a developer write to learn what addresses have slaves present on the I2C bus?
   - `I2C_List = i2c.scan()`

8. What can be used to `catch` an exception and print it out?
   - `except Exception as e: print(e)`

9. What statement can be written to force the application to exit?
   - `sys.exit(0)`

10. What type of setup can be used to fully test and validate the drivers created in an application?
    - A test suite or test harness

Chapter 4

1. What are the three main components that are part of nearly every test harness?
   - A test execution engine
   - A repository of tests
   - A test reporting mechanism

2. What are the advantages of using a test harness?
   - Automating testing, which then frees up developers to focus on other activities.
   - Performing regression testing, which can verify that recent changes haven't broken other pieces of code.
   - Increased code quality.

3. What are a few examples of faults that we would want a test harness to test for?
   - Non-responsive slave device
   - Invalid response
   - I2C bus errors

4. What are some of the architectures that a test harness can follow?
   - PC to embedded device
   - Embedded device monitor to embedded device target
   - Self-contained embedded device target and tester

5. What are the four operations that we need our module tests to perform?
   - Test setup
   - Test execution
   - Test cleanup
   - Test reporting

Chapter 5

1. In which folder in the kernel can you find all the MicroPython-supported architectures?
    - The `ports/` folder

2. Which microcontroller architecture has the most supported development boards?
    - STM32

3. What three types of files can be found in a development board's board folder?
    - Supported board folders
    - STM32 derivative linker files
    - STM32 derivative pin maps

4. What are a few features that make the `STM32L475E_IOT01A` board interesting for MicroPython?
    - Arduino headers
    - On-board Wi-Fi
    - On-board Bluetooth
    - A built-in DFU bootloader
    - The PMOD expansion header

5. Which board kernel file can be modified to change the pin designation that is used to control a pin in a MicroPython script?
    - `pins.csv`

6. What function must be defined in order to customize the startup code initialization?
    - `MICRO_BOARD_EARLY_INIT`

7. What steps should be followed to customize the startup code?
    1. Update the board's `mpconfigboard.h` module with the `MICROPY_BOARD_EARLY_INIT` definition along with the function name that will be called.
    2. Create a module to contain the code.
    3. Define the function that will be executed.
    4. Add the custom startup code.

8. Which compiler tool is used to generate `.mpy` files and to convert Python scripts to frozen modules?
    - `mpy-cross`

9. What are the advantages of using a frozen module?
   - The Python module cannot be modified without flashing the kernel.
   - The module is compiled into byte code, which keeps the source code away from prying eyes.
   - Updating the application scripts is faster because there are fewer modules to update.
   - If something goes wrong with the filesystem and it gets set back to default, the compiled modules will still be present and can be called as part of the default script to get the system into a safe state.
   - You can put the compiled module into zero-wait RAM if it has some speed-critical functionality, which will ensure it executes as efficiently as possible.
   - The compiled module can now also be stored and executed from the flash memory, which will free up RAM for the Python compiler and the scripts that are stored on the filesystem.

10. What command is used to compile the kernel with frozen modules?
    - `make BOARD= B_L475E_IOT01A FROZEN_MPY_DIR=boards/ B_L475E_IOT01A /script`

Chapter 6

1. What files is used to modify what USB classes are supported on startup by the MicroPython board?
   - `boot.py`

2. What are some reasons we would use generated data in our development rather than a live sensor?
   - Less code to write initially
   - No need to troubleshoot sensor code
   - A simpler hardware setup

3. At what chart refresh rate does the user interface start to become sluggish?
   - 100 milliseconds

4. What are some reasons for using the MicroPython UART for communication over using USB?
   - It's useful to gain experience with the UART, which can be used to interface with other sensors and devices.

5. What Python function is used to convert a floating-point number into a string?
    - `str()`

6. What module is used to create command-line arguments?
    - `args`

7. What are some new features that could be added to the visualizer to enhance its capabilities?
    - Add a configuration file.
    - Add a data packet checksum.
    - Save the incoming data stream.
    - Add two-way communication.
    - Use USB instead of a UART.

Chapter 7

1. What are the technologies that are typically used in gesture-control applications?
    - IR LEDs and photodiodes
    - Cameras

2. What four main gestures were covered in this chapter?
    - Forward
    - Backward
    - Left
    - Right

3. What three analog engines are provided in the APDS-9660?
    - Proximity detection
    - Gesture detection
    - RGB color detection

4. What is the difference between a driver and an integrated application module?
    - A driver provides access to all functionality within a chip for use generically by the application. A driver requires a developer to create a higher-level module to use the data from the driver to perform useful work. An integrated application module integrates some driver functionality into the application module so that they are highly integrated and coupled together.

5. What method was used to determine the gesture direction?
    - Using four of the last five data points with the last data point thrown out. The separation distance between each axis diode was calculated to determine on which axis the gesture direction was. The direction of the axis counts was then used to determine in which direction the gesture was.

Chapter 8

1. What library do we use to create tasks within MicroPython?
    - `uasyncio`

2. What MicroPython image do we use when flashing the ESP32?
    - Generic-SPIRAM with support for BLE but no LAN or PPP

3. What tool is used to flash the ESP32 with MicroPython?
    - `esptool.py`

4. Which MicroPython module can be used to generically control I/O across any MicroPython port?
    - `machine`

5. What methods can be used to push scripts to the ESP32?
    - WebREPL
    - Anaconda terminal

Chapter 9

1. What skill areas are traditionally covered within embedded systems?
    - Architecture design
    - Code analysis
    - Defect management/debugging
    - Documentation
    - Language skills
    - Processes and standards
    - Testing tools

2. Why are intelligent systems now required in the industry?
   - To solve problems that are not easy for a human to code for
   - To scale system behaviors and results based on new data and situations
   - To perform tasks that are easy for a human but traditionally difficult for computers
   - To decrease system costs in certain applications
   - And because it's cool and cutting edge

3. What are the benefits of moving machine learning from the cloud to the edge?
   - Bandwidth
   - Power
   - Cost
   - Latency
   - Reliability
   - Security

4. What image dataset is most commonly used in machine learning algorithm development?
   - CIFAR-10

5. What tools are used to train and deploy a machine learning model on an embedded system?
   - A dataset
   - Machine learning libraries and frameworks
   - TFLu
   - CMSIS-NN

Other Books You May Enjoy

If you enjoyed this book, you may be interested in these other books by Packt:

Hands-On Embedded Programming with Qt

John Werner

ISBN: 978-1-78995-206-3

- Understand how to develop Qt applications using Qt Creator on Linux
- Explore various Qt GUI technologies to build resourceful and interactive applications
- Understand Qt's threading model to maintain a responsive UI
- Get to grips with remote target load and debug using Qt Creator
- Become adept at writing IoT code using Qt
- Learn a variety of software best practices to ensure that your code is efficient

Hands-On Embedded Programming with C++17
Maya Posch

ISBN: 978-1-78862-930-0

- Choose the correct type of embedded platform to use for a project
- Develop drivers for OS-based embedded systems
- Use concurrency and memory management with various microcontroller units (MCUs)
- Debug and test cross-platform code with Linux
- Implement an infotainment system using a Linux-based single board computer
- Extend an existing embedded system with a Qt-based GUI
- Communicate with the FPGA side of a hybrid FPGA/SoC system

Leave a review - let other readers know what you think

Please share your thoughts on this book with others by leaving a review on the site that you bought it from. If you purchased the book from Amazon, please leave us an honest review on this book's Amazon page. This is vital so that other potential readers can see and use your unbiased opinion to make purchasing decisions, we can understand what our customers think about our products, and our authors can see your feedback on the title that they have worked with Packt to create. It will only take a few minutes of your time, but is valuable to other potential customers, our authors, and Packt. Thank you!

Index